PHILOSOPHY, POLITICS AND SOCIETY

Philosophy, Politics and Society

A COLLECTION EDITED BY

PETER LASLETT

*Fellow of Trinity College, Cambridge
and University Lecturer in History*

OXFORD
BASIL BLACKWELL
1970

ISBN 0 631 04870 7

First Printed 1956
Reprinted 1957, 1963, 1967, 1970

PRINTED IN GREAT BRITAIN BY OFFSET LITHOGRAPHY BY
BILLING AND SONS LTD., GUILDFORD AND LONDON

CONTENTS

INTRODUCTION

IT is one of the assumptions of intellectual life in our country that there should be amongst us men whom we think of as political philosophers. Philosophers themselves and sensitive to philosophic change, they are to concern themselves with political and social relationships at the widest possible level of generality. They are to apply the methods and the conclusions of contemporary thought to the evidence of the contemporary social and political situation. For three hundred years of our history there have been such men writing in English, from the early seventeenth to the twentieth centuries, from Hobbes to Bosanquet. To-day, it would seem, we have them no longer. The tradition has been broken and our assumption is misplaced, unless it is looked on as a belief in the possibility that the tradition is about to be resumed. For the moment, anyway, political philosophy is dead.

This calls for a certain sententiousness, and it would be easier still to be sententious about the reasons for it. We could point to events in the political arena itself, and gravely claim that they have become too serious for philosophic contemplation. Horrific is the adjective for the politics of the twentieth century, as they have been carried on between the powers, in Russia, in Germany and elsewhere. Faced with Hiroshima and with Belsen, a man is unlikely to address himself to a neat and original theory of political obligation. This argument has its force, though it happens to contradict one of the traditional explanations of why certain great thinkers of the past addressed themselves to political philosophy. It was the horror of the fall of Rome, it has so often been said, which produced in the mind of St. Augustine the political philosophy of the *City of God*, just as it was the terror of the English Civil War which called forth the *Leviathan* of Thomas Hobbes and the Revolution which made Locke write on *Civil Government*. Though each of these two later statements happens to be untrue, it may still be the case that we have no political philosophy because politics have become too serious to be left to philosophers.

There are those who would say that it is the sociologists who have done this thing. And first amongst them are the Marxists, who have erected a system in which statements of sociological description and determinism tend to fill the function of philosophic analysis.

This view would not be easy to defend, for a political philosophy of the traditional sort could be built up on the Marxian sociology, and the debate between the Marxists and their critics is carried on to a certain extent within the conventions of traditional political philosophy. Nevertheless, the claim must be allowed a certain validity, for neither Marx nor Lenin described himself as a political philosopher and the expounders of their political doctrine to-day carry on their effort to dismiss all political philosophizing as determined, sociologically determined. Marxists are quite simply not interested in the perennial debates which exercised the political philosophers in the past, and their immensely successful political following in the twentieth century has apparently found little occasion to present them with philosophical problems of the political sort. They have got on without it and they have frightened everybody else.

The academic sociologists have had a somewhat similar impact. Post-Marxian, post-Freudian as they tend to be, they seem to alternate between an attitude which proclaims that political philosophy is impossible and an urgent pleading for a new political philosophy which will give them guidance and make sense of their conclusions. The first of these moods is to be seen at its most extreme in the late Karl Mannheim's sociology of knowledge, in which not simply political activity and political thinking are shown to be sociologically determined, but all thinking and all knowing as well. Such relativism could only lead, as lead it did, to a surrender to dogma or to an appeal to the 'thinkers', whoever they may be, for a new synthesis at 'a higher level', wherever that may lie. Meanwhile the social scientists have maintained a continuing Œdipus relationship with the natural scientists, whose children they are or would like to be. Sometimes identifying themselves entirely with the scientific attitude and proclaiming with Radcliffe-Brown that their only object is a natural science of society, at other times they insist that their activity is also a humanist activity which must have its philosophy and philosophers. In view of the enormous prestige of natural science in our day, this ambivalence is not surprising, nor is it surprising that the humanists themselves, the philosophers, historians and so on, should be uncertain how to treat the social scientists. The academic debate in our country on the status of sociology and the validity of its results is still unresolved. Under such circumstances it is only natural that the social and political philosopher should feel inhibited. The area of his activity has been taken over by the sociologists, who do not seem to be

doing anything with it, or at any rate, nothing of philosophic
interest.

So far we have concerned ourselves with the difficulties and dis-
couragements which face the political philosopher in our day. We
could develop all this much further, but it would not, I think, tell
us who killed Cock Robin. It is not only the world of politics and
the methods of studying it which have been transformed in the last
half-century; philosophy and philosophers have changed too. So
striking and so complete is the difference between the philosopher's
world of our own day and that of Bosanquet's time, or even of
Harold Laski's, that it is really very easy to point to the culprit.
The Logical Positivists did it. It was Russell and Wittgenstein, Ayer
and Ryle who convinced the philosophers that they must withdraw
unto themselves for a time, and re-examine their logical and
linguistic apparatus. And the result of this re-examination has been
radical indeed. It called into question the logical status of all ethical
statements, and set up rigorous criteria of intelligibility which at
one time threatened to reduce the traditional ethical systems to
assemblages of nonsense. Since political philosophy is, or was, an
extension of ethics, the question has been raised whether political
philosophy is possible at all.

When this philosophical development is added to the other
influences we have described, it will be seen why it should be that
the winter has set in for the political philosopher. In a climate such
as this it can be no surprise that so much of the young growth of
political speculation should have been blasted as it burgeoned, or
that the plant itself should show such evident signs of having
withered and died. It is an object of this present collection of essays
to illustrate the effect of all this, and more particularly of contemporary philosophy, on writing about politics in our country since
the end of the war. Like the collections on which it is modelled,
those edited by Professor Flew under the title *Logic and Language*,
the contributions come from British writers, although the situation
in which they write is by no means confined to this country. It is
hoped that students and teachers of politics, political theory, and to
some extent of law and the social sciences generally, will find here
a representative selection of contemporary theoretical writing about
politics, undertaken by men who are for the most part themselves
philosophers, though none of them political philosophers in the old
sense.

It is possible that what has been said so far may have been

misleading. Whatever may have been the intention of the Marxists and the other sociologists, it was, perhaps, never intended by the analytic philosophers of the early twentieth century that a traditional area of philosophic inquiry should be permanently closed. 'Temporarily railed off pending examination and repair' is rather the sort of notice which they might have felt necessary to put up to mark the field of political philosophy. With their new general survey map of philosopher's language clasped in their hands, and with their analytical tools considerably sharper, they might enter these regions again with a much modester and more realistic attitude to what they might accomplish in them. It is true that in the earlier phase of the movement, the linguistic philosophers talked as if the only function of philosophy in the future was to be the exposure of linguistic confusions. Even if this were to be the case, the task of passing judgments of this sort on the propositions of political philosophy would still remain to be done. But in recent years there have been signs that our philosophers were preparing to take up their responsibilities towards political discussions once more. It is on these small signs that some might wish to base an expectation of a rebirth of traditional political philosophy.

It is for these and other reasons that the actual impact of contemporary philosophy on political and social theory is exceedingly difficult to represent in a compendium of this sort. The essays reprinted or first presented here do not, for the most part, undertake to expound the content of recent analytical writing and its relevance to political philosophy. Rather they are examples of what can still be done in the light of the new philosophical attitude. If the reader wishes to know what is implied for general political theory by the logical analysis of Wittgenstein's *Tractatus*, or by the account given of the will and will language in Gilbert Ryle's *Concept of Mind*, it is to these books that he must turn. In the second of the essays, however, that by Mr. Weldon on *Political Principles*, he will find a terser form of the argument of Mr. Weldon's book, *The Vocabulary of Politics* (Pelican, 1953). These are the only attempts known to me at a general consideration in contemporary logical terms of the conventional content of political philosophy. Mr. Weldon, of course, speaks for himself alone, and it would be very difficult for any individual to stand as a representative of a whole body of thinkers in a rapidly developing school of opinion. The student of politics who wishes to know how his interests are affected by to-day's philosophy must acquaint himself at first hand with what the philosophers are saying.

It is hoped that the contents of this volume will encourage him to do this. The complaint that the philosophy of our time has no sort of relevance outside its chosen area, a highly restricted area, is very often heard, especially amongst those who study politics and political thinking. But it will be noticed that the subjects represented here range widely over the field, from the interpretation of Plato to the contemporary theory of international law. It is remarkable that each study is in the form of a reformulation of an inherited position, rather than of an attempt to establish entirely novel positions as a part of a complete attitude. Still, the arguments used are cogent and penetrating, and the reformulated claim is subtler, much more effective as a tool of analysis. It has to be admitted that the editor's area of choice was severely limited, and in only one field, that of jurisprudence, has any considerable body of work been published since 1945.[1] A survey of our philosophical periodicals for the purposes of this collection gives the impression that their editors have often included articles on political subjects merely out of a sense of their conventional duty. Their contributors, too, sometimes give the feeling that they have turned their attention to politics only because the curriculum of their university requires it. It would be wrong, then, in my opinion, to claim that philosophizing about politics is felt to be an urgent and exciting opportunity for the contemporary thinker, as compared with epistemology. Nevertheless, what has been accomplished is substantial enough to justify the bringing together within one convenient cover a set of typical exercises which would otherwise remain scattered in their various files.

Editorial policy has been a difficult problem, as might be expected when the task has been to draw a circle round a hole. There have been more accidental obstacles. Two pieces which might have found a place here have already been included in Professor Flew's first collection, Miss Macdonald on *The Language of Political Theory*

[1] Professor H. L. Hart has written a brief but illuminating survey of this material in the *American Journal of Comparative Law*, Vol. 2, no. 3 (1953). To the contributions listed there, several must now be added, in particular Mr. Richard Wollheim's article on 'The Nature of Law' in *Political Studies*, Vol. 2 (1954). It is regretted that it has only been possible to include Doctor Glanville Williams's rather earlier study in a volume devoted to political theory generally. For the same reasons it proved impracticable to reprint his much longer essay on 'Language and the Law' (*Law Quarterly Review*, Vols. 61–2, 1945–6), which is more frequently quoted by philosophers, but it is good to know that he now contemplates publishing it as a separate book.

and Professor Hart on *The Ascription of Responsibility and Rights*.[1]
An obvious omission is a contribution from Professor Karl Popper,
perhaps the most influential of contemporary philosophers who have
addressed themselves to politics, but his occasional writings have
been reserved for a collection of their own. Professor Oakeshott's
remarkable inaugural lecture on *Political Education*, with which this
volume begins, must, of course, be exempted from the remarks which
have been made about the linguistic philosophers and their effect
on political theory, for he is not of their number. His distrust of
rationalism, however, and the whole tendency of his political
doctrine, makes its presence within this context particularly illuminating. For this and for the decision to include something of his own
on a theme still less related to the rest, the editor alone is responsible.

So is he for the arbitrary definition of political philosophy with
which this Introduction began. It might be urged against the claim
that this pursuit is to all appearances dead, that books expounding
its content continue to be published and to serve the function of
their distinguished predecessors, and some of them important books,
such as Mr. J. D. Mabbott's *The State and the Citizen*. It might also
be argued that even if it were dead, we, in whose presence the
decease occurred, would not be in a position to certify it, for that
must be left to posterity. A plausible case might be made for
supposing that there is abroad in the world a movement growing
every day more powerful for the restoration of a philosophy of all
humanity, a philosophy on the Stoic model, which represents not
the extinction of political philosophy but its metamorphosis. The
evidence for this would be taken from international organization,
the recognition of the insufficiency in the contemporary world of
the nation state and the concept of sovereignty and in such
documents—notably once more legal documents—as the Universal
Declaration of Human Rights. Indeed, though the point is too
obvious to press, 'philosophy' is like all other abstract words,
capable of a great variety of definitions, and anyone who chose
could legitimately call the exercises which form the body of this
work political philosophy, since they are written by philosophers on
political subjects.

In defence of the definition we have used it must be maintained
that it is a statement of vulgar prejudice, where vulgar means on the
part of people at large, and prejudice a persistent belief in the
existence of something, whether or not there is evidence for it.

[1] Nos. IX and X in *Logic and Language*, ed. A. G. N. Flew, Oxford, Blackwell, 1951.

Now there is no escaping the fact that the people, the statesmen, that is the lawyers, the administrators, the citizens and the soldiers, do believe what we claimed. They do expect that certain people somewhere in their society can give an unequivocal answer to such questions as—Why should I obey the call up? is a Jamaican as good as an Englishman? Is there such a thing as Socialist morality and should I adopt it? And they ask not only normative questions like this, but analytic and predictive questions as well—What is the State? or, Will the Labour Party ever win another General Election? The conspicuous feature of the answers they feel entitled to be given to their questions is that they should be general and systematic. They feel entitled to reject answers beginning with 'It depends what you mean by . . .', where it is implied that there is no one general meaning which can be given to the question, or beginning with 'You must ask a particular specialist who . . .', given when it is obvious that no such special body of knowledge is as yet forthcoming or likely in principle to be built up. In fact they expect philosophic answers to their questions, where philosophy means what it meant to Aristotle and the whole succession down to Samuel Alexander in our country, a complete, coherent view of all knowledge and experience, what used to be called a Weltanschauung.

The philosophical movement unsatisfactorily named Logical Positivism is perhaps too easily supposed to be purely destructive. But if they have not, as their critics often claim, put an end to philosophy as a pursuit, they have radically revised the identity of the philosopher as a person. It could be argued, and I should myself incline to this position, that the philosopher of vulgar prejudice never existed. What little has been done by this school on the history of their doctrine goes to show that it has a long and respectable lineage, going back at least to Locke and Hobbes, even to Ockham and the medieval nominalists. As applied specifically to political philosophers, this line is worth pursuing. It could be maintained that there have in fact been only two political philosophers whose thinking corresponds at all closely to the philosophy of vulgar prejudice, Aristotle himself and Thomas Hobbes. In the case of Locke, certain aspects of whose thinking are crucial for contemporary philosophers, the conflict between the epistemologist and the political theorist is quite apparent and from our point of view very interesting. In fact there was no coherent body of Lockeian thought which related the *Essay on Human Understanding* on the one hand with the *Essay on Civil Government* on the other, and what goes for its founder goes for the liberal political tradition as a whole.

The intellectual light of the mid-twentieth century is clear, cold and hard. If it requires those who undertake to answer questions about politics to do so without being entitled to call themselves political philosophers, we must answer them nevertheless. It has been granted that there is nothing in the name itself, except that to use it in the sense given to it by vulgar prejudice is to claim a prestige in the world at large to which we should do better not to pretend. The questions will continue to be asked, and in answering them we should take account of the philosophical situation as it is, getting all the advantage we can of those exact and subtle methods which have given precision to epistemological inquiry, and shown up so much of its traditional discussion as meaningless.

Some may think it an exaggeration, even a distortion, to proclaim that political philosophy is dead, even with the expectation of its imminent revival. But it is surely better to do this than to proceed as if all the intermediate linkages between our knowledge of the material world and the rights and wrongs of political decisions were certain and secure. Some such assumption, an entirely unjustifiable one unless Revelation is invoked, would be necessary to sanction, for example, a concept of Natural Law which would make of modern Stoicism a genuine political philosophy of the traditional sort. This is the crux, and it might help us to recognize it if we ceased to analyse the classics of political philosophy as if these linkages must have been certainly established for their authors. This is one of the ways in which we have been able to convince ourselves that our situation is new and peculiar. Because of it we have not stopped to ask ourselves to what extent the situation has been a universal one. If this collection does anything in such directions as these, it will have achieved its purpose.

Editor's note

I should like to thank the writers of these articles for their co-operation, and the publishers for permission to reprint. Some of the authors, and especially Mr. Bambrough, have helped with criticism and advice, and I am indebted to many other people for guidance too. Professor Oakeshott's lecture first appeared as a pamphlet published by Bowes & Bowes. The contribution by Mr. Rees is from *Mind* (1950), that by Mr. Quinton from *Analysis* (1954), and those by Professor Gallie and Mr. Mayo come from *Philosophy* (1949 and 1950). Dr. Glanville Williams wrote his article for *The British Yearbook of International Law* (1945), and Mr. Weldon's, Mr. Bambrough's and the editor's are published for the first time. Miss Macdonald's paper is reprinted from *The Proceedings of the Aristotelian Society* for 1947–8.

PHILOSOPHY, POLITICS AND SOCIETY

I

POLITICAL EDUCATION

AN INAUGURAL LECTURE DELIVERED AT THE LONDON SCHOOL OF
ECONOMICS AND POLITICAL SCIENCE ON MARCH 6, 1951

by Michael Oakeshott

Fellow of Gonville and Caius College, Cambridge
Professor of Political Science in the University of London

THE two former occupants of this Chair, Graham Wallas and
Harold Laski, were both men of great distinction; to follow
them is an undertaking for which I am ill-prepared. In the first of
them, experience and reflection were happily combined to give a
reading of politics at once practical and profound; a thinker without
a system whose thoughts were nevertheless firmly held together by
a thread of honest, patient inquiry; a man who brought his powers
of intellect to bear upon the inconsequence of human behaviour
and to whom the reasons of the head and of the heart were alike
familiar. In the second, the dry light of intellect was matched with
a warm enthusiasm; to the humour of a scholar was joined the
temperament of a reformer. It seems but an hour ago that he was
dazzling us with the range and readiness of his learning, winning
our sympathy by the fearlessness of his advocacy and endearing
himself to us by his generosity. In their several ways, ways in which
their successor cannot hope to compete with them, these two men
left their mark upon the political education of England. They were
both great teachers, devoted, tireless, and with sure confidence in
what they had to teach. And it seems perhaps a little ungrateful
that they should be followed by a sceptic; one who would do better
if only he knew how. But no one could wish for more exacting or
more sympathetic witnesses of his activities than these two men.
And the subject I have chosen to speak about to-day is one which
would have their approval.

B

I

The expression 'political education' has fallen on evil days; in the wilful and disingenuous corruption of language which is characteristic of our time it has acquired a sinister meaning. In places other than this, it is associated with that softening of the mind, by force, by alarm, or by the hypnotism of the endless repetition of what was scarcely worth saying once, by means of which whole populations have been reduced to submission. It is, therefore, an enterprise worth undertaking to consider again, in a quiet moment, how we should understand this expression, which joins together two laudable activities, and in doing so play a small part in rescuing it from abuse.

Politics I take to be the activity of attending to the general arrangements of a set of people whom chance or choice has brought together. In this sense, families, clubs, and learned societies have their 'politics'. But the communities in which this manner of activity is pre-eminent are the hereditary co-operative groups, many of them of ancient lineage, all of them aware of a past, a present, and a future, which we call 'states'. For most people, political activity is a secondary activity—that is to say, they have something else to do besides attending to these arrangements. But, as we have come to understand it, the activity is one in which every member of the group who is neither a child nor a lunatic has some part and some responsibility. With us it is, at one level or another, a universal activity.

I speak of this activity as 'attending to arrangements', rather than as 'making arrangements', because in these hereditary co-operative groups the activity is never offered the blank sheet of infinite possibility. In any generation, even the most revolutionary, the arrangements which are enjoyed always far exceed those which are recognized to stand in need of attention, and those which are being prepared for enjoyment are few in comparison with those which receive amendment: the new is an insignificant proportion of the whole. There are some people, of course, who allow themselves to speak

> As if arrangements were intended
> For nothing else but to be mended,

but, for most of us, our determination to improve our conduct does not prevent us from recognizing that the greater part of what we have is not a burden to be carried or an incubus to be thrown off, but an inheritance to be enjoyed. And a certain degree of shabbiness is joined with every real convenience.

Now, attending to the arrangements of a society is an activity which, like every other, has to be learned. Politics make a call upon knowledge. Consequently, it is not irrelevant to inquire into the kind of knowledge which is involved, and to investigate the nature of political education. I do not, however, propose to ask what information we should equip ourselves with before we begin to be politically active, or what we need to know in order to be successful politicians, but to inquire into the kind of knowledge we unavoidably call upon whenever we are engaged in political activity and to get from this an understanding of the nature of political education.

Our thoughts on political education, then, might be supposed to spring from our understanding of political activity and the kind of knowledge it involves. And it would appear that what is wanted at this point is a definition of political activity from which to draw some conclusions. But this, I think, would be a mistaken way of going about our business. What we require is not so much a definition of politics from which to deduce the character of political education, as an understanding of political activity which includes a recognition of the sort of education it involves. For, to understand an activity is to know it as a concrete whole; it is to recognize the activity as having the source of its movement within itself. An understanding which leaves the activity in debt to something outside itself is, for that reason, an inadequate understanding. And if political activity is impossible without a certain kind of knowledge and a certain sort of education, then this knowledge and education are not mere appendages to the activity but are part of the activity itself and must be incorporated in our understanding of it. We should not, therefore, seek a definition of politics in order to deduce from it the character of political knowledge and education, but rather observe the kind of knowledge and education which is inherent in any understanding of political activity, and use this observation as a means of improving our understanding of politics.

My proposal, then, is to consider the adequacy of two current understandings of politics, together with the sort of knowledge and kind of education they imply, and by improving upon them to reach what may perhaps be a more adequate understanding at once of political activity itself and the knowledge and education which belong to it.

2

In the understanding of some people, politics are what may be called an empirical activity. Attending to the arrangements of a society is waking up each morning and considering, 'What would I like to do?' or 'What would somebody else (whom I desire to please) like to see done?', and doing it. This understanding of political activity may be called politics without a policy. On the briefest inspection it will appear a concept of politics difficult to substantiate; it does not look like a possible manner of activity at all. But a near approach to it is, perhaps, to be detected in the politics of the proverbial oriental despot, or in the politics of the wall-scribbler and the vote-catcher. And the result may be supposed to be chaos modified by whatever consistency is allowed to creep into caprice. They are the politics attributed to the first Lord Liverpool, of whom Acton said, 'The secret of his policy was that he had none', and of whom a Frenchman remarked that if he had been present at the creation of the world he would have said, '*Mon Dieu, conservons le chaos*'. It seems, then, that a concrete activity, which may be described as an approximation to empirical politics, is possible. But it is clear that, although knowledge of a sort belongs to this style of political activity (knowledge, as the French say, not of ourselves but only of our appetites), the only kind of education appropriate to it would be an education in lunacy—learning to be ruled solely by passing desires. And this reveals the important point; namely, that to understand politics as a purely empirical activity is to misunderstand it, because empiricism by itself is not a concrete manner of activity at all, and can become a partner in a concrete manner of activity only when it is joined with something else—in science, for example, when it is joined with hypothesis. What is significant about this understanding of politics is not that some sort of approach to it can appear, but that it mistakes for a concrete, self-moved manner of activity what is never more than an abstract moment in any manner of being active. Of course, politics are the pursuit of what is desired and of what is desired at the moment; but precisely because they are this, they can never be the pursuit of merely what recommends itself from moment to moment. The activity of desiring does not take this course; caprice is never absolute. From a practical point of view, then, we may decry the style of politics which approximates to pure empiricism because we can observe in it an approach to lunacy. But from a theoretical point of view, purely empirical politics are not something difficult to achieve or proper to be avoided, they are merely impossible; the product of a misunderstanding.

3

The understanding of politics as an empirical activity is, then, inadequate because it fails to reveal a concrete manner of activity at all. And it has the incidental defect of seeming to encourage the thoughtless to pursue a *style* of attending to the arrangements of their society which is likely to have unfortunate results; to try to do something which is inherently impossible is always a corrupting enterprise. We must, if we can, improve upon it. And the impulse to improve may be given a direction by asking, 'What is it that this understanding of politics has neglected to observe?' What (to put it crudely) has it left out which, if added in, would compose an understanding in which politics are revealed as a self-moved manner of activity? And the answer to the question is, or seems to be, available as soon as the question is formulated. It would appear that what this understanding of politics lacks is something to set empiricism to work, something to correspond with specific hypothesis in science, an end to be pursued more extensive than a merely instant desire. And this, it should be observed, is not merely a good companion for empiricism; it is something without which empiricism in action is impossible. Let us explore this suggestion, and in order to bring it to a point I will state it in the form of a proposition: that politics appear as a self-moved manner of activity when empiricism is preceded and guided by an ideological activity. I am not concerned with the so-called ideological *style* of politics as a desirable or undesirable manner of attending to the arrangements of a society; I am concerned (at present) only with the contention that when to the ineluctable element of empiricism is added a political ideology, a self-moved manner of activity appears, and that consequently this may be regarded in principle as an adequate concept of political activity.

As I understand it, a political ideology purports to be an abstract principle, or set of related abstract principles, which has been independently premeditated. It supplies in advance of the activity of attending to the arrangements of a society a formulated end to be pursued, and in so doing it provides a means of distinguishing between those desires which ought to be encouraged and those which ought to be suppressed or redirected.

The simplest sort of political ideology is a single abstract idea, such as Freedom, Equality, Maximum Productivity, Racial Purity, or Happiness. And in that case political activity is understood as the

enterprise of seeing to it that the arrangements of a society conform
to or reflect the chosen abstract idea. It is usual, however, to recognize the need for a complex scheme of related ideas, rather than a
single idea, and the examples pointed to will be such systems of ideas
as: 'the principles of 1789', 'Liberalism', 'Democracy', 'Marxism', or
the Atlantic Charter. These principles need not be considered
absolute or immune from change (though they are frequently so
considered), but their value lies in their having been premeditated.
They compose an understanding of *what* is to be pursued independent of *how* it is to be pursued. A political ideology purports to
supply in advance knowledge of what 'Freedom' or 'Democracy'
or 'Justice' is, and in this manner sets empiricism to work. Such a
set of principles is, of course, capable of being argued about and
reflected upon; it is something that men compose for themselves,
and they may later remember it or write it down. But the condition
upon which it can perform the service assigned to it is that it owes
nothing to the activity it controls. 'To know the true good of the
community is what constitutes the science of legislation', said
Bentham; 'the art consists in finding the means to realize that good'.
The contention we have before us, then, is that empiricism can be
set to work (and a concrete, self-moved manner of activity appear)
when there is added to it a guide of this sort.

Now, there is no doubt about the sort of knowledge which
political activity, understood in this manner, calls upon. What is
required, in the first place, is knowledge of the chosen political
ideology—a knowledge of the ends to be pursued, a knowledge of
what we want to do. Of course, if we are to be successful in pursuing
these ends we shall need knowledge of other sorts also—a knowledge, shall we say, of economics and psychology. But the common
characteristic of all the kinds of knowledge required is that they may
be, and should be, gathered in advance of the activity of attending
to the arrangements of a society. Moreover, the appropriate sort of
education will be an education in which the chosen political ideology
is taught and learned, in which the techniques necessary for success
are acquired, and (if we are so unfortunate as to find ourselves
empty-handed in the matter of an ideology) an education in the skill
of abstract thought and premeditation necessary to compose one for
ourselves. The education we shall need is one which enables us to
expound, defend, implement, and possibly invent a political ideology.

In casting around for some convincing demonstration that this
understanding of politics reveals a self-moved manner of activity,

we should no doubt consider ourselves rewarded if we could find an example of politics being conducted precisely in this manner. This at least would constitute a sign that we were on the right track. The defect, it will be remembered, of the understanding of politics as a purely empirical activity was that it revealed, not a manner of activity at all, but an abstraction; and this defect made itself manifest in our inability to find a *style* of politics which was anything more than a distant approximation to it. How does the understanding of politics as empiricism joined with an ideology fare in this respect? And without being over-confident, we may perhaps think that this is where we wade ashore. For we would appear to be in no difficulty whatever in finding an example of political activity which corresponds to this understanding of it: half the world, at a conservative estimate, seems to conduct its affairs in precisely this manner. And further, is it not so manifestly a possible style of politics that, even if we disagree with a particular ideology, we find nothing technically absurd in the writings of those who urge it upon us as an admirable style of politics? At least its advocates seem to know what they are talking about: they understand not only the manner of the activity but also the sort of knowledge and the kind of education it involves. 'Every schoolboy in Russia', wrote Sir Norman Angel, 'is familiar with the doctrine of Marx and can recite its catechism. How many British schoolboys have any corresponding knowledge of the principles enunciated by Mill in his incomparable essay on Liberty?' 'Few people', says Mr. E. H. Carr, 'any longer contest the thesis that the child should be educated *in* the official ideology of his country'. In short, if we are looking for a sign to indicate that the understanding of politics as empirical activity preceded by ideological activity is an adequate understanding, we can scarcely be mistaken in supposing that we have it to hand.

And yet there is, perhaps, room for doubt; doubt first of all whether in principle this understanding of politics reveals a self-moved manner of activity; and doubt, consequentially, whether what have been identified as examples of a style of politics corresponding exactly to this understanding have been properly identified.

The contention we are investigating is that attending to the arrangements of a society can begin with a premeditated ideology, can begin with independently acquired knowledge of the ends to be pursued. It is supposed that a political ideology is the product of intellectual premeditation and that, because it is a body of principles not itself in debt to the activity of attending to the arrangements of a society, it is able to determine and guide the direction of that activity. If, however, we consider more closely the character of a political ideology, we find at once that this supposition is falsified. So far from a political ideology being the quasi-divine parent of political activity, it turns out to be its earthly stepchild. Instead of an independently premeditated scheme of ends to be pursued, it is a system of ideas abstracted from the manner in which people have been accustomed to go about the business of attending to the arrangements of their societies. The pedigree of every political ideology shows it to be the creature, not of premeditation in advance of political activity, but of meditation upon a manner of politics. In short, political activity comes first and a political ideology follows after; and the understanding of politics we are investigating has the disadvantage of being, in the strict sense, preposterous.

Let us consider the matter first in relation to scientific hypothesis, which I have taken to play a role in scientific activity in some respects similar to that of an ideology in politics. If a scientific hypothesis were a self-generated bright idea which owed nothing to scientific activity, then empiricism governed by hypothesis could be considered to compose a self-contained manner of activity; but this certainly is not its character. The truth is that only a man who is already a scientist can formulate a scientific hypothesis; that is, an hypothesis is not an independent invention capable of guiding scientific inquiry, but a dependent supposition which arises as an abstraction from within already existing scientific activity. Moreover, even when the specific hypothesis has in this manner been formulated, it is inoperative as a guide to research without constant reference to the traditions of scientific inquiry from which it was abstracted. The concrete situation does not appear until the specific hypothesis, which is the occasion of empiricism being set to work, is recognized as itself the creature of knowing how to conduct a scientific inquiry.

Or consider the example of cookery. It might be supposed that an ignorant man, some edible materials, and a cookery book compose together the necessities of a self-moved activity called cooking. But nothing is further from the truth. The cookery book is not an independently generated beginning from which cooking can spring; it is nothing more than an abstract of somebody's knowledge of how to cook: it is the stepchild, not the parent of the activity. The book, in its turn, may help to set a man on to dressing a dinner, but if it were his sole guide he could never, in fact, begin:

the book speaks only to those who know already the kind of thing to expect from it and consequently how to interpret it.

Now, just as a cookery book presupposes somebody who knows how to cook, and its use presupposes somebody who already knows how to use it, and just as a scientific hypothesis springs from a knowledge of how to conduct a scientific investigation and separated from that knowledge is powerless to set empiricism to work, so a political ideology must be understood, not as an independently premeditated beginning for political activity, but as knowledge (in an abstracted and generalized form) of a traditional manner of attending to the arrangements of a society. The catechism which sets out the purposes to be pursued merely abridges a concrete manner of behaviour in which those purposes are already hidden. It does not exist in advance of political activity, and by itself it is always an insufficient guide. Political enterprises, the ends to be pursued, the arrangements to be established (all the normal ingredients of a political ideology), cannot be premeditated in advance of a manner of attending to the arrangements of a society; *what* we do, and moreover what we want to do, is the creature of *how* we are accustomed to conduct our affairs.

On August 4, 1789, for the complex and bankrupt social and political system of France was substituted the Rights of Man. Reading this document we come to the conclusion that somebody has done some thinking. Here, displayed in a few sentences, is a political ideology: a system of rights and duties, a scheme of ends—justice, freedom, equality, security, property, and the rest—ready and waiting to be put into practice for the first time. 'For the first time?' Not a bit of it. This ideology no more existed in advance of political practice than a cookery book exists in advance of knowing how to cook. Certainly it was the product of somebody's reflection, but it was not the product of reflection in advance of political activity. For here, in fact, are disclosed, abstracted and abridged, the common law rights of Englishmen, the gift not of independent premeditation or divine munificence, but of centuries of the day-to-day attending to the arrangements of an historic society. Or consider Locke's *Second Treatise on Government*, read in America and in France in the eighteenth century as a statement of abstract principles to be put into practice, regarded there as a preface to political activity. But so far from being a preface, it has all the marks of a postscript, and its power to guide derived from its roots in actual political experience. Here, set down in abstract terms, is a brief conspectus of the manner in which Englishmen were accustomed to go about the business of attending to their arrangements —a brilliant abridgement of the political habits of Englishmen. Or consider this passage from a contemporary continental writer: 'Freedom keeps Europeans in unrest and movement. They wish to have freedom, and at the same time they know they have not got it. They know also that freedom belongs to man as a human right.' And having established the end to be pursued, political activity is represented as the realization of this end. But the 'freedom' which can be pursued is not an independently premeditated 'ideal' or a dream; like scientific hypothesis, it is something which is already intimated in a concrete manner of behaving. Freedom, like a recipe for game pie, is not a bright idea; it is not a 'human right' to be deduced from some speculative concept of human nature. The freedom which we enjoy is nothing more than arrangements, procedures of a certain kind: the freedom of an Englishman is not something exemplified in the procedure of Habeas Corpus, it *is*, at that point, the availability of that procedure. And the freedom which we wish to enjoy is not an 'ideal' which we premeditate independently of our political experience; it is what is already intimated in that experience.

On this reading, then, the systems of abstract ideas we call 'ideologies' are abstracts of some kind of concrete activity. Most political ideologies, and certainly the most useful of them, are abstracts of the political traditions of some society. But it sometimes happens that an ideology is offered as a guide to politics which is an abstract, not of political experience, but of some other manner of activity— war or the conduct of industry, for example. And here the model we are shown is not only abstract, but is also misleading on account of the irrelevance of the activity from which it has been abstracted. This, I think, is one of the defects of the model provided by the Marxist ideology. But the important point is that, at best, an ideology is an abbreviation of some manner of relevant concrete activity.

We are now, perhaps, in a position to perceive more accurately the character of what may be called the ideological *style* of politics, and to observe that its existence offers no ground for supposing that the understanding of political activity as empiricism guided solely by an ideology is an adequate understanding. The ideological style of politics is a confused style. Properly speaking, it is a traditional manner of attending to the arrangements of a society which has been abridged into a doctrine of ends to be pursued, the abridgement (together with the necessary technical knowledge) being erroneously regarded as the sole guide relied upon. In certain circumstances an abridgement of this kind may be valuable; it gives sharpness of outline and precision to a political tradition which the occasion may make seem appropriate. When a manner of attending to arrangements is to be transplanted from the society in which it has grown up into another society (always a questionable enterprise), the simplification of an ideology may appear as an asset. If, for example, the English manner of politics is to be planted elsewhere in the world, it is perhaps appropriate that it should first be abridged into something called 'democracy' before it is packed up and shipped abroad. There is, of course, an alternative method: the method by which what is exported is the detail and not the abridgement of the tradition and the workmen travel with the tools—the method which made the British Empire. But it is a slow and costly method. And, particularly with men in a hurry, *l'homme à programme* with his abridgement wins every time; his slogans enchant, while the resident magistrate is seen only as a sign of servility. But whatever the apparent appropriateness on occasion of the ideological style of politics, its defect becomes apparent when we consider the sort of knowledge and the kind of education it encourages us to believe is sufficient for the activity of attending to the arrangements of a society. For it suggests that a knowledge of the chosen political ideology, and a political education confined to learning a catechism, can take the place of a tradition of political behaviour. The wand and the book come to be regarded as themselves potent, and not merely the symbols of potency. The arrangements of a society are made to appear, not as manners of behaviour, but as pieces of machinery to be transported about the world indiscriminately. The complexities of the tradition which have been squeezed out in the process of abridgement are taken to be unimportant, if not actually suspect: the 'rights of man' are believed to exist insulated from a manner of attending to arrangements. And because, in fact, the abridgement is never by itself sufficient, we are encouraged to fill it out, not with our suspect political experience, but with experience drawn from other (often irrelevant and misleading) activities, such as war, the conduct of industry, or Trade Union negotiation.

4

The understanding of politics as the activity of attending to the arrangements of a society under the sole guidance of an independently premeditated ideology is, then, no less a misunderstanding than the understanding of it as a purely empirical activity. Wherever else politics may begin, they cannot begin in ideological activity. And in an attempt to improve upon this understanding of politics, we have already observed in principle what needs to be recognized in order to have an intelligible concept. Just as scientific hypothesis cannot appear, and is impossible to operate, except within an already existing tradition of scientific investigation, so a scheme of ends for political activity appears within, and is valuable only when it is related to, an already existing tradition of how to attend to our arrangements. In politics, the only self-moved manner of activity detectable is one in which empiricism and the ends to be pursued are recognized as dependent, alike for their existence and their operation, upon a traditional manner of behaviour.[1]

Politics is the activity of attending to the general arrangements of a collection of people who, in respect of their common recognition of a manner of attending to its arrangements, compose a single community. To suppose a collection of people without recognized traditions of behaviour, or one which enjoyed arrangements which intimated no direction for change and needed no attention, is to suppose a people incapable of politics. This activity, then, springs neither from instant desires, nor from general principles, but from the existing traditions of behaviour themselves. And the form it takes, because it can take no other, is the amendment of existing arrangements by exploring and pursuing what is intimated in them. The arrangements which constitute a society capable of political activity, whether they are customs or institutions or laws or diplomatic decisions, are at once coherent and incoherent; they compose a pattern and at the same time they intimate a sympathy for what does not fully appear. Political activity is the exploration of that

---

[1] In terms of the analogy of scientific inquiry, my argument so far has been as follows: Mere empiricism is not a manner of inquiry at all; it is devoid of direction and incapable of reaching significant conclusions. Empiricism guided by hypothesis approaches more nearly to a concrete manner of inquiry capable of reaching conclusions. But hypotheses in a 'scientific' inquiry are not any suppositions that may happen to occur to an inquirer; they are the suppositions which a man educated in the manners of 'scientific' inquiry will recognize as capable of leading to 'scientific' conclusions. Consequently, 'scientific inquiry' can appear as a self-moved or concrete activity only when these three components are recognized; and only when the dependence of empirical research upon the formulation of specific hypotheses, and the dependence of both upon the traditions and manners of 'scientific' inquiry, are also recognized.

sympathy; and consequently, relevant political reasoning will be the convincing exposure of a sympathy not yet followed up and the convincing demonstration that now is the opportune moment for recognizing it. For example, the legal status of women in our society was for a long time (and perhaps still is) in comparative confusion, because the rights and duties which composed it intimated rights and duties which were nevertheless not recognized. And, on the view of things I am suggesting, the only relevant reason to be advanced for the technical 'enfranchisement' of women was that in all or most other important respects they had already been enfranchised. Arguments (either for or against) drawn from abstract natural right, from 'justice', or from some general concept of feminine personality, must be regarded as either irrelevant, or as unfortunately disguised forms of the one valid argument; namely, that there was an incoherence in the arrangements of the society which pressed convincingly for remedy. In politics, then, every enterprise is a consequential enterprise, the pursuit, not of a dream, or of a general principle, but of an intimation. What we have to do with is something less imposing than logical implications or necessary consequences: but if the intimations of a tradition of behaviour are less dignified or more elusive than these, they are not on that account less important. Of course, there is no piece of mistake-proof apparatus by means of which we can elicit the intimation most worth while pursuing; and not only do we often make gross errors of judgment in this matter, but also the total effect of a desire satisfied is so little to be forecast, that our activity of amendment is often found to lead us where we would not go. Moreover, the whole enterprise is liable at any moment to be perverted by the incursion of an approximation to empiricism in the pursuit of power. These are imperfections which can never be eliminated. But it is to be believed that our mistakes will be less frequent and less disastrous, and our achievements more manageable, if we escape the illusion that politics can ever be anything more than the pursuit of intimations:[1] a conversation, not an argument.

[1] I do not know why this expression should cause offence or incredulity. We are concerned with human activity, and to surmise the focal point from fragmentary glimpses of directions being followed, to perceive the order of a sum in advance of completing the process of addition, to guess from a few moves of a game the strategy being followed and the moves to come, are all common enough experiences; and I do not understand why they should be absent from politics or insignificant in political activity. Indeed, as I listened to a collection of party politicians discussing the possibility of the emergence within English politics of a new 'cause' which might give a new turn to political enterprise and a new alignment to political opinion, it did not seem so very far-fetched to describe their manner of thinking as the 'pursuit of intimations'.

Now, every society which is intellectually alive is liable, from time to time, to abridge its tradition of behaviour into a scheme of abstract ideas; and on occasion political discussion will be concerned, not (like the debates in the *Iliad*) with isolated transactions, nor (like the speeches in Thucydides) with policies and traditions of activity, but with general principles. And in this there is no harm; perhaps even some positive benefit. It is possible that the distorting mirror of an ideology will reveal important hidden passages in the tradition, as a caricature reveals the potentialities of a face; and if this is so, the intellectual enterprise of seeing what a tradition looks like when it is reduced to an ideology will be a valuable part of political education. But to make use of abridgement as a technique for exploring the intimations of a political tradition, to use it, that is, as a scientist uses hypothesis, is one thing; it is something different, and something inappropriate, to allow political activity itself to appear as the activity of amending the arrangements of a society so as to make them agree with the provisions of an ideology. For when this happens a character has been attributed to an ideology which it is unable to sustain, and we find ourselves directed by a false and a misconceived guide: false, because in the abridgement, however skilfully it has been performed, a single intimation is exaggerated and proposed for unconditional pursuit and the benefit to be had from observing what the distortion reveals is lost when the distortion itself is given the office of a criterion; misconceived, because the abridgement itself never, in fact, provides the whole of the knowledge used in political activity.

There will be some people who, though in general agreement with this understanding of political activity, will suspect that it confuses what is, perhaps, normal with what is necessary, and that important exceptions (of great contemporary relevance) have been lost in a hazy generality. It is all very well, it may be said, to observe in politics the activity of exploring and pursuing the intimations of a tradition of behaviour, but what light does this throw upon a political crisis such as the Norman Conquest of England, or the establishment of the Soviet régime in Russia? It would be foolish, of course, to deny the possibility of serious political crisis. But if we exclude (as we must) a cataclysm which for the time being made an end of politics by altogether obliterating a current tradition of behaviour, there is little to support the view that even the most serious political upheaval carries us outside this understanding of politics. A tradition of behaviour is not a fixed and inflexible manner of doing things; it is a flow of sympathy. It may be temporarily disrupted by the incursion of a foreign influence, it may be diverted, restricted, arrested, or become dried-up, and it may reveal so deep-seated an incoherence that (even without foreign assistance) a crisis appears. And if, in order to meet these crises, there were some steady, unchanging, independent guide to which a society might resort, it would no doubt be well advised to do so. But no such guide exists; we have no resources outside the fragments, the vestiges, the relics of its own tradition of behaviour which the crisis has left untouched. For even the help we may get from the traditions of another society (or from a tradition of a vaguer sort which is shared by a number of societies) is conditional upon our being able to assimilate them to our own arrangements and our own manner of attending to our arrangements. The hungry and helpless man is mistaken if he supposes that he overcomes the crisis by means of a tin-opener: what saves him is somebody else's knowledge of how to cook, which he can make use of only because he is not himself entirely ignorant. In short, political crisis (even when it seems to be imposed upon a society by changes beyond its control) always appears *within* a tradition of political activity; and salvation comes from the unimpaired resources of the tradition itself. Those societies which retain, in changing circumstances, a lively sense of their own identity and continuity (which are without that hatred of their own experience which makes them desire to efface it), are to be counted fortunate, not because they possess what others lack, but because they have ready mobilized what none is without and all, in fact, rely upon.

In political activity, then, men sail a boundless and bottomless sea; there is neither harbour for shelter nor floor for anchorage, neither starting-place nor appointed destination. The enterprise is to keep afloat on an even keel; the sea is both friend and enemy; and the seamanship consists in using the resources of a traditional manner of behaviour in order to make a friend of every hostile occasion.[1]

---

[1] This paragraph, which I thought was innocent (and obvious) enough not to excite comment, has been fastened upon by critics, and perhaps will bear further elucidation. It is asked: Why travel if there is no prefigured and final destination? But it may be replied: Why suppose that the analogy of a journey towards a prefigured destination is relevant? It is clearly irrelevant in science, in art, in poetry and in human life in general, none of which have prefigured final destinations and none of which are (on that account) considered to be 'pointless' activities. Of course, the politician (like the astronomer or the architect) may set before himself immediate tasks to be achieved; but this does not make the activity of politics itself a teleological activity. And further, the activity of governing and being governed is, after all, only one among many human activities, and to describe the enterprise as 'keeping afloat and on an even keel' is to assign it an office neither to be overrated nor despised.

A depressing doctrine, it will be said—even by those who do not make the mistake of adding in an element of crude determinism which, in fact, it has no place for. A tradition of behaviour is not a groove within which we are destined to grind out our helpless and unsatisfying lives: Spartam nactus es; hanc *exorna*. But in the main the depression springs from the exclusion of hopes that were false and the discovery that guides, reputed to be of superhuman wisdom and skill, are, in fact, of a somewhat different character. If the doctrine deprives us of a model laid up in heaven to which we should approximate our behaviour, at least it does not lead us into a morass where every choice is equally good or equally to be deplored. And if it suggests that politics are *nur für die Schwindelfreie*, that should depress only those who have lost their nerve.

5

The sin of the academic is that he takes so long in coming to the point. Nevertheless, there is some virtue in his dilatoriness; what he has to offer may, in the end, be no great matter, but at least it is not unripe fruit, and to pluck it is the work of a moment. We set out to consider the kind of knowledge involved in political activity and the appropriate sort of education. And if the understanding of politics I have recommended is not a misunderstanding, there is little doubt about the kind of knowledge and the sort of education which belongs to it. It is knowledge, as profound as we can make it, of our tradition of political behaviour. Other knowledge, certainly, is desirable in addition; but this is the knowledge without which we cannot make use of whatever else we may have learned.

Now, a tradition of behaviour is a tricky thing to get to know. Indeed, it may even appear to be essentially unintelligible. It is neither fixed nor finished; it has no changeless centre to which understanding can anchor itself; there is no sovereign purpose to be perceived or invariable direction to be detected; there is no model to be copied, idea to be realized, or rule to be followed. Some parts of it may change more slowly than others, but none is immune from change. Everything is temporary. Nevertheless, though a tradition of behaviour is flimsy and elusive, it is not without identity, and what makes it a possible object of knowledge is the fact that all its parts do not change at the same time and that the changes it undergoes are potential within it. Its principle is a principle of *continuity*: authority is diffused between past, present, and future; between the old, the new, and what is to come. It is steady because, though it moves, it is never wholly in motion; and though it is tranquil, it is never wholly at rest. Nothing that ever belonged to it is completely lost; we are always swerving back to recover and make something topical out of even its remotest moments: and nothing for long remains unmodified. Everything is temporary, but nothing is arbitrary. Everything figures by comparison, not with what stands next to it, but with the whole. And since a tradition of behaviour is not susceptible of the distinction between essence and accident, knowledge of it is unavoidably knowledge of its detail: to know only the gist is to know nothing. What has to be learned is not an abstract idea, or a set of tricks, not even a ritual, but a concrete, coherent manner of living in all its intricateness.

It is clear, then, that we must not entertain the hope of acquiring this difficult understanding by easy methods. Though the knowledge we seek is municipal, not universal, there is no short cut to it. Moreover, political education is not merely a matter of coming to understand a tradition, it is learning how to participate in a conversation: it is at once initiation into an inheritance in which we have a life interest, and the exploration of its intimations. There will always remain something of a mystery about how a tradition of political behaviour is learned, and perhaps the only certainty is that there is no point at which learning it can properly be said to begin. The politics of a community are not less individual (and not more so) than its language, and they are learned and practised in the same manner. We do not begin to learn our native language by learning the alphabet, or by learning its grammar; we do not begin by learning words, but words in use; we do not begin (as we begin in reading) with what is easy and go on to what is more difficult; we do not begin at school, but in the cradle; and what we say springs always from our manner of speaking. And this is true also of our political education; it begins in the enjoyment of a tradition, in the observation and imitation of the behaviour of our elders, and there is little or nothing in the world which comes before us as we open our eyes which does not contribute to it. We are aware of a past and a future as soon as we are aware of a present. Long before we are of an age to take interest in a book about our politics we are acquiring that complex and intricate knowledge of our political tradition without which we could not make sense of a book when we come to open it. And the projects we entertain are the creatures of our tradition. The greater part, then—perhaps the most important part—of our political education we acquire haphazard in finding our

way about the world into which we are born, and there is no other way of acquiring it. There will, of course, be more to acquire, and it will be more readily acquired, if we have the good fortune to be born into a rich and lively political tradition and among those who are well educated politically; the lineaments of *political* activity will earlier become distinct: but even the most needy society and the most cramped surroundings have some political education to offer, and we take what we can get.

But if this is the manner of our beginning, there are deeper recesses to explore. Politics are a proper subject for academic study; there is something to think about and it is important that we should think about the appropriate things. Here also, and everywhere, the governing consideration is that what we are learning to understand is a political tradition, a concrete manner of behaviour. And for this reason it is proper that, at the academic level, the study of politics should be an historical study—not, in the first place, because it is proper to be concerned with the past, but because we need to be concerned with the detail of the concrete. It is true that nothing appears on the present surface of a tradition of political activity which has not its roots deep in the past, and that not to observe it coming into being is often to be denied the clue to its significance; and for this reason genuine historical study is an indispensable part of a political education. But what is equally important is not what happened, here or there, but what people have thought and said about what happened: the history, not of political ideas, but of the manner of our political thinking. Every society constructs a legend of its own fortunes which it keeps up to date and in which is hidden its own understanding of its politics; and the historical investigation of this legend—not to expose its errors but to understand its pre-judices—must be a pre-eminent part of a political education. It is, then, in the study of genuine history, and of this quasi-history which reveals in its backward glances the tendencies which are afoot, that we may hope to escape one of the most insidious current mis-understandings of political activity—the misunderstanding in which institutions and procedures appear as pieces of machinery designed to achieve a purpose settled in advance, instead of as manners of behaviour which are meaningless when separated from their con-text: the misunderstanding, for example, in which Mill convinced himself that something called 'Representative Government' was a 'form' of politics which could be regarded as proper to any society which had reached a certain level of what he called 'civilization'.

Nevertheless, to be concerned only with one's own tradition of political activity is not enough. A political education worth the name must embrace, also, knowledge of the politics of other contemporary societies. It must do this because some at least of our political activity is related to that of other people and not to know how they go about attending to their own arrangements is not to know the course they will pursue and not to know what resources to call upon in our own tradition, and because to know only one's own tradition is not to know even that. But here again two observations must be made. We did not begin yesterday to have relations with our neighbours; and we do not require constantly to be hunting outside the tradition of our politics to find some special formula or some merely *ad hoc* expedient to direct those relations. It is only when wilfully or negligently we forget the resources of understanding and initiative which belong to our tradition that, like actors who have forgotten their part, we are obliged to gag. And secondly, the only knowledge worth having about the politics of another society is the same kind of knowledge as we seek of our own tradition. Here also, *la verité reste dans les nuances*; and a comparative study of institutions, for example, which obscured this would provide only an illusory sense of having understood what nevertheless remains a secret. The study of another people's politics, like the study of our own, should be an œcological study of a tradition of behaviour, nor an anatomical study of mechanical devices or the investigation of an ideology. And only when our study is of this sort shall we find ourselves in the way of being stimulated, but not intoxicated, by the manners of others. To range the world in order to select the 'best' of the practices and purposes of others is a corrupting enterprise and one of the surest ways of losing one's political balance; but to investigate the concrete manner in which another people goes about the business of attending to its arrangements may reveal significant passages in our own tradition which might otherwise remain hidden.

There is a third department in the academic study of politics which must be considered—what, for want of a better name, I shall call a philosophical study. Reflection on political activity may take place at various levels: we may consider what resources our political tradition offers for dealing with a certain situation, or we may abridge our political experience into a doctrine, which may be used, as a scientist uses hypothesis, to explore its intimations. But beyond these, and other manners of political thinking, there is a range of reflection the object of which is to consider the place of political activity itself on the map of our total experience. Reflection of this sort has gone on in every society which is politically conscious and intellectually alive; and so far as European societies are concerned, the inquiry has uncovered a variety of problems which each generation has formulated in its own way and has tackled with the technical resources at its disposal. And because political philosophy is not what may be called a 'progressive' science, accumulating solid results and reaching conclusions upon which further investigation may be based with confidence, its history is specially important: indeed, in a sense, it has nothing but a history, which is a history of the problems philosophers have detected and the manner of solution they have proposed, rather than a history of doctrines and systems. The study of this history may be supposed to have a considerable place in a political education, and the enterprise of understanding the turn which contemporary reflection has given to it, an even more considerable place. Political philosophy cannot be expected to increase our ability to be successful in political activity. It will not help us to distinguish between good and bad political projects; it has no power to guide or to direct us in the enterprise of pursuing the intimations of our tradition. But the patient analysis of the general ideas which have come to be connected with political activity—ideas such as nature, artifice, reason, will, law, authority, obligation, etc.—in so far as it succeeds in removing some of the crookedness from our thinking and leads to a more economical use of concepts, is an activity neither to be overrated nor despised. If we pursue it, at least we may hope to be less often cheated by ambiguous statement and irrelevant argument.

Abeunt studia in mores. The fruits of a political education will appear in the manner in which we think and speak about politics and in the manner in which we conduct our political activity. To select items from this prospective harvest must always be hazardous, and opinions will differ about what is most important. But for myself I should hope for two things. The more profound our understanding of political activity, the less we shall be at the mercy of plausible but mistaken analogy, the less we shall be tempted by a false or irrelevant model. And the more thoroughly we understand our own political tradition, the more readily its whole resources are available to us, the less likely we shall be to embrace the illusions which wait for the ignorant and the unwary: the illusion that in politics we can get on without a tradition of behaviour, the illusion that the abridgement of a tradition is itself a sufficient guide, and the illusion that in politics there is anywhere a safe harbour, a destination to be reached or even a detectable strand of progress. 'The world is the best of all possible worlds, and *everything* in it is a necessary evil.'

II

POLITICAL PRINCIPLES
by T. D. Weldon
Fellow of Magdalen College, Oxford

I

IT is not the job of philosophy to provide new information about politics, biology, physics or any other matter of fact. Philosophical problems are entirely second order problems. They are problems, that is, which are generated by the language in which facts are described and explained by those whose function it is to construct and defend scientific, historical and other types of theory.

This is not a revolutionary statement, indeed it is rather platitudinous. As Professor Ryle puts it in his introduction to *The Concept of Mind*, 'The philosophical arguments which constitute this book are intended, not to increase what we know about minds, but to rectify the logical geography of the knowledge we already possess'. The point, however, needs constant repetition, since it is still widely believed that philosophers do, or ought to do, something different from this. Political philosophers in particular are thought to be concerned with the establishment and the demolition of political principles, and it is therefore to be expected that their conclusions will have a direct bearing on the decisions of politicians. They should be qualified to give advice and helpful criticism on actual plans for the framing of legislation, the reform of electoral systems, the government of colonial empires and so on.

This is a strange view. Indeed, one has only to ask 'What qualifications have philosophers as a class for carrying out such a task?' to see that it is a silly view. But philosophers themselves have encouraged it and it dies hard.

But if philosophers are to make no claim to improve either the theories or the methods of those who are engaged on scientific or political activities, is there really anything left for them to do? Are they doomed to technological unemployment? Some have feared that this might indeed be the case. The development of knowledge during the past 400 years is sometimes misrepresented as the gradual partitioning of the old philosophical empire among greedy physicists, biologists and psychologists, and now the last fortress is threatened. The sociologists have laid siege to Moral and Political Philosophy. This is an alarming picture, but fortunately it is based on a complete misunderstanding. No territory has been lost, since none was ever held. What is true is that, especially in the seventeenth and eighteenth centuries, the same man often did two different jobs. Descartes and Leibniz were philosophers as well as physicists. But with the expansion of our knowledge this is no longer practicable and there is no good reason for rejecting the advantages derived from the division of labour in the making of theories any more than in the making of pins.

It is common knowledge that scientific experts such as Sir Arthur Eddington who talk profound sense within their own branch of knowledge, frequently lapse into pompous nonsense when they attempt to discourse on their own theorizing; when, that is to say, they turn from physics or biology to what is solemnly designated 'The Relation of Science to Reality'. Their first order talk is admirable, their second order talk is frequently pathetic. And why should it not be so? They are not expected to construct and repair for themselves all the complex apparatus they use in their laboratories.

The purpose of philosophy, then, is to expose and elucidate linguistic muddles; it has done its job when it has revealed the confusions which have occurred and are likely to recur in inquiries into matter of fact because the structure and use of language are what they are. This does not mean that either natural or technical ways of talking are inherently defective and in need of extensive reconstruction. Sometimes, indeed, they are more open to abuse than they need be, but there are usually compensating advantages to be gained from these defects. Any language is liable to lead to paradox and confusion unless it is studied and employed with reasonable care, but this is not an argument for mistrusting language. Motor cars and safety razors are not fool proof.

2

This prospectus for political philosophy has been widely criticized, both on the ground that the aim which it proposes is trivial and on the ground that it is subversive. To some extent these attacks cancel one another, but they are also in part complementary. I shall first consider very briefly the arguments by which they are separately supported and then go at greater length into the genuine discomfort from which, as it seems to me, they originate.

The argument from triviality is itself rather a trivial affair. Essentially it is that to restrict philosophy to the consideration and analysis of linguistic use is to debase the subject. It is comparable, as one critic has put it, to fiddling while Rome burns. This criticism, however, depends on a somewhat elementary misconception of what is at issue. Nobody has ever supposed that the study of French or English grammar is a substitute for philosophical inquiry; but no important philosopher has ever held that the logical grammar of scientific or natural discourse is unimportant. With what was Plato concerned in the *Theaetetus* and *Sophist*—or Kant in the *Critique of Pure Reason*? Indeed, it is senseless to attempt an inquiry into the use of any language without knowing what that use is, for second order talk presupposes at least competence to handle first order talk.

The idea that philosophical analysis is subversive or sceptical is no better founded. The purpose of philosophy, as already stated, is not to establish or to demolish physical, economic, political or any other principles. It is to clarify their meaning, or to examine their logical force.

These objections, then, fail, but that is by no means all that there is to be said about them. Both spring from a conviction, not always clearly expressed, that there is rather more in this process of analysis than is at first sight apparent. This suspicion is to some extent justified, for though second order talk is not directly concerned with the validity of the first order principles whose logical force it examines, it is a serious overstatement to say that the psychological attitude of those who adhere to such principles is quite unaffected by such examination. To say that political philosophy is concerned with linguistic analysis and with nothing else at least suggests that, since it has no aim except clarification, it can have no effect on actual political beliefs. And this is not true.

'Modern political philosophers do not preach', we say. 'That was the heresy of the nineteenth century. We are plain, honest men who tidy up muddles and have no axe to grind.' Up to a point this is perfectly correct, but the case is somewhat analogous to that of David Hume, from whom modern empiricism chiefly derives its inspiration. What Hume set out to do was not to make scientific or psychological discoveries, but to analyse such concepts as cause, identity, probability and so on. But in spite of the apparent innocence of this project, his philosophical conclusions gave rise to misgiving and indignation among those who claimed special knowledge in virtue of intuition or revelation into theological and metaphysical truth.

In the same sort of way, talk about linguistic analysis and language games, though it is not revolutionary talk about facts (since it is not about facts) has a strongly deflating tendency from a psychological point of view. It inevitably (and quite rightly, in my opinion) deflates a great deal of talk which purports to be about facts, even though they are admittedly facts of a rather special and peculiar type.

As this is a mystifying pronouncement, I will try to elucidate it in the light of some political theorizing which was popular in the nineteenth and early twentieth centuries.

It was necessary for philosophers to make up their minds on the relation between what they claimed to be doing and the investigations of empirical scientists. They might have followed the path pointed out by Hume, but for a number of reasons most of them did not do so. Instead of recognizing that philosophy was a second order study, they attempted to protect it from the 'encroachments' of the scientists by maintaining that it was a first order study of an *a priori* or non-empirical kind. In pursuit of this aim they invented on the one hand a sort of para-science known as 'The Theory of Knowledge' and a para-politics known by various names. 'Political Philosophy', 'Political Theory' and 'Political Science' were all called into service, though this uncertainty in nomenclature itself suggested uncertainty as to the nature of the truths which were to be discovered.

The belief which supported the whole movement was that important discoveries might be made concerning both the 'laws' of nature and the rules of human behaviour by thinking alone. These truths were of such a kind that no evidence gained by observation and experiment could either confirm or refute them. In the philosophical language of the time, they were expressed in *synthetic a priori* propositions. What emerged from this belief was a highly sophisticated language game which teachers played regularly with their pupils and with one another. The purpose of playing the game in this country, as far as it was para-politics, was to give an *a priori* endorsement to the moral and political principles which the educational system inaugurated by Dr. Arnold impressed on the minds of those who were destined to be rulers. Controversies were little if at all concerned with those principles themselves. These were taken over with suitable adaptations from what was accepted as Christian ethics, and the primary aim of moral and political philosophy was to find their foundations. This mattered, or was thought to matter, because, as F. H. Bradley pointed out to Henry Sidgwick, if you chose the wrong foundations (e.g. Utilitarianism), you might find yourself committed to approving conduct which you knew to be wrong.

Hence it was common ground that one could prove the rightness of discipline, thrift, tolerance and other respectable virtues by non-empirical reasoning. It was unnecessary and indeed perilous to consult anthropologists, psychologists or economists on such matters. Philosophers were the only certified consultants, and they alone were qualified to expound the true basis of moral laws and, in the light of this exposition, to appraise political institutions. It is worth noticing that similar high-minded and high-handed proceedings were carried out by the para-scientists. H. W. B. Joseph proved that Einstein was talking nonsense and was neither surprised by nor suspicious of the simplicity of the argument by which he did the trick.

Now the obvious criticism of the whole of this philosophical procedure was that developed by the Viennese Circle in the nineteen-twenties. It was that, since the philosophers had avowedly excluded all factual inquiries from their field of study, their investigations were either linguistic or 'metaphysical' and worthless. In the end, I think this criticism is justified, but the matter is not as simple as the early positivists supposed. As far as political philosophy is concerned, while it is true that this was generally regarded as an *a priori* inquiry, those who practised it certainly believed that they were somehow concerned with what goes on in human associations. They talked little about actual political institutions, but dealt with ghostly or abstract entities, the State, the Individual, Society, the General Will, the Common Good, and so on.

This raises an interesting question which is worth mentioning though I cannot go further into it here, namely, How were these fictitious entities of para-politics supposed to help?, What job were they supposed to do? The answer, I think, lies in a problem which underlies Locke's notion of abstract ideas. What was correctly noted in the seventeenth century and repeated and developed by Kant in the eighteenth century, was the real importance of blueprints, diagrams and models in engineering and other practical activities and their consequent perfectly legitimate force as explanatory techniques. The abstract ideas of political philosophy were supposed to have the same logical power. They had indeed no such power, but the reason why they had not deserves more attention than it has so far received.

But whatever is the answer here, it is certainly true that abstract entities like the State and the Individual are roughly treated by philosophical analysis. This, however, does not affect the issue as regards political principles since the political theories which postulate such entities, as we have seen, take political principles for granted and attempt to provide a philosophical foundation for them. It is a mistake, therefore, to suppose that criticism of a political theory commits us to a rejection of the principles which that theory claims to underwrite; but that this is so becomes clear only when some attention is given to the logical status of political principles themselves.

3

Generally speaking, to cite a principle is to put a stop to demands for reasons and explanation, but the closure is not always of universal application or completely efficacious. Two important truisms are involved here. The first is that demands for reasons and explanations have to stop somewhere; and the second, that no empirical explanation is ever complete.

This needs further explanation, but when it is understood, it is possible to see how it comes about that the application of analysis to political theories tends to give the impression of a confidence trick. It gives rise to the uneasy suspicion that, under the pretence of disposing of political ideologies, the philosopher is trying to recommend his own political principles for general consumption. Although, as will appear, this suspicion is not entirely without foundation, the proceeding is not a discreditable one.

There are plenty of English words and phrases which are commonly employed as explanation stoppers. Some of them, for instance, 'intuition' and 'revelation', suggest that the finality of the principle which is being cited is vouched for by a special method of understanding; others, like 'self-evident', 'indubitable', suggest a special kind of lucidity or intelligibility in what is asserted; others again, like 'obviously' and 'of course', are less specific and less restricted in their use. All, however, have a well recognized linguistic function akin to that performed by 'Keep out' notices. They resemble 'This part of the College is closed to visitors'. Such notices are used arbitrarily. They register decisions, but not always decisions deliberately formulated by a governing body or other formally constituted authority. What is interesting and important about them from our point of view is that they are used with widely varying degrees of confidence and in more or less localized contexts.

This can best be elucidated by reference to the use of principles in the physical sciences, and it is convenient to consider these as they were in the Newtonian era. This avoids introducing modern complications and brings out the analogy (and the lack of it) with political principles which I shall consider later on.

It is self-evident (or apparent to intuition) that perceptual space has three and only three dimensions; and that perceptual time has one and only one dimension. What is the cash value of this principle? Shortly and dogmatically, it is equivalent to 'I cannot envisage any state of affairs in which I should need more (or less) than "above-below", "to the right of—to the left of", "in front of—behind", "before—after" in order to describe the spatio-temporal arrangement of what I observe. I cannot attach any definite meaning to the statement that cuttlefish or the inhabitants of Mars need more or get along with less.'

Two points are to be noted here. It would be incorrect to say that the stop is final. I cannot say 'I know for certain that statements like this are and always will be without significance for any intelligent being whatever'; but it is final in the sense that neither I nor, as far as I know, any other human being has any use for them now. This statement is quite unaffected by the technical terminology which modern physicists make use of for their own special purposes.

Hence, it is possible to be clear about the use of 'self-evident principles' in this context. 'Self-evident' means simply that there is no point (because no clearly assignable meaning) in demands for further explanation or elucidation here. 'How do you know that space has three and only three dimensions?' is an empty question. It can be answered only by re-wording the statement (as I did). Otherwise one can say no more than 'That is how things are'. It is not indeed necessarily meaningless to say, 'They might be otherwise', but to us at present it is in fact meaningless since we are quite unable to say how they might be otherwise. This being so it is reasonable to call 'Space has three and only three dimensions' a linguistic convention, and it does no harm to say that such principles are expressed in *synthetic a priori* propositions provided we recognize that what is at issue is simply a decision that demands for further explanations are here out of place. There is, however, nothing ultimate or inviolable about such decisions. They can be revoked if circumstances alter. New facts such as those inquiries into extra-sensory perception and para-normal psychology are said to reveal, may well lead to a revision of the self-evident principles which are at present generally accepted and which are implicit in our normal use of perception words and personal pronouns.

Few if any other principles of what may roughly be called Newtonian science have the same logical power as the spatio-temporal axiom. But there are others of a somewhat weaker type which are still powerful enough to make the use of 'self-evident' etc., in connection with them intelligible. Take, for instance, the statement 'Everything that happens has a cause'. It is easy to see that this is a principle of a different order. It was an important part of Kant's aim in the *Analytic of Principles* to demonstrate that this difference, though real, was not fundamental; to show, in fact, that the principles of Newton were as ultimate (for human beings) as those of Euclid. But he was quite clear that proof was needed, and few philosophers would now hold that his attempt to provide it was successful. And this is hardly surprising since we handle without difficulty the concepts 'luck', 'chance' and 'accident' in our ordinary discourse. It does not matter that they may ultimately be discarded as useless, that the language of a perfectly intelligent being might not include such words. We still have in our present state a significant employment for 'It was a complete accident I met him yesterday'.

It is, however, convenient for many purposes, notably for a great deal of scientific experimental procedure, to ignore this and to establish some sort of regularity principle such as the conservation of energy, which is treated as unquestionable in a wide but still restricted area of inquiry.

In addition to these types of principle there are others, e.g. the inverse square law, for which a much more restricted claim is made. They are not deemed to be 'self-evident' or 'a priori' at all, but still they are firmly established and are accepted without question. It is, however, possible to see how things might be otherwise than as they are in these respects.

What this comes to is that for purposes of physical investigations, principles can be established, i.e. stop words and phrases can be used with a definite and statable force, either at the level of universal (so far as we know) human characteristics, built in physical limitations; or at the very much lower level of 'We find it convenient for our purposes to accept this as a principle for the time being'; and there are intermediate stages between these.

4

How do political principles compare with those which I considered in the last section? It is at once clear that all political associations have principles. To put it differently, in any State and political party there are some statements which are generally accepted as being beyond question, and of which no explanations are to be demanded. Thus in a Communist State it is pointless to ask for reasons why the means of production should not be privately owned. The only answer which can be given is 'Because profits involve the robbery (or exploitation) of man by man'. It does not require a genius to see that 'because' here is misleading. What is offered is not a reason but simply a restatement of the principle in question. The same may be said of 'explanations' of the rejection of birth-control on principle in Roman Catholic States and of nationalization in the United States (because it restricts freedom of enterprise).

But these principles all seem to correspond to the least powerful level of physical principles. There is nothing but a practical reason (which may still be quite a good one) for giving them the high grade stop sign of 'self-evident' or 'intuitively obvious'. Further reasons and explanations can be asked for, since things might be otherwise, though in a particular association at a particular point in time it may be useless and even perilous to ask for them.

Do any statements of political principles achieve a logically higher grade than this? I do not think that they do and I am not clear that it makes sense to say they ought to do so. Universality was indeed claimed for the Law of Nature (which is in effect a statement of political principles) but it is difficult to see how the claim might be substantiated. Some philosophers would certainly maintain that very general principles such as those enunciated by Kant or those embodied in the American Declaration of Independence have the logical force required; but the trouble here is that, as they stand, they are far too vague to qualify, and, if they are made precise, it can no longer be claimed with much plausibility that they are, or even might be, generally acceptable to all human beings. This, however, is a debatable point and I am not concerned to argue it here. My contention is simply that to assert any proposition as a principle is logically to put it outside discussion in some more or less precisely defined context. Hence it is difficult to see how any principle can significantly claim absolute or non-contextual validity. Furthermore, it appears that (1) political principles have a much more restricted context than some at any rate of the principles which are found in the physical sciences; (2) the adoption of any proposition as a political principle is a matter for decision. Such decision may be reached consciously and deliberately by a controlling authority, but this is by no means always the case.

Now this may easily be mistaken for a first order statement about political associations and as such it has a familiar ring. It may be thought simply to amount to the following:

i. any association possesses some principles (or rules of behaviour. The distinction is unimportant in the present context);

ii. a significant change in the rules constitutes a revolution;

iii. governing classes think poorly of revolutions;

iv. governing classes sanctify what they deem to be the basic or important rules (or principles) by making inquiries into them or demands for explanations of them illegitimate.

This is roughly the Marxist account, and as a partial statement of what tends to happen it is moderately accurate. But my reason for introducing it here is to emphasize that it is irrelevant to the philosophical question in which I am interested. What I am asking is 'Do associations have to have fundamental or basic principles about which no questions may be asked, and, if so, why?' Is this a logical 'must'—part of the meaning of the word 'association', or is it just an empirical fact about associations which may or might be otherwise?

It is safe to say, dogmatically, that the second of these answers is correct. It is indeed part of the meaning of 'association' that there should always be some rules; but there might (logically) be an association in which all the rules were open to question all the time, in which, that is, no propositions had the status of principles. There is, however, an excellent reason why no actual association should be like that, for it is a psychological truism that every man, since life is short, and he has to act in order to stay alive, normally desists from demands for explanations fairly quickly. To appreciate the desirability of doing so is part of the process called 'growing up'.

A similar point to this, which may help to explain what I have in mind, has been emphasized in epistemological discussions in recent years. 'The cat is on the mat' and 'There is a bottle of beer in the cupboard' are basic in the sense that they call for no explanation or inquiry at common-sense level (explanation stops there): but they can be questioned (since no empirical explanation is final) and are in fact challenged by opticians, physiologists and logicians, from different points of view. It is indeed a commonplace that the same table looks different to different people at the same time and to the same person at different times. This can be simply explained when we take into account the relevant conditions (light, perspective, positions of observers and so on). Certainly such differences should not lead us to suppose either that there is really no table there or that no statement made about the table by any observer is ever true. All that is involved is the unmysterious fact that everybody sees things from his own point of view. This, however, is itself a 'self-evident' epistemological principle. I cannot give any precise meaning to 'I might feel your toothache'.

So, epistemologically considered, is 'Everyone has his own sentiments, adopts his own attitudes, formulates his own value judgments, decides on his own political principles'. These ways of speaking differ only idiomatically. I do not mean that anyone sits down, excogitates propositions like 'The private ownership of the means of production is intolerable' and then decides that this proposition is 'self-evident', 'a revealed truth' or some equivalent phrase. There are all sorts of explanations, historical, psycho-analytical, historical, etc., of the fact that this particular individual attaches 'Keep off' notices, or confers immunity from further inquiry on one set of propositions rather than another. All that matters politically is that he does confer it, and confers it where he does. He may or may not have good and statable reasons for conferring it, but these justify and do not entail the conferring.

It is therefore not at all a surprising truth that groups of people who live together tend to confer this status on the same sets of propositions. Recalcitrants either conceal their preferences or end by being forced to be free in Wormwood Scrubbs or Broadmoor. It is also unsurprising that psychological stops are frequently, but not always, accompanied by linguistic stops. It is pointless in this country to ask whether freedom is a good thing. The linguistic job of the 'revelation' and 'intuition' family of words is largely to bring about this agreement.

I hope that this examination disposes of the point at issue, namely

'Does linguistic analysis of "political principles" beg an important question?' More specifically, 'Does it aim at selling a favoured ideology under the pretence of being down to earth and anti-ideological?' The answer is 'No, except in an accidental and perfectly blameless way'.

Everyone can decide what are his own political principles. This really says no more than 'All men are human'. And it is no part of the job of philosophy to criticize language in the sense of recommending an ideally antiseptic language which can give rise to no confusions and create no paradoxes. Russell, indeed, has yearned for this, but it is still not a sensible aim. The job is to reveal the confusions and misunderstandings which may follow from the careless or uncriticized use of language as it is. Philosophically in the context in which I am now talking, it is to show that there is nothing logically disreputable about my own or anyone else's political intuitions, revelations, value judgments or whatever else you prefer to call them. Any particular set of them may be (and should be) criticized on non-philosophical grounds. They may be, and often are, of shady origin, lead to unforeseen and undesired consequences, be internally incoherent, be accepted without argument and under threats from a self-styled arbiter of faith and morals, and so on. But what I am interested in here is solely their logical function as stop signs.

If this point is agreed, I see no reason why a philosopher or a clergyman or a communist should not advocate his own views. And there is in particular no reason why anyone who is engaged in second order talk about politics should not use his own first order principles as examples. He naturally feels more comfortable with them than he does with those of other people. Certainly in choosing these as examples he is not performing as a philosopher, but he is not acting as a crook either.

What is dishonest is to misstate the logical character of such pronouncements and to claim special status for them; that is, to pretend that they are like the highest grade of physical principles when they are in fact like the lowest. Some writers even claim that political principles are, in some unexplained sense, logically superior even to *synthetic a priori* statements about perceptual space. I do not pretend to know what this means.

Such irresponsible up-grading inevitably leads to trouble in talk about 'Fundamental human rights'—but even this kind of talk is innocuous when the logical grammar of it is understood. Such

D

understanding, however, is unlikely to be popular with contemporary 'dealers in magic and spells'.

5

The points to which I wish to direct attention in this paper may be summarized as follows:

1. To claim for a statement that it asserts a political principle is to claim for it exemption from questioning in a particular context. Linguistically such claims are often made by employing such words as 'intuition', 'self-evident', 'obviously', etc. These function as stop signs, in the same sort of way as 'Keep off the grass' notices.

2. Such notices do not have to be set up anywhere in particular, indeed, they do not (logically) have to be used at all. But there are overwhelming practical reasons for using them and, in any actual society, for having a wide measure of agreement as to their location.

3. Anyone who is occupied with second order or philosophical talk about political institutions tends to use his own principles as instances.

4. This practice may encourage the reader to suppose that these principles are being recommended for more general adoption. So they are. But this recommendation has nothing to do with the author's activity as a philosopher. For this purpose any set of principles would do equally well.

5. Nevertheless, the importance of such second order talk should not be underrated. It is inevitably much resented by those who claim that their private principles are not simply the product of human decisions but have some logically superior status.

6. It is a philosophical obligation on those who make such a claim to explain clearly what this superior status is or might be.

III

NATURAL RIGHTS

by Margaret Macdonald

Late Reader in Philosophy, Bedford College, University of London

DOCTRINES of natural law and natural rights have a long and impressive history from the Stoics and Roman jurists to the Atlantic Charter and Roosevelt's Four Freedoms.[1] That men are entitled to make certain claims by virtue simply of their common humanity has been equally passionately defended and vehemently denied. Punctured by the cool scepticism of Hume; routed by the contempt of Bentham for 'nonsense upon stilts'; submerged by idealist and Marxist philosophers in the destiny of the totalitarian state; the claim to 'natural rights' has never been quite defeated. It tends in some form to be renewed in every crisis in human affairs, when the plain citizen tries to make, or expects his leaders to make, articulate his obscure, but firmly held, conviction that he is not a mere pawn in any political game, nor the property of any government or ruler, but the living and protesting individual for whose sake all political games are played and all governments instituted. As one of Cromwell's soldiers expressed it to that dictator: 'Really, sir, I think that the poorest he that is in England hath a life to live as the greatest he.'[2]

It could, perhaps, be proved hedonistically that life for most ordinary citizens is more *comfortable* in a democratic than a totalitarian state. But would an appeal for effort, on this ground, have been sanctioned between 1939–45? However true, it would have been rejected as inefficient because *uninspired*. Who could be moved to endure 'blood and toil, tears and sweat' for the sake of a little extra comfort? What, then, supplied the required inspiration? An appeal to the instinct of national self-preservation? But societies have been known to collapse inexplicably almost without waiting to be physically defeated. No doubt there are several answers, but at least one, I suggest, was an appeal to the values of freedom and equality among men. An appeal to safeguard and restore, where necessary, the Rights of Man, those ultimate points at which

---

[1] Freedom of Speech and Worship; Freedom from Want and Fear of all persons everywhere.

[2] *Clarke Papers*, vol. 1, p. 301.

authority and social differences vanish, leaving the solitary individual with his essential human nature, according to one political theory, or a mere social fiction, according to another.

All this sounds very obscure. And the doctrine of natural law and of the natural rights of men is very obscure—which justifies the impatience of its opponents. It seems a strange law which is un-written, has never been enacted, and may be unobserved without penalty, and peculiar rights which are possessed antecedently to all specific claims within an organized society. Surely, it will be said, the whole story now has only historical interest as an example of social mythology? Nothing is so dead as dead ideology. All this may be true,[1] but nevertheless the doctrine is puzzling. For if it is sheer nonsense why did it have psychological, political and legal effects? Men do not reflect and act upon collections of meaningless symbols or nonsense rhymes.

There seems no doubt that the assertions of certain Greek philoso-phers about the 'natural' equality of men and their consequent right to freedom caused intelligent contemporaries to become uneasy about the institution of slavery;[2] that doctrines of the primal Rights of Man were significantly connected with the French and American Revolutions. It even seems probable that the Communist Manifesto owed much of its success not to its 'scientific' analysis of capitalist society, but to its denouncement of a wage slavery degrading to human nature and its appeal to all workers to assert their equal brotherhood. A major crime of capitalist society for Marx and Engels was that it had destroyed all ties between men other than naked self-interest and had 'resolved personal worth into exchange value'. Only after the proletarian revolution would *human* history begin and men treat each other as equal human beings, not as exploiter and exploited. The object of the transfer of class power is to end class power and to reveal or restore some essential human nature at present disguised by distorting social relationships.

So even if the theory were dead, the puzzle of its effects would remain, and suggest that it had been introduced to solve a genuine problem of political and social philosophy. And it is interesting, therefore, to inquire what the problem was; whether it has found an alternative solution, or is bogus and insoluble.

Why should people have supposed, and, as I believe, continue to

[1] It is not quite true, for the doctrines of natural law and consequent natural rights flourish in Catholic social philosophy. See e.g. *The Rights of Man and Natural Law* by Jacques Maritain; 1944.

[2] Cf. *The Open Society*, by K. Popper; vol. 1, esp. pp. 58–9.

suppose, in obscure fashion, that they have 'natural' rights, or rights as human beings, independently of the laws and governments of any existing society? It is, surely, partly at least, because no existing social compulsion or relationship is self-justifying. Men may always ask why they should or should not endure it and expect a convincing answer. And, ultimately, it would seem, they may challenge the dictates of all existing governments and the pressures of every society if they find them eqally oppressive, i.e. if they deny what the individual considers his fundamental 'right'. But since, *ex hypothesi*, this 'right' is denied by every existing law and authority, it must be a right possessed independently of them and derived from another source. If, e.g., the laws of every existing society condemn a human being to be a slave, he, or another on his behalf, may yet hold that he has a 'right' to be free. What sort of proposition is this and how is such a claim to be justified? This seems to be one most important problem which the doctrine of natural rights tried to solve.

Natural Law, Natural Laws and Natural Rights

There are an indefinite number of different types of propositions and other forms of human utterance. I will, for my present purpose, notice three. (1) Tautological or analytic propositions which state rules for the uses of symbols or which follow from such rules within a linguistic or logical system. (2) Empirical or contingent propositions which state matter of fact and existence. Propositions which describe what does or may occur in the world and not the symbolic techniques employed in such description. (3) Assertions or expressions of value. With the help of this classification it may be possible to show that some of the difficulties of the doctrine of natural rights have been due to an attempt to interpret propositions about natural rights as a curious hybrid of types (1) and (2) of the above classification.

For in the theory which conceived of natural rights as guaranteed by a 'natural' law, the position seems to have been considered in the following terms. The 'rights' of a slave, e.g. derive from the laws in any society which govern his artificial status as a slave. Yet he has a right to be free. But in virtue of what status and law? Only it seems by his status of being a man like other men. This, however, is a natural status as opposed to one determined by social convention. Every man is human 'by nature'; no human being is 'by nature' a slave of another human being. There must then be an essential human nature which determines this status and a law governing the relations of human beings as such, independently of the laws of all particular societies concerning their artificial relationships. But essential human nature or human 'essence' is constituted by those propertie‹ expressed in the definition of 'human being'. And what is expressed or entailed by a definition is a necessary or analytic proposition. Thus by a logical fusion of the characteristics of two different types of proposition, statements about natural rights tended in this theory to be represented as statements of a necessary natural fact.

But not even statements of actual fact, necessary or contingent. For another element intervened. Though the slave had an actual 'right' to be free, he was not free, because no existing law admitted his right. Because laws were imperfect, he was not free though he 'ought' to be. And this introduces into the situation a further complication. By nature a man must be that which yet he is not. Or, it follows from the definition of 'human being' that every human being is, or must be, free—or possess any other 'natural' right though his freedom is ideal and not real. But the ideal as well as the actual is natural fact.

Thus the Roman lawyers who gave the earliest authoritative statements of the doctrine of natural law, conceived of natural law as an ideal or standard, not yet completely exemplified in any existing legal code, but also as a standard fixed by nature to be discovered and gradually applied by men. And the good lawyer kept his eye on this standard as the good gardener keeps his eye fixed on the prize rose which he is hoping to reproduce among his own blooms next summer. For the lawyer, said Ulpian, is not merely the interpreter of existing laws but also the priest or guardian of justice, which is the 'fixed and abiding disposition to give every man his right'.[1] This standard was not determined by men, but by nature, or, sometimes, by God. It was fact and not fancy.

The institution of slavery showed that no existing code was perfectly just. Thus natural *law* is only imperfectly realized in positive *laws*. And it is significant that the lawyers and later political theorists who adopted this distinction talked only of natural *law* and *the* Law of Nature, never of natural laws and laws of nature. But what is most characteristic of legal codes and systems is that they consist of many laws, regulating the different relations of men as debtor and creditor, property owner and thief, employer and

[1] Sabine: *History of Political Theory*, p. 170.

employee, husband and wife, etc. But natural law was not conceived of as consisting of ideal regulations corresponding to all positive laws. Indeed, if completely realized, some positive laws would be abolished, e.g. those relating to slave owner and slave. Natural law was not formulated in natural *laws*. It was neither written nor customary and might even be unknown. But it applies, nevertheless, to all men everywhere whether they are debtors or creditors, masters or servants, bond or free. But how is it discovered?

It seems probable that the concept of natural law influenced the later conception of natural or scientific laws obtained by the observation of natural events. For natural law applies impartially to all men in all circumstances, as the law of gravitation applies to all bodies. But the law of gravitation is obtained by deduction from the observation of bodies in sense perception. Are the Law of Nature and the Rights which it implies known by similar observation of the nature of man? The law of gravitation, like all other laws of nature, states a uniformity exemplified in the actual movements of natural bodies. But no existing society may observe the Law of Nature or guarantee natural rights. These cannot, therefore, have been learned from observation of the actual practice of existing societies.

'Man is born free', said Rousseau, 'and everywhere he is in chains.' What sort of proposition is this? Did Rousseau observe ten or ten million babies immediately after birth and record when the infant limbs were manacled? The law of nature applies to all men equally, said Cicero. For if we had not been corrupted by bad habits and customs 'no one would be so like his own self as all men would be like others'.[1] But since everyone everywhere has been subjected to customs and laws of varying degrees of imperfection, where and when did Cicero observe our uncorrupted nature? How can facts about nature be discovered which have never been observed or confirmed by observation?

The answer lies in the peculiar status given to reason in the theory. Propositions about natural law and natural rights are not generalizations from experience nor deductions from observed facts subsequently confirmed by experience. Yet they are not totally disconnected from natural fact. For they are known as entailed by the intrinsic or essential nature of man. Thus they are known by reason. But they are entailed by the proposition that an essential property of men is that they have reason. The standard of natural law is set by reason and is known because men have reason. But that men

[1] *Laws*, Bk. 1, 10, 28–9 (trans. C. W. Keyes).

have reason, i.e. are able to deduce the ideal from the actual, is a natural fact. And it is by having this specific, and natural, characteristic of being rational that men resemble each other and differ from the brutes. Reason is the great leveller or elevator. According to Sir Frederick Pollock, 'Natural law was conceived to be an ultimate principle of fitness with regard to the nature of man as a rational and social being which is, or ought to be, the justification of every form of positive law'.[1] 'There is, in fact', said Cicero, 'a true law—namely right reason—which is in accordance with nature, applies to all men and is unchangeable and eternal.'[2] And for Grotius, too, 'The law of nature is a dictate of right reason'.[3]

Let it be admitted that all or most human beings are intelligent or rational. And that what is known by reason is certainly true. But, also, what can be known by unaided reason is what *must* be true, and perhaps what *ought* to be but never what *is* true of matter of fact. And statements which are logically certain are tautological or analytic and are neither verified nor falsified by what exists. Statements about what ought to be are of a peculiar type which will be discussed later, but it is certain that they say nothing about what *is*. Because it is confused on these distinctions, the theory of natural law and natural rights constantly confounds reason with right and both with matter of fact and existence. The fact that men do reason is thought to be somehow a natural or empirical confirmation of what is logically deduced by reason as a standard by which to judge the imperfections of what exists.

The Social Contract

Though the Roman lawyers conceded that a man might be entitled by natural law to that which he was denied by every positive law, they do not seem to have related this to any particular doctrine of legal and political authority. But in the seventeenth century the doctrines of natural law and natural rights were directly connected with the contract theory of the State. Because he is rational, Locke emphasized, man is subject to the law of nature even before the establishment of civil society. And he never ceases to be so subject. By right of the law of nature men lived in a state of freedom, equality and the possession of property 'that with which a man hath mixed his labour'. True, this picture differs from that of Hobbes whose 'natural man' is constantly at war, possesses only the

[1] The History of the Law of Nature; *Essays in the Law*, 1922.
[2] *Republic*, Bk. 3, p. 22 (trans. Sabine and Smith).   [3] Bk. 1, ch. 1, sec. x, 1.

right to preserve his life, if he can, but usually finds it short and nasty. Nevertheless, even Hobbes's unpleasant savages have sufficient sense, or reason, to enable them to escape their 'natural' predicament. Locke's natural individualists are peaceful property owners who nevertheless sometimes dispute and want an impartial arbitrator. Civil society is formed by compact that natural rights may be better preserved. Man did not enter society, said Paine, to become *worse* than he was before by surrendering his natural rights but only to have them better secured. His natural rights are the foundation of all his civil rights. It was essential for the social contract theorists to deny that all rights are the gift of civil society, since existing societies denied certain rights which they affirmed. In order to claim them, therefore, it was supposed that they had been enjoyed or were such as would be enjoyed by rational creatures in a 'natural' as opposed to an established society. The Declaration of the French Revolutionary Assembly enunciated the Rights of Man and of citizens; the two being distinct.

His 'natural' rights attach, by virtue of his reason, to every man much as do his arms and legs. He carries them about with him from one society to another. He cannot lose them without losing himself. 'Men are born free and equal', said the French Assembly, 'in respect of their *natural* and *imprescriptible* rights of liberty, property, security and resistance of oppression.'[1] The framers of the American Declaration of Independence declare as self-evident truths that all men are created equal, that they are endowed by their creator with certain inalienable rights, among which are Life, Liberty and the Pursuit of Happiness and that governments are instituted to secure these rights.[2] The free people of Virginia proclaimed[3] that the rights with which men enter society they cannot by any compact deprive themselves or their posterity.

These were self-evident truths about a state which men might have left or not yet attained but which was 'natural' to them as opposed to accidental or conventional. A person is accidentally a native of England, France, America; a Red Indian, negro or Jew. His social environment is determined by accident of birth. He may change his family by adoption and his citizenship by naturalization. And he is accidentally, or conventionally, a doctor, soldier, employer, etc. These conventionalities determine his civic and legal

[1] Declaration of the Rights of Man and of Citizens, by the National Assembly of France, 1791.
[2] Declaration of Independence of the United States of America—July 4, 1776.
[3] The Virginia Declaration of Rights—June 12, 1776.

rights in a particular society. But he is not accidentally human. Humanity is his essence or nature. There is no essence of 'being Greek' or 'being English'; of 'being a creditor' or 'being an old age pensioner' all of which properties, however, might be the basis of civil rights. The nature of man determines his 'natural' rights. And since, though not accidental, it also seemed to be a matter of fact that men exist and are rational, rights claimed on account of this fact seemed also to be natural and to follow from the essence of man, even though they might be denied. But the essence of man is expressed in the definition of the word 'man'. So that the statement 'Men have natural rights' is equivalent to the prepositional function 'x is human entails x has natural rights' which is a tautology. Again the ambiguity inherent in the theory between what is necessary and what is natural, is revealed. It is hard to believe that a barren tautology generated the ardours of that time in which it was good to be alive and to be young was 'very heaven'.[1] But what is meant by the nature or essence of man by 'being rational' or 'having reason'?

Rights and Reason

" 'Man' equals 'rational animal' Df." is the fossil preserved in logic text books since Aristotle. It was never accompanied by any adequate account of the meaning of 'rational' which was, however, generally assumed to include the capacity to abstract and generalize by the use of symbols in speech and writing; to formulate and understand general propositions and laws and to perceive necessary or logical connections between propositions. It is true that Aristotle himself used the term 'reason' more widely to include the practical intelligence manifested in various skills and the appropriate behaviour of the well-trained character in various moral situations. But usually reason is conceived to be the capacity by which men understand abstractions. This was certainly Kant's view. To be rational is to be able to think abstractly. And the most characteristic activities of men, including living in societies, are due to this capacity to use reason. It is peculiar to men and shared by no other animal. Hence the basis of the equality of men for the exponents of natural law, and of their intrinsic worth for Kant is the fact that they all have reason. Men share all other characteristics with the brutes and might themselves have them in varying degrees, but reason was alike in all

---

[1] Wordsworth in *The French Revolution.*

men, it was man's defining characteristic. Hence it is the foundation, too, of his natural rights, as a human being.

It is probable that other animals do not abstract and generalize for they do not use symbols. But neither is it true that all men do this with equal skill. Reason, in this sense, is no less or no more invariable among human beings than sense perception, and the rights of man might as well depend upon eyesight as upon rationality. But if the term reason is to be used more widely to include non-verbal manifestations of intelligence, knowing-how as well as knowing-that,[1] then intelligence does not set an unbridgeable gulf between men and other living creatures. For in many activities, those, e.g. of hunting, building, fighting, and even social organization, other creatures display skill, adaptability of means to ends, and other characteristics which are evidence of intelligence in men. And as for social life, ants use tools, domesticate other insects, and live a highly organized social life. Bees and wasps manage their affairs by a complicated system of government. Moreover, many of the most characteristic human activities depend very little on abstract thought or use of symbols, e.g. cooking, sewing, knitting, carpentry. And at a higher level the excellence of pictures, sculptures, symphonies, is not due to their expression of abstract thought. But where in this variety are we to find the constant factor by which to determine human rights? What passport will admit to the Kingdom of Ends?

What may be agreed is that only at a certain level of intellectual development do men claim natural rights. Savages do not dream of life, liberty and the pursuit of happiness. For they do not question what is customary. Neither do the very depressed and downtrodden. It was not the slaves who acclaimed their right to be free but the philosophers and lawyers. Marx and Engels were not themselves wage slaves of the industrial system. It is generally agreed that the doctrines of natural rights, natural law and the social contract, are individualistic. To claim rights as an individual independently of society, a man must have reached a level of self-consciousness which enables him to isolate himself in thought from his social environment. This presupposes a considerable capacity for abstraction. To this extent natural rights, or the ability to claim natural rights, depends on reason. But it does not follow from this that reason alone constitutes the specific nature of man or that the

---

[1] See Presidential Address to the Aristotelian Society by Professor G. Ryle, 1945, and *The Concept of Mind*, 1949, ch. II.

worth of human beings is determined solely by their I.Q.s. Reason is only one human excellence.

But the Aristotelian dream of fixed natures pursuing common ends dies hard. It reappears in M. Maritain's account of the Rights of Man cited earlier. He says, e.g.:

> . . . there is a human nature and this human nature is the same in all men . . . and possessed of a nature, constituted in a given determinate fashion, man obviously possesses ends which correspond to his natural constitution and which are the same for all—as all pianos, for instance, whatever their particular type and in whatever spot they may be, have as their end the production of certain attuned sounds. If they do not produce these sounds, they must be attuned or discarded as worthless . . . since man has intelligence and can determine his ends, it is up to him to put himself in tune with the ends necessarily demanded by his nature.[1]

And men's rights depend upon this common nature and end by which they are subject to the natural or 'unwritten' law. But this seems to me a complete mistake. Human beings are not like exactly similar bottles of whisky each marked 'for export only' or some device indicating a common destination or end. Men do not share a fixed nature, nor, therefore, are there any ends which they must necessarily pursue in fulfilment of such nature. There is no definition of 'man'. There is a more or less vague set of properties which characterize in varying degrees and proportions those creatures which are called 'human'. These determine for each individual human being what he *can* do but not what he *must* do. If he has an I.Q. of 85 his intellectual activities will be limited; if he is physically weak he cannot become a heavyweight boxer. If a woman has neither good looks nor acting ability she is unlikely to succeed as a film star. But what people may do with their capacities is extremely varied, and there is no one thing which they must do in order to be human. It would be nonsense to say: 'I am not going to be an actress, a school teacher, a postman, a soldier, a taxpayer, but simply a human being.' For what is the alternative? A man may choose whether he will become a civil servant or a schoolmaster; a conservative or a socialist, but he cannot choose whether he will be a man or a dog. There is certainly a sense in which it is often said that in the air-raid shelter or in the battle people forgot that they were officers or privates, assistant secretaries or typists, rich or poor, and remembered only that they were all human beings, i.e. all liable to die without regard to status. But that is always true. They did not remember that they were something *in addition* to being the

Loc. cit., p. 35.

particular human being they each were and which they might be
without being any particular individual. And, as individuals, when
the 'All Clear' sounded, each returned to pursue his or her own
ends, not the purpose of the human race. Certainly, many human
beings may co-operate in a joint enterprise to achieve a particular
end which each chooses. But that cannot be generalized into the
spectacle of all human beings pursuing one end. There is no end
set for the human race by an abstraction called 'human nature'.
There are only ends which individuals choose, or are forced by
circumstances to accept. There are none which they *must* accept.
Men are not created for a purpose as a piano is built to produce
certain sounds. Or if they are we have no idea of the purpose.

It is the emphasis on the individual sufferer from bad social
conditions which constitutes the appeal of the social contract theory
and the 'natural' origin of human rights. But it does not follow
that the theory is true as a statement of verifiable fact about the
actual constitution of the world. The statements of the Law of
Nature are not statements of the laws of nature, not even of the
laws of an 'ideal' nature. For nature provides no standards or ideals.
All that exists, exists at the same level, or is of the same logical type.
There are not, by nature, prize roses, works of art, oppressed or
unoppressed citizens. Standards are determined by human choice,
not set by nature independently of men. Natural events cannot tell
us what we ought to do until we have made certain decisions, when
knowledge of natural fact will enable the most efficient means to be
chosen to carry out those decisions. Natural events themselves have
no value, and human beings as natural existents have no value either,
whether on account of possessing intelligence or having two feet.

One of the major criticisms of the doctrine of natural rights is that
the list of natural rights varies with each exponent. For Hobbes,
man's only natural right is self-preservation. More 'liberal' theorists
add to life and security; liberty, the pursuit of happiness and sometimes property. Modern socialists would probably include the right
to 'work or adequate maintenance'. M. Maritain enumerates a list
of nine natural rights which include besides the rights to life, liberty,
and property of the older formulations, the right to pursue a religious vocation, the right to marry and raise a family, and, finally,
the right of every human being to be treated as a person and not as
a thing.[1] It is evident that these 'rights' are of very different types
which would need to be distinguished in a complete discussion of

[1] *Loc. cit.*, p. 60.

the problem. My aim in this paper, however, is only to try to understand what can be meant by the assertion that there are some rights to which human beings are entitled independently of their varying social relationships. And it seems difficult to account for the wide variations in the lists of these 'rights' if they have all been deduced from a fixed human nature or essence, subject to an absolutely uniform 'natural law'. Nor is the disagreement one which can be settled by more careful empirical observation of human beings and their legal systems. The doctrine seems to try to operate by an analogy which it is logically impossible to apply.

The word 'right' has a variety of uses in ordinary language, which include the distinction between 'legal right' and 'moral right'. 'A has a legal right against B' entails B has a duty to A which will be enforced by the courts. A has a claim against B recognized by an existing law. No person has a legal right which he cannot claim from some other (legal) person and which the law will not enforce. That A has a moral right against B likewise entails that B has a duty to A. But it is not necessarily a duty which can be legally enforced. A has a right to be told the truth by B and B has a corresponding duty to tell A the truth. But no one, except in special circumstances recognized by law, can force B to tell the truth, or penalize him, except by censure, if he does not. No one can, in general, claim to be told the truth, by right, under penalty. But a creditor can claim repayment of a debt or sue his debtor.

When the lawyers said that a slave had a right in natural law to be free, they thought of a legal right not provided for by any existing statute, enactment or custom and to whose universal infringement no penalties attached. But this, surely, is the vanishing point of law and of legal right? It indicates that there just wasn't a law or legal right by which a slave might demand his freedom. But perhaps there was a moral right and a moral obligation. The slave ought to be free and maybe it was the duty of every slaveholder to free his slaves and of legislators to enact laws forbidding slavery. But until this happened there was no law which forbade a man to keep slaves. Consequently, there is no point in saying there was 'really' a natural law which forbade this. For the natural law was impotent. Statements about natural law were neither statements of natural fact nor legal practice.

So, does it follow that a 'natural' right is just a 'moral' right? Kant said, in effect, that to treat another human being as a person, of intrinsic worth, an end in himself, is just to treat him in accordance with the moral law applicable to all rational beings on account of their having reason. But this is not quite the sense in which the term 'natural rights' has been historically used. Declarations of the Rights of Man did not include his right to be told the truth, to have promises kept which had been made to him, to receive gratitude from those he had benefited, etc. The common thread among the variety of natural rights is their *political* character. Despite their rugged individualism, no exponent of the Rights of Man desired to enjoy them, in solitude, on a desert island. They were among the articles of the original Social Contract; clauses in Constitutions, the inspiration of social and governmental reforms. But 'Keep promises'; 'Tell the truth'; 'Be grateful' are not inscribed on banners carried by aggrieved demonstrators or circulated among the members of an oppressed party. Whether or not morality can exist without society, it is certain that politics cannot. Why then were 'natural rights' conceived to exist independently of organized society and hence of political controversies? I suggest that they were so considered in order to emphasize their basic or fundamental character. For words like freedom, equality, security, represented for the defenders of natural rights what they considered to be the fundamental moral and social values which should be or should continue to be realized in any society fit for intelligent and responsible citizens.

When the contract theorists talked of the rights as human beings which men had enjoyed in the state of nature, they seemed to be asserting unverifiable and nonsensical propositions since there is no evidence of a state of nature in which men lived before the establishment of civil societies. But they were not simply talking nonsense. They were, in effect, saying 'In any society and under every form of government men ought to be able to think and express their thoughts freely; to live their lives without arbitrary molestation with their persons and goods. They ought to be treated as equal in value, though not necessarily of equal capacity or merit. They ought to be assured of the exclusive use of at least some material objects other than their own bodies; they ought not to be governed without some form of consent. And that the application of these rights to the particular conditions of a society, or their suspension, if necessary, should be agreed with them'. The exponents of the natural Rights of Man were trying to express what they deemed to be the fundamental conditions of *human* social life and government.

And it is by the observance of some such conditions, I suggest, that human societies are distinguished from ant hills and beehives.

This, however, has frequently been denied by utilitarian, idealist and marxist philosophers who, though differing in other respects, agree in holding that the rights of an individual must be determined only by the needs and conveniences of society as a whole. Surely, they say, there can be no 'natural' right to life in any society when a man may be executed as a criminal or killed as a conscripted soldier. And very little right to liberty exists when external danger threatens the state. 'The person with rights and duties', says the evolutionist utilitarian Ritchie, 'is the product of society and the rights of the individual must, therefore, be judged from the point of view of society as a whole and not the society from the point of view of the individual.'[1] It is the duty of the individual to preserve society for his descendants. For individuals perish but England remains. But the plain man may well ask why he must preserve a society for his descendants if it neither is, nor shows any prospect of being, worth living in? Will his descendants thank him for this consideration? All that seems to follow from Ritchie's view is that at any time the members of a society may agree to sacrifice some goods in order to achieve a certain result. And the result will include the restoration of basic rights. Does the ordinary citizen consider that he has no right to life and liberty because he agrees to (or does not protest against) the suspension of those rights in an emergency? He would be very unlikely to approve of such suspension if he thought the result would be the massacre or enslavement of himself, his contemporaries and possibly his children and descendants at the arbitrary will of a ruler or government. To suspend, or even to forfeit rights, as a criminal does, also temporarily, is not to deny rights. Nor is it to deny that such practices must be justified to the individuals required to submit to them. Though it may be much more useful to society that a man should remain a slave and even that he may be happier in that condition, it is not possible to prove to him that he has no right to be free, however much society wants his slavery. In short, 'natural rights' are the conditions of a good society. But what those conditions are is not given by nature or mystically bound up with the essence of man and his inevitable goal, but is determined by human decisions.

[1] Ritchie: *Natural Rights*, p. 101.

Propositions and Decisions

Assertions about natural rights, then, are assertions of what ought to be as the result of human choice. They fall within class 3 of the division stated on page 37, as being ethical assertions or expressions of value. And these assertions or expressions include all those which result from human choice and preference, in art and personal relations, e.g. as well as in morals and politics. Such utterances in which human beings express choices determined by evaluation of better and worse have been variously interpreted, and it is, indeed, difficult to introduce a discussion of the topic without assuming an interpretation. I have tried, e.g. to avoid the use of the words 'proposition' and 'statement' in referring to these utterances since these words emphasize a relation between what is asserted and a fact by which it is verified or falsified. And this leads either to the attempts of the natural law and natural rights theories to find a 'natural' fact which justifies these assertions or to a search for non-sensible entities called 'Values' as the reference of ethical terms. Yet, of course, it is, in some sense, true that 'No one ought to be ill-treated because he is a Jew, a negro or not able to count above ten.' Alternatively, to talk of 'expressions of value' sounds as though such utterances are sophisticated ways of cheering and cursing. Just as the blow becomes sublimated into the sarcastic retort so our smiles of delight at unselfish action and howls of woe at parricide become intellectualized into apparent judgments about good and evil, right and wrong, without, however, losing their fundamentally emotive character.[1] On this view, value judgments do not state what is true or false but are expressions of feeling, sometimes combined with commands to do or forbear. But whatever its emotional causes and effects, an articulate utterance does not seem to be simply a substitute for a smile or a tear. It *says* something. But I cannot hope in a necessarily brief discussion to do justice to the enormous variety of value utterances. So I will plunge, and say that value utterances are more like records of *decisions* than propositions.[2] To assert that 'Freedom is better than slavery' or 'All men are of equal worth' is not to state a fact but to *choose a side*. It announces *This is where I stand*.

I mentioned earlier that in the late war propaganda appeals to defend our comforts and privileges would have been rejected as uninspiring but that appeals to defend the rights of all men to

[1] Cf. A. J. Ayer: *Language, Truth and Logic*, ch. 6.
[2] Dr. K. R. Popper makes a similar distinction in an interesting discussion of value judgments in *The Open Society*, vol. 1, ch. 5.

freedom and equality obtained the required response, at least in all but the depraved and cynical. I now suggest that they did so because they accorded with our decisions about these ultimate social values. For whether or not we were more or less comfortable as a result, we should not choose to act only upon orders about which we had not in some way been consulted; to suppress the truth; to imprison without trial or to permit human individuals or classes of individuals to be treated as of no human value.

Two questions suggest themselves on this view. Firstly, if ethical judgments, and particularly the ethical judgments which concern the fundamental structure of society are value decisions, who makes these decisions and when? Is this not, as much as the natural law theory, the use of an analogy without application? I did safeguard myself to some extent by saying that these assertions are 'more like' decisions than they are like propositions. They are unlike propositions because they are neither tautologies nor statements of verifiable fact. But it is also true that if asked when we decided in favour of free speech or democratic government or many of our social values we could not give a date. It is, therefore, suggested that we no more record a decision by a value assertion than we signed a Social Contract. Nevertheless, I think the analogy does emphasize important differences between value and other assertions. For, if intelligent, we do choose our politics as we choose our friends or our favoured poems, novels, pictures, symphonies, and as we do not choose to accept Pythagoras's theorem or the law of gravitation. And when challenged we affirm our decision or stand by our choice. We say, 'I did not realize how much I valued free speech until I went to Germany in 1936', indicating that a choice had been made, but so easily that it had seemed scarcely necessary to record its occurrence.

For, indeed, the fundamental values of a society are not always recorded in explicit decisions by its members, even its rulers, but are expressed in the life of the society and constitute its quality. They are conveyed by its 'tone' and atmosphere as well as its laws and Statutory Rules and Orders. The members of a society whose values are freedom and equality behave differently, walk, speak, fight differently from the members of a slave society. Plato expressed this nastily in the Republic[1] when he said that in a democracy even the horses and asses behaved with a gait expressive of remarkable freedom and dignity, and like everyone else became 'gorged

[1] Book 8, 563.

with freedom'. Suspicion, fear and servility are absent, or, at least, inconspicuous in such a society. And no one who visited Germany after 1933 needs to be reminded of the change of atmosphere.

Decisions concerning the worth of societies and social institutions are not made by an *élite*, by rulers or a governing class but, explicitly or by acceptance, by those who live and work in the society and operate its institutions. But these decisions may be changed by the effective propaganda of a minority who have reached other decisions of whose value they desire to convince the majority. Perhaps, ultimately, men get the societies and governments which they choose, even if not those which they deserve, for they may deserve better than passion, indolence or ignorance permits them to choose.

This leads to a second question. Upon what grounds or for what reasons are decisions reached? Consider the expression of the doctrine of equality; that all human beings are of equal worth, intrinsic value, or are ends in themselves. Is there an answer to the question, Why? On what *evidence* is this assertion based? How can such a decision be maintained despite the obvious differences between human beings? The answer of the natural law theorists and of Kant was that the 'natural' fact that all men have reason proves that they are of intrinsic worth, and are thus entitled to the Rights of Man. It is not clear, however, whether imbeciles and lunatics forfeit human rights. No one can deny that they are human beings. A person who becomes insane does not thereby become a mere animal. But if statements about the possession by anything of a natural characteristic is related to a decision of worth as evidence for a conclusion, then it would be illogical to retain the decision when the characteristics were absent or had changed. It is irrational to continue to believe a proposition when evidence shows that it is false. I affirm that no natural characteristic constitutes a *reason* for the assertion that all human beings are of equal worth. Or, alternatively, that *all* the characteristics of *any* human being are equally reasons for this assertion. But this amounts to saying that the decision of equal worth is affirmed of all human beings *whatever their particular characteristics*. It does not follow that they are of equal *merit* and that their treatment should not vary accordingly, in ways compatible with their intrinsic value. But even a criminal, though he has lost merit and may deserve punishment, does not become worthless. He cannot be cast out of humanity.

I am aware that this view needs much more elaboration, and especially illustration than can be given in very limited space. I can, therefore, indicate only in a general way the type of value assertions and the manner in which they are related to each other and to other assertions. They are not related as evidence strengthening a conclusion. For decisions are not true or false and are not deduced from premises. Do we, then, decide without reason? Are decisions determined by chance or whim? Surely, it will be said, the facts have some relevance to what is decided? To say that decisions are made without reason looks like saying that we choose by tossing a coin; opening the *Works of Shakespeare* or *The Bible* at random and reading the first sentence; or shutting our eyes and sticking a pin into the list of starters to pick the Derby winner. These seem very irrational methods of choice. Nevertheless, we do sometimes choose by a not very dissimilar procedure. If two candidates for a post are of exactly equal merit, the selectors may well end by plumping for one or the other. This, it may be said, was justified because there was 'nothing to choose between them', not that the decision bore no relation to their merits. But there are some choices into which merit hardly enters. Those involving personal relations, for instance. It would seem absurd to try to prove that our affections were not misplaced by listing the characteristics of our friends. To one who asked for such 'proof' we should reply, with Montaigne:[1]

If a man urge me to tell him wherefore I loved him, I feel it cannot be expressed but by answering, because it was he, because it was myself. . . . It is not one especial consideration, nor two, nor three, nor four, nor a thousand. It is I wot not what kind of quintessence of all this commixture which seized my will.

Yet it is also correct to say that our decisions about worth are not merely arbitrary, and intelligent choices are not random. They cannot be proved correct by evidence. Nor, I suggest, do we try to prove them. What we do is to support and defend our decisions. The relation of the record of a decision to the considerations which support it is not that of proof to conclusion. It is much more like the defence of his client by a good counsel.

Consider an analogous situation in art. Suppose one were trying to defend a view that Keats is a greater poet than Crabbe. One would compare passages from each writer, showing the richness and complexity of the imagery and movement of Keats's verse and the monotonous rhythm, moral platitudes and poverty-stricken images of Crabbe. One would aid the effect by reading passages aloud for their comparable musical effects; would dwell on single lines and passages which show the differences between the evocative language

---

[1] *Essays* (trans. John Florio), *Of Friendship*.

of Keats and the conventional 'poetic diction' of Crabbe. The 'Season of mists and mellow fruitfulness' of the one and the 'finny tribes', etc., of the other. One might eventually resort to the remarks of the best critics on both writers. In short, one would employ every device to 'present' Keats, to build up a convincing advocacy of his poetry. And the resistance of Crabbe's defender might collapse, and he would declare the case won with the verdict 'Keats is the better poet'. But nothing would have been *proved*. Crabbe's supporter might still disagree. He would dwell on Crabbe's 'sincerity'; his genuine sympathy with the poor and excuse his poetic limitations as due to a bad tradition for which he was not responsible. He might add that Crabbe was one of Jane Austen's favourite poets. And if he so persisted he would not be *wrong*, i.e. he would not be believing falsely that Crabbe was a better poet than Keats but much more persuasion would be needed to induce him to alter his decision.

Compare with this the correct attitude to the proof of a scientific law. If the empirical evidence is conclusive then a person who rejects the conclusion is either stupid or biased. He is certainly believing a false proposition. We do not 'defend' the law of gravitation but all instructed persons accept the proof of the law.

On the other hand, we do not refer to Mill's proof but to his 'magnificent defence' of civil liberty. For a successful defence involves much more than statement of facts. The facts of the case are known to both the prosecuting and defending counsel. The question is, should the accused be condemned or acquitted? The skilful lawyer uses these facts, but he uses them differently from the scientist. He marshals them so as to emphasize those which favour his client. He interprets those which appear unfavourable in terms of legal decisions in similar cases which would benefit the accused. He chooses language which does not merely state, but impress: he uses voice, gesture, facial expression, all the devices of eloquence and style in order to influence the decision of the jury in favour of his client. His client may still lose, but he would admit that he has a better chance of winning if he briefs a good counsel.

But, it may be asked, is this a recommendation to take fraudulent advocacy as our model for defending the rights of man? Not at all. Lawyers and art critics are not frauds, but neither are they scientists. They are more like artists who use material with results which impress and convince but do not *prove*. There is no conceivable method of *proving* that Keats is a better poet than Crabbe or that freedom is better than slavery. For assertions of value cannot be subjected to demonstrative or inductive methods. It is for this reason that such assertions have been regarded as simple expressions of feeling or emotion like cries of pain and anger. But we do not defend or support a cry of pain or shout of joy though it may be related to a cause. If our value choices are defensible their defence requires other methods.

The lawyer says: 'I agree that my client was on the premises; I deny that his being there in those circumstances constitutes a *trespass*. This may be confirmed from *Gower v. Flint* where this ruling was given in similar circumstances.' The critic says: 'You agree that Keats's imagery is *rich* and *complex*; his language *original* and *powerful*: that Crabbe, on the contrary, is *frigid* and *conventional* in language; *meagre* in imagery, etc. etc.' The lawyer supports his plea from previous decisions. The critic likewise appeals not to physical or psychological facts about the occurrences of marks on paper, internal pictures, etc., but to previous decisions *evaluating* these and other occurrences. Rich and powerful poetry is good; frigid and meagre versifying is bad. If we stand by our previous decisions it does not follow that we *must* on account of them make a further decision now, but they are certainly relevant. Incorporated into a system of skilful advocacy they may win a favourable verdict. But, on the other hand, we may reject our former decisions. Elaborate imagery; lyrical quality, are dismissed as *barbarous* or *sentimental*; our choice is now for the *plain* and *elegant* statement. Such a complete change in systems of evaluation seems to occur in different ages. The eighteenth century listened to Shakespeare, but gave the palm to Pope. The Victorians saw Georgian houses but chose sham Gothic. So we may present the authoritarian with an attractive picture of a free and democratic society, and if he already values independence, experimentation, mutual trust, he may agree that these values are realized in such a society. But he may call independence, insolence; experimentation, rash meddling; and the picture will fail in its effect.

There are no certainties in the field of values. For there are no true or false beliefs about values, but only better or worse decisions and choices. And to encourage the better decisions we need to employ devices which are artistic rather than scientific. For our aim is not intellectual assent, but practical effects. These are not, of course, absolutely separate, for intellectual assent to a proposition or theory is followed by using it. But values, I think, concern only behaviour. They are not known, but accepted and acted upon.

Intellectuals often complain that political propaganda, e.g. is not conducted as if it were scientific argument. But if moral values are not capable of scientific proof it would be irrational to treat them as if they were. The result of a confusion of logical types is to leave the field of non-scientific persuasion and conviction to propagandists of the type of the late Dr. Goebbels.

IV

THE THEORY OF SOVEREIGNTY RESTATED

by W. J. Rees

Sometime Research Fellow of Bedford College, University of London

THERE is a tendency among present-day political theorists to work without the aid of the concept of sovereignty. This is due partly to the logical difficulties inherent in the concept, and partly to the fact that certain modern political developments, such as the growth of democracy, federalism and public law, have made the concept a difficult one to apply in present conditions. The purpose of this article will be to re-examine the traditional use of the concept, and to inquire whether it still cannot be used in such a way as to avoid the objections now usually raised against it.

I

The strength of the logical objection to the traditional theory can be seen if we merely examine the following traditional questions: (1) Is it necessary that there should be a sovereign, or an ultimate source of authority or power, in every state? (2) Is it necessary that the authority or power of the sovereign should be indivisible? (3) Is it necessary that the authority or power of the sovereign should be unlimited? and (4) Where is the sovereign located? It is notorious that no unambiguous answer is possible to these questions. What then is the point of asking them, and what is the point of a concept which merely enables us to ask pointless questions? Nor is the criticism obviously exaggerated. The evidence of some three and a half centuries of political theory is largely on the side of the critics.

There are, however, two different reasons why it may not be possible to give a straight answer to a seemingly straight question. In the first place, the question may not be a genuine question. This may be either because it involves a logical contradiction, e.g. What is there outside the universe? or because we do not know what information would be relevant to determining the answer to the question, e.g. Is everything twice as big to-day as it was yesterday? But in the second place, the question may be more than one question.

This would be the case when the terms in which the question is stated are capable of having more than one meaning, e.g. 'Is justice the interest of the stronger?' where 'justice' may mean 'legal justice' or 'ideal justice', and where the answer may be different according to the sense in which the word is used.

The traditional questions about sovereignty, it seems to me, are questions of the latter and not of the former kind. They cannot be satisfactorily answered, not because they are not genuine questions, but because each question consists of several questions which have never been clearly distinguished. Once the proper distinctions are drawn, therefore, they may be replaced by other questions to which unambiguous answers can always be given. To show that this is so, all that is necessary is to analyse the possible meanings of the terms we are using.

In the traditional questions about sovereignty, the words which have been most often used ambiguously are the words 'sovereign' and 'state'. My first task, therefore, must be to analyse the different meanings which different philosophers, and sometimes the same philosophers, have given to these two words. I shall take, first of all, the word 'sovereign'.

1. The word has been used by some as equivalent to a *supreme legal authority*. Those who have used the word in this way have not usually thought it necessary to define what they mean by authority, or to say how authority is to be distinguished from power or influence. It is clear, however, from the way in which they have written, that they have meant to draw some important distinction between these concepts. 'Let us notice in the first place', writes Lord Lindsay, 'that the doctrine of sovereignty is properly concerned with the question of authority. It is not properly concerned with questions of force or power as such'.[1] This is predominantly the sense in which the word was used by John Austin, and by the lawyers of the Austinian school. I shall call this, sovereignty in the legal sense.

A word of further explanation, however, is needed. Theorists who have adopted the doctrine of the separation of powers have used the word 'sovereign' to mean either (*a*) a supreme legislative authority, as for instance in the case of Dicey, or (*b*) a supreme legislative or executive authority, as in the case of Lord Bryce. Those who have denied the separation of powers, on the other hand, have used the word to mean (*c*) a supreme legal authority, irrespec-

[1] *The Modern Democratic State*, vol. i, pp. 217–18.

tive of whether it is the authority of a Parliament, a Ministry, or a Court; that is, they have used it to mean what would, on a separationist view, be regarded as a supreme legislative, executive or judicial authority.[1] In order to avoid over-burdening the present analysis, and in order also not to prejudge the case for or against the doctrine of the separation of powers, I shall use the words 'supreme legal authority' in this latter sense. I shall use them, that is to say, in what a separationist may regard as a generic sense, and what an anti-separationist may regard as the only appropriate sense. This will preclude any direct discussion of sovereignty in senses (*a*) and (*b*) above, but that will not affect my general argument. If the separationist view is the correct one, and if clear answers can be given to the traditional questions, using the present generic sense, then the same answers can always be given to the same questions, using senses (*a*) or (*b*). If, however, the separationist view is not the correct view, then the need to discuss senses (*a*) and (*b*) does not arise in any case.

2. The word 'sovereign' has been used by others to mean a *supreme legal authority in so far as it is also a completely moral authority*. This is sovereignty as understood by Rousseau and the Hegelians. 'The Sovereign', says Rousseau, 'merely by virtue of what it is, is always what it should be'. 'Sovereignty', says Bosanquet, 'is the exercise of the General Will', which 'is expressed in law, in so far as law is what it ought to be'.[2] It is, therefore, a species of sovereignty in the previous sense. For that reason, it is not always clear that a person who uses the word in this way is using it necessarily in a way which is different from the previous one. But we can, in fact, be sure that a different sense is involved wherever there is clear evidence that the writer would, in addition, deny the title of sovereign to a supreme legal authority which is not, in his opinion, a completely moral authority. When the word is used in this way, I shall say that it is used in the moral sense.

3. For another group of philosophers the word has meant *a supreme coercive power exercised by a determinate body of persons possessing a monopoly of certain instruments of coercion*. They have not usually defined what they mean by coercive power, nor clearly stated how it is to be distinguished from legal authority or political influence. But it has been generally understood that power in this sense is to be distinguished from legal authority at least in one

---

[1] Cf. Finer: *The Theory and Practice of Modern Government*, vol. i, chap. 1.
[2] *The Philosophical Theory of the State*, pp. 232 and 107.

respect, namely, that its exercise may sometimes be extra-legal. In this sense, the sovereign is a determinate body of persons capable of *enforcing* decisions against any likely opposition, no matter who *makes*, or *otherwise carries out*, those decisions. Usually such a body consists of a professional police or a standing army; usually, too, the decisions which it enforces are those of Parliaments, Ministries and Courts, but they may be the analogous decisions of persons who have no legal authority to make such decisions, although such persons may acquire such legal authority in virtue of their decisions being enforced, e.g. the dissolution of the Long Parliament by Cromwell, or the overthrow of the Directory by Napoleon. This use of the word 'sovereign' is implied in Lord Bryce's concept of the Practical Sovereign, which he defined as 'the strongest force in the State, whether that force has or has not any recognized legal supremacy'.[1] T. H. Green also wrote as if he thought the word should ordinarily be used in this or some similar sense: 'the term "sovereign" is best kept to the ordinary usage in which it signifies a determinate person or persons charged with the supreme coercive function of the state'.[2] I shall call this, sovereignty in the institutionally coercive sense.

4. The word has again been used by some as equivalent to a *supreme coercive power exercised habitually and co-operatively by all, or nearly all, the members of a community*. Locke speaks variously of this kind of supreme coercive power as 'the force of the community', 'the force of the majority', and 'all the force of all the people', in such a way as to imply a distinction between this and the coercive power of a professional police or a standing army.[3] T. H. Green, although he did not favour the usage, held that the word *could* be used in this, or a very similar, way. 'A majority of citizens *can* be conceived as exercising a supreme coercive power. . . . But as the multitude is not everywhere supreme, the assertion of its sovereignty has to be put in the form that it is sovereign "de jure".' (p. 109.) This is also a meaning of the word which has sometimes, though not necessarily always, been implied both by those who have spoken of the 'sovereignty of the people', and by those who have spoken of the 'tyranny of the majority'. When the word is used in this way, it will be convenient to say that it is used in the socially coercive sense.

[1] *Studies in History and Jurisprudence*, p. 511.
[2] *Lectures on the Principles of Political Obligation*, p. 103.
[3] For examples see *Treatise*, Book II, paras. 3, 88, 89, 96, 130, 131.

5. It may now be noted that these four different senses of the word 'sovereign' refer to supreme authorities or powers, each of a different kind. But the fact that they are sovereigns of a different kind does not mean that they cannot, in some cases, be subordinated one to another according to some principle of subordination other than those already indicated. Some philosophers have, indeed, held that they can be so subordinated, and have tried to show accordingly which of these sovereigns is 'really sovereign'. By so doing, they have used the word 'sovereign' in yet another sense. They have used it in a sense which is equivalent to what one might call the *strongest political influence*, where political influence is to be distinguished, in some way yet to be determined, both from legal authority and from coercive power. Many things may be regarded as sovereign in this sense, but usually this kind of sovereignty has been attributed to the popular majority, irrespective of whether the popular majority be also regarded as the coercive sovereign or not. The following examples from Locke and Dicey will indicate how the concept has been generally used. 'Though in a constituted commonwealth', writes Locke, 'there can be but one supreme power, which is the legislative, to which all the rest are and must be subordinate, yet the legislative power being only a fiduciary power to act for certain ends, there remains still in the people a supreme power to remove or alter the legislative, when they find the legislative act contrary to the trust reposed in them'. (para. 149.) 'The plain truth', says Dicey, 'is that as a matter of law Parliament is the sovereign power in the state. . . . It is, however, equally true that in a political sense the electors are the most important part of, we may even say are actually, the sovereign power, since their will is under the present constitution sure to obtain ultimate obedience'.[1] This I shall call sovereignty in the influential sense.

6. There is, finally, a usage of the word 'sovereign' which would make it equivalent to a *permanently supreme authority, power or influence*—the significant word in this case being the word 'permanent'. It seems to be a matter of custom among political theorists to make statements such as the following: 'Force is not sovereign in the state, for no state can be perpetually ruled by force alone.' Those who make such statements as this would not usually deny that a state may for some time be ruled by force alone; force may well be sovereign for some time, assuming some meaning of the word 'sovereign' already given. But if now the title of sovereign is to be

[1] *The Law of the Constitution*, 8th edn., p. 73.

denied to a 'sovereign' of this kind, clearly the word has once again shifted its meaning. It has shifted its meaning to the extent that a sovereign, in any of our previous senses, is no longer to be called sovereign unless it continues to exist for an indefinitely long time. Duguit says of Bodin, for instance, that 'he defines sovereignty as "the absolute and perpetual power in the state" ';[1] and Professor Laski, with this definition apparently in mind, argues against Bodin as follows: 'The government which acts as its (Professor Laski means the state's) sovereign organ never, as a matter of history, has the prospect of permanence if it consistently seeks to be absolute. Civil War and Revolution in the England of the seventeenth century, 1789 in France, 1917 in Russia, are all of them footnotes to the problem of sovereignty'.[2] I shall call this, sovereignty in the permanent sense.

So much for the word 'sovereign'. It is necessary now to consider the word 'state'.

The word 'state' has been used by philosophers in at least three different ways. (1) To some, it has meant a *politically organized society*. 'The state', says Sorley, 'is not something separate from the citizen, and it is not something separate from the community or society to which it belongs. It is this society organized as a whole and able to act as a unity'.[3] This is the sense of the word 'state' which we usually have in mind when we are dealing with matters of international politics, e.g. when we speak of small and large states, backward states, industrial states, European states, etc. (2) To others, it has meant a *politically organized society in so far as it is ideally organized*. This, in the main, is the Hegelian use of the term. 'By the State, then', says Bosanquet, 'we mean Society as a unit, recognized as rightly exercising control over its members through absolute physical power'. (p. 184.) Since this is a species of the state in the previous sense, it is not always clear that a person who uses the term in this way is using it in a sense which is different from the previous one. But, as with the moral sense of the word 'sovereign', we can be sure that a different sense is involved whenever the writer is prepared to deny the title of state to a politically organized society which is not, in his opinion, ideally organized. (3) More often in ordinary speech, however, and sometimes in political theory, the word 'state' has meant *government as an institution*. 'The state', says Professor R. M. MacIver, 'exists within society, but it is

---

[1] *Law in the Modern State*, trans. F. and H. Laski, p. 9.   [2] *Grammar of Politics*, p. 49.
[3] Creighton and others: *The Theory of the State*, p. 32.

not even the *form* of society'; it is 'a structure not coeval and co-extensive with society, but built within it as a determinate order for the attainment of specific ends'.[1] This is the sense of the word which we usually have in mind when we are discussing matters of domestic politics, e.g. when we speak of state enterprise, state employees, the revenues of the state, the machinery of the state, etc.

It may be that the words 'sovereign' and 'state' have been used in some senses other than these which I have indicated, but these at least are definite, it seems to me, as far as the history of political theory is concerned. Admittedly some of these senses are arbitrary, in that they are not the senses which are implied in the common use of the words by persons who are not political theorists; but to determine which is arbitrary and which is not is a question which need not concern us here, since it would not in any case affect any of the conclusions which may be derived from the foregoing analysis.

We are now in a position to answer the first of the traditional questions about sovereignty, namely, Is it necessary that there should be a sovereign in every state?

1. If we are using the word 'sovereign' in the legal sense, it is not *logically* necessary that there should exist a sovereign in every state, on any of the three definitions of the word 'state', since it is clearly not self-contradictory to say that there does not exist in a state a supreme legal authority. But it is, however, *causally* necessary that there should exist a sovereign in every state, on any of our three definitions. I am now using the word 'cause' in the sense in which it is normally used in the practical sciences, and which has been defined by Collingwood to mean 'an event or state of things which it is in our power to produce or prevent, and by producing or preventing which we can produce or prevent that whose cause it is said to be'. In this sense it is causally necessary that a sovereign should exist in every state, since, in practice, government can only be carried on by means of laws, and laws can only be effectively administered if there exists some final legal authority beyond which there is no further legal appeal. In the absence of such a final legal authority no legal issue could ever be certainly decided, and government would become impossible.

2. If, however, we take the word 'sovereign' in the moral sense, and if, in addition, we use the word 'state' in its second, or Hegelian, sense, then it is *logically* necessary that there should exist a sovereign

---

[1] *The Modern State*, pp. 5 and 40.

in every state. For if the supreme legal authority which exists in a 'state' is not a completely moral authority, that 'state' is not an ideally organized society, that is, it is not a state on the present definition. This is an analytical proposition derived solely from the definitions of the terms used. But on any other use of the word 'state', of course, it is neither logically nor causally necessary that there should exist in any state a sovereign in this sense.

3. It is not *logically* necessary that there should exist in a state, on any of the three definitions, a sovereign in the coercive sense, since again, it is not self-contradictory to say that there does not exist in a state a supreme coercive power. But it is, nevertheless, *causally* necessary, in the present state of society, that there should exist in the state—senses (1) and (2)—a sovereign either in the socially coercive or in the institutionally coercive sense. Since it is a fact that many men in their present state are prone to disobey the law, it is necessary, if laws are to be effective, that they should be capable of being enforced. But laws can only be enforced in one of two ways: either by the habitual and co-operative exercise of coercive power in support of the law by indeterminate but exceedingly numerous persons in society, or else by the exercise of coercive power by a determinate body of persons, who are fewer in number, but who possess a monopoly of the instruments of coercion. Assuming, for the time being, that these two ways represent genuine practical alternatives, it is not causally necessary that there should exist in the state, as now defined, a sovereign in both the above senses, but only that there should exist a sovereign in the one sense or the other. But if, however, we are using the word 'state' in the third sense, the same facts would need to be stated rather differently. In this case we should have to say that it is causally necessary that an institutionally coercive sovereign should exist in the state, if there does not exist in society a sovereign of the socially coercive kind. That is, the state must possess a monopoly of the instruments of coercion, as long as there does not exist in society a sufficiently large number of persons capable of co-operating to enforce the state's decisions.

4. If now we use the word 'sovereign' in the influential sense, it is neither logically nor causally necessary that there should exist a sovereign in every state. This is true on any use of the word 'state', since the strongest political influence may be exercised by bodies which exist, or events which occur, outside the boundaries of the state, e.g. the influence of another powerful state, or of international

economic events, etc. If we use the word 'state' in sense (3), moreover, there is the additional reason that the strongest political
influence may be that of public opinion, which itself lies outside the
state as the state is now being defined.

5. It is, finally, neither logically nor causally necessary that there
should exist in the state, on any of the given definitions, a sovereign
in the permanent sense. In order, for instance, that the King in
Parliament may be the legal sovereign to-day, it does not seem to
be either logically or causally necessary that he should continue to
be the legal sovereign for an indefinitely long time.

Summing up now the above argument, it is possible to say (*a*) that
it is necessary, *in the sense of logically necessary*, that there should exist
a sovereign in every state, if we use the word 'sovereign' in the
moral sense and the word 'state' in the sense of a political society
ideally organized. It is also possible to say (*b*) that it is necessary, *in
the sense of causally necessary*, that there should exist a sovereign in
every state, if we use the word 'sovereign' in the legal sense or
generically in the coercive sense, and if we use the word 'state' in
any of the three senses indicated. On no other usages of the words
'sovereign' and 'state' can it be said to be necessary that a sovereign
should exist in every state.

The three remaining traditional questions may be dealt with more
briefly, since we shall no longer be concerned with the variations in
the meaning of the word 'state'. The answers may be given in three
groups corresponding to the three traditional questions.

1. To the question, Is it necessary that the sovereign, if it exists,
should be indivisible? the following answers may be given: (*a*) If
by the word 'sovereign' we mean the legal sovereign, it is in one
sense logically necessary that the sovereign should be indivisible,
since it would be self-contradictory to hold that there could be more
than one final decision on any one legal question; but it is neither
logically nor causally necessary that the sovereign should be indivisible in the sense that every legal question should be finally decided
by one and the same legal authority. This is equally true, if by the
word 'sovereign' we mean a moral sovereign, since sovereignty of
this kind is only a special case of sovereignty in the legal sense. (*b*)
The same would also be true, *mutatis mutandis*, if by the word
'sovereign' we meant the institutionally coercive sovereign, the
socially coercive sovereign or the influential sovereign. It is, in one
sense, logically necessary that these sovereigns should be indivisible,
since it would be self-contradictory to say of any two coercive

powers which were of the same kind, or of any two political influences, that they were both at one and the same time the strongest. But it is neither logically nor causally necessary that these sovereigns should be indivisible in the sense that the power or influence in question may not be divided between two or more bodies. (*c*) If, however, we use the word 'sovereign' in the permanent sense, no questions about indivisibility arise, other than those already answered in connection with its other meanings. The additional qualification of permanence now introduced does not affect the present issue.

2. The answers to the third of the traditional questions, namely the question, Is it necessary that the authority or power or influence of the sovereign should be unlimited? will depend on what political theorists have meant when they have used the word 'unlimited'. The word has been used in at least two different ways. (*a*) Some have used it as equivalent to 'omnipotent'.[1] When it is used in this way, it is clearly neither logically nor causally necessary that sovereignty, in any sense, should be unlimited. In the United States, for instance, there exists no legal authority which can legally deprive any State within the Union of its equal representation in the Senate. Standing armies everywhere are dependent on other persons for their supplies of arms and equipment, and the larger the army the greater its dependence, in this respect, on the rest of the population. Equally, there are few political groups which can successfully influence legislation without compromising to some extent with rival groups. On no usage of the word 'sovereign', therefore, is it necessary that sovereignty should be unlimited in this sense. (*b*) The word 'unlimited' has often been used, however, in a weaker sense, to mean 'exceedingly great' or 'superior to any other'.[2] When the word is used in this way, it is logically necessary that sovereignty, in any sense of the word, should be unlimited. But to say that it is, is now to utter rather a pointless tautology. It is simply to say that a supreme legal authority must be supreme, and so on, *mutatis mutandis*, for any other use of the word 'sovereign'.

3. The fourth of the traditional questions, namely, Where is the sovereign located? may now be easily dealt with, since it resolves itself into a series of entirely empirical questions requiring straightforward historical, legal or sociological answers. It is not necessary here, therefore, to establish what the correct answers are in this case,

---

[1] E.g. Laski, op. cit., pp. 51–3; Popper, *The Open Society and its Enemies*, vol. i, p. 107.
[2] E.g. Bryce, op. cit., pp. 522–3; Laird, *The Device of Government*, pp. 83 ff.

F

but merely to indicate what kinds of answers would be appropriate. It would be appropriate, for instance, though not necessarily true, to say that the sovereign was located in the King in Parliament, or the Cabinet, or the House of Lords (legal or moral sense), or in the bulk of the people or in the army (coercive sense), or in the electoral majority or in the economically dominant class (influential sense), or nowhere, because no such sovereign at present exists (moral or permanent or any other sense). Needless to say, this question, or rather these series of questions, may still be difficult to answer, but if so, that is now due to insufficient empirical evidence, rather than to any ambiguity or other logical impropriety in the question. Not all questions which are difficult to answer are logically improper questions.

Answers have now been given to the traditional questions about sovereignty. If these are satisfactory, and I trust they are, then the traditional questions are not pointless questions, however much they may require analysis, and the theory of sovereignty may still be used in such a way as to present at least a consistent theory of politics.

2

The analysis which has now been given, I submit, removes the ambiguities in the traditional theory. Unfortunately, however, it does so only at the expense of making the theory so complicated that it is no longer economical or serviceable to use. The dilemma with which we are faced, therefore, if we wish to retain the concept of sovereignty, is very great. If we preserve the traditional simplicity of the concept, it is too ambiguous to be of service, but if we draw the distinctions necessary to avoid these ambiguities, the analysis of the concept becomes so complicated that its use is no longer helpful. Is there, then, any way of overcoming this difficulty? Is it possible to recommend a use of the concept which will both remove the ambiguities of the traditional theory and preserve it as a useful instrument of political analysis? It seems to me that this is possible, and I shall now endeavour to show how I think this can best be done.

In the first place, the use of the word 'sovereign' in the permanent sense may, with every advantage, be abandoned altogether. If the word 'permanent' is taken literally to mean 'lasting for an indefinitely long time', then this usage is objectionable for two reasons. (1) If we are referring to states which have existed in the past, the concept is so imprecise that no two historians could easily agree as to whether or not a sovereign in this sense did or did not exist in any given state. Did such a sovereign exist, for instance, in the Roman Empire? Some would say not. (2) If we are referring to contemporary states, it is impossible to *know* that a sovereign in this sense exists in any state, for even though it is conceivably possible that some existing 'sovereign' may last for an indefinitely long time, it cannot possibly be *known* that it will. Nor is it easy to see what other use of the word 'permanent' would justify the retention of the concept. It may be, of course, that some theorists have meant by 'permanent' the same thing as 'stable', but, although it is causally necessary that a sovereign should be stable, this does not justify a separate use of the word 'sovereign'. The fact that a certain characteristic belonging to a thing is a *causally necessary* characteristic, in the sense of causal necessity used here, does not justify our making it a *definitional* characteristic of that thing. A well-drained soil is necessary to grow most plants and vegetables, but the fact that it is not well-drained does not mean that we no longer call it soil.

In the second place, the concept of the sovereign as the moral sovereign may also be abandoned without loss. All the issues which can be discussed with the help of this concept can be discussed more adequately and more usefully with the aid of the concept of obligation. If we define the state in such a way as to identify it with the ideal state, then we can quite logically speak of the sovereignty of the state in the moral sense, but this simply means that we are defining the state and the sovereign in such a way that no organization is a state, and no authority a sovereign, unless we recognize a moral obligation to obey them. There is nothing logically objectionable about this, so long as it is understood that this is simply a way of approaching the problems of political obligation. But in practice this method of approach is objectionable for two reasons. (1) Since the definition of the state is arbitrary, the method is liable to slip from being a method of approaching problems of political obligation to being a method of justifying any state or political régime which happens to exist. This occurs whenever the meanings of the words 'state' and 'sovereign' slip from their announced meanings into one or other of their more familiar meanings. (2) It tends to prejudge certain questions of ethical theory. The concept of the sovereign as a moral authority tends to establish a strong *presumption* in favour of the view that there are certain moral standards which are the same for all persons, at least within any given political group. But although it may well be true that an objective theory of some kind in ethics is the correct one, this is a question to be examined in the light of our moral experience as a whole, and not one to be prejudged in the interest of a political theory.

This leaves four other concepts, the value of which needs now to be determined.

There is no doubt that the concept of legal sovereignty is valuable in any discussion of the legal aspects of the state's activity. On any definition of the state, as we have seen, it is causally necessary that a sovereign of this kind should exist in every state, and the question, Where is the legal sovereign located? is a fundamental question for every lawyer. Indeed, no contemporary political theorist seems to be prepared to deny the utility of the concept in this limited field, and those who have attacked the use of the concept have done so simply because its utility is confined to this particular field. Since its utility is confined to this field, it is argued, the concept is worthless for more general political purposes. This is a criticism which may fairly be levelled against anyone who maintains that this use of the word 'sovereign' is its only 'proper' use, and who then ignores its other, allegedly 'improper' uses. For, in that case, the theory of sovereignty becomes predominantly a legal theory without relevance to political issues, except in so far as these also happen to be legal issues. But suppose we allow, as certainly we should, that there can be more than one 'proper' use of the word 'sovereign'. What then becomes of this criticism? A theory of sovereignty which permits a number of proper usages of the word 'sovereign', may easily allow that the concept of legal sovereignty is only useful within a limited field, without thereby limiting its own utility to the same field.

But there is a further requirement which needs to be met if the concept is to be worth using at all, and that is to define more precisely what is meant by supreme legal authority. To exercise authority, in its widest sense, is to determine a person's actions in certain intended ways by means of a rule. It is possible, however, to distinguish different kinds of authority by distinguishing the different ways in which different rules, and sometimes the same rules, may oblige a person to act. In this way, the following kinds of authority may be distinguished: (1) authority of a moral kind, where a rule obliges a person to act in virtue of its being accepted by his own conscience, (2) authority of a customary kind, where a rule obliges him to act in virtue of his desire not to incur the disapproval of some other person or persons, e.g. the authority of a tribal chief or of a father of a family, and (3) authority of a coercive kind, where a rule obliges a person to act in virtue of its being enforced, usually with a penalty attached, in the event of disobedience. There are, however, two further sub-species of this latter kind of authority: (*a*) authority of the kind where the rule is usually enforced by a coercive power, but not by a supreme coercive power, e.g. the authority of a schoolmaster (in some respects), of a trade union, or of an umpire at a cricket match; and (*b*) legal authority in the strict sense, where the rule, whether it takes the form of a written regulation or of an unwritten convention, is enforced either directly by the exercise of a supreme coercive power, or indirectly by a serious threat of the exercise of such power, e.g. the authority of a king, of a parliament, or of a judge. Legal authority, therefore, is one species of authority, and, when exercised, may be defined as the determination of a person's actions in certain intended ways by means of a law, law being defined as an unwritten convention or a written regulation, enforceable either directly by the exercise of a supreme coercive power, or indirectly by a serious threat of the exercise of such power. From this standpoint the definition of what is meant by the exercise of legal sovereignty presents no further difficulty. To exercise legal sovereignty, or supreme legal authority, is to determine the actions of persons in certain intended ways by means of a law as previously defined, where the actions of those who exercise the authority, in those respects in which they do exercise it, are not subject to any exercise by other persons of the kind of authority which they are exercising.

The definition of law given above is not yet entirely satisfactory since the concept of supreme coercive power, as yet undefined, occurs in the definition. This will be remedied in due course. Leaving the matter for the time being in abeyance, the definitions now given differ in two respects from the definitions given by Austin: (1) the definition of law is wider and designed to include customary law as well as case law and statute law, and (2) legal sovereignty is defined in terms of law rather than vice versa. The latter point has important implications, in that it enables us to reduce constitutional law, as it exists in either the United States or in Great Britain, to positive law. This is theoretically important, since it enables us to bring the theory of legal sovereignty into line with the more fundamental aspects of constitutional and federal government. Moreover, it enables us to do this without necessarily abandoning the command theory of law, since anyone who wishes to hold that theory may still claim that, although judges and legislative assemblies say what the rules are, it is the command of the *coercive* sovereign (*not* the legal sovereign, as Austin seems to have thought) which gives those rules the status of law.

As to the concept of coercive sovereignty, it is clear that this is no less important than the concept of legal sovereignty. Where it is necessary that a legal sovereign should exist, it is also necessary, as we have seen, that a coercive sovereign should exist. There is, in fact, a functional connection between them. Human nature being what it now is, it is necessary, if certain rules are to be obeyed, that they should be capable of being enforced; and, in order that they may be capable of being enforced, it is necessary that there should exist some body of persons sufficiently strong to enforce such rules against any likely opposition within the community. It is this functional connection which was recognized in our definition of law and of legal sovereignty, both of which were defined, at least partly, in terms of supreme coercive power. There is little doubt, it seems to me, that the utility of the concept is great, and that its use in political theory is fully justified.

There are separate objections, however, which might be raised against both what I have called the institutionally coercive sovereign and the socially coercive sovereign. These require to be considered.

It might be objected that the concept of the institutionally coercive sovereign is itself ambiguous. As it has been usually employed, this is certainly a fair criticism. Very often, the sovereign in this sense has been understood to be, not the army or the professional police, but the person who has the legal or effective control of the army or the police, i.e. not Cromwell's army, but Cromwell. This is a practice based on one of two different kinds of confusion. The first is the identification of a whole with a part, or of a group with a member. When the army, commanded by Cromwell, enforces the decisions of Parliament, Cromwell is a *member* of the coercive sovereign and may himself be called sovereign only by a metaphor. The second confusion is to identify coercive sovereignty with legal sovereignty. When Cromwell's army enforces the decisions of Cromwell as against the decisions of Parliament, or even the decisions of Parliament as dictated by Cromwell, Cromwell is not the coercive sovereign; he is simply appropriating legal sovereignty. Provided these two confusions are removed, however, the concept is no longer ambiguous.

The utility of the concept of the socially coercive sovereign might be questioned on the ground that no such coercive power can in fact exist. There is no doubt, however, that there have been historical examples of a supreme coercive power of this kind, notably the police system known as the frankpledge system in medieval England, and similar systems elsewhere. There are, nevertheless, fairly definite conditions under which a coercive power of this kind may be exercised. It can be exercised only, (1) if all or nearly all adult men can be effectively organized for police duties, (2) if all or nearly all men have access to certain kinds of arms and are trained in their use, and (3) if there do not exist serious social cleavages within the community. Where any one of these conditions, and more especially the third, is lacking, law can only be maintained in the last resort by a professional police or armed force. Very often, however, the two coercive systems may exist side by side within the same community. It is often the case, as in England for many centuries, that the socially coercive power performs the coercive functions necessary in the case of those breaches of the law on which society is not deeply divided, such as crimes committed against the common law in times of peace, while the institutionally coercive power is held in reserve to deal with possible large-scale breaches of the law, such as a riot or a threatened revolt or uprising. Of more theoretical interest, it is the existence side by side of these two coercive systems which enables us to regard customary law as genuine law, and thus justify the wide definition of law previously given.

There is no doubt, therefore, that these two concepts of coercive sovereignty are useful. Since they represent, however, two species of a single genus, the theory of sovereignty may be simplified without loss of comprehensiveness or clarity, if we use the word 'sovereign' in a generic sense only. Traditionally, in order to simplify the theory, it has been the custom to confine the use of the word 'sovereign' to one or other of the relevant species. This is what was recommended by T. H. Green, for instance, when he said that 'the term "sovereignty" is best kept to the ordinary usage in which it signifies a determinate person or persons charged with the supreme coercive function of the state'. But this is simply a further example of the common error of assuming that some one possible meaning of the word 'sovereign' is a 'proper' meaning, while all other possible meanings are to be ignored. In this case, indeed, the error is committed twice over. Not only is it assumed that one generic usage rather than another (i.e. the coercive rather than the legal usage) is the proper usage, but also it is assumed that, within this genus, the word is properly confined to one of the species. There is no solution of our problem along these lines. The only solution lies in accepting both usages, or, if the requirements of simplification are over-riding, in accepting only a generic usage. In this case, there is everything to be said for retaining only the generic usage.

This means that it is necessary now to define what is meant by supreme coercive power, and, in particular, to distinguish coercive power from legal authority and from political influence. To exercise power, in a social and political sense, is to determine the actions of persons in certain intended ways. There are, however, different species of power, and these may be distinguished according to the means used to determine persons' actions. We thus have the following species. (1) Power in the sense of authority, especially legal authority, where the means used is the formulation of, or the reference to, a rule of law, e.g. 'the powers of the President', 'the powers of local authorities', etc. This species of power we have already considered. (2) Coercive power, where the means used consists either in the direct use of physical force, or else in a serious threat of the use of force, e.g. 'the power of the police'. (3) Power in the sense of influence, where the means used may be any means other than the employment of a rule of law or of physical force, e.g. 'the power of the priest'. In all these cases, of course, one often finds, in addition, figurative expressions in which the power is ascribed to the means used rather than to the persons using it, e.g. 'the power of the law', 'the power of the bayonet', 'the power of money', etc.

It is now possible, however, to define coercive power. Coercive power, when it is exercised, is the determination of a person's actions in certain intended ways, either by the direct use of physical force, or else by a serious threat of the use of force. Only a further step is therefore necessary in order to define what is meant by the exercise of coercive sovereignty. A person or a body of persons may be said to exercise coercive sovereignty, or supreme coercive power, if it determines the actions of persons in certain intended ways by means of force or the threat of force, and if the actions of the persons who exercise the power, in those respects in which they do exercise it, are not themselves capable of being similarly determined.

This leaves one more concept to be considered, namely, that of the influential sovereign. The most serious objection which might be raised against the retention of this concept is that it is seldom possible to determine the existence of an influence, and never possible to determine its strength, even when we know that it exists. In the case of legal authority and coercive power we can directly observe certain written rules and punitive instruments; we can observe the ways in which these are being used, and thereby discover chains of authority and power. But how does one determine the existence of an influence and, more especially, the strength of an influence? The objection is one of fundamental importance, since, if there is no means of doing this, the concept is obviously pointless.

It does not seem to me, however, that this objection is finally convincing. The determination of degrees of influence is a job which economists, historians, anthropologists and politicians have often to undertake, and one which they often undertake quite successfully. There are two ways in which this can be done. (1) By means of experimental methods, i.e. by deliberately changing the supposed determinants with the view to observing the concomitant changes, if any, in the behaviour of the persons whose actions are supposed to be influenced. In order to test the extent of the influence which slum surroundings have upon children, it is possible to remove a number of children from these surroundings and observe the changes, if any, in their behaviour. (2) By means of historical abstraction, i.e. by abstracting past variations in the supposed determinants and correlating these with the variations, if any, in the behaviour of the persons or bodies of persons whose activities are supposed to be influenced. In order to determine the influence of economic factors on the techniques of instrumental music, it is not necessary to change the economic system here and now; it is possible by means of abstraction to isolate past economic changes and to correlate these with past changes, similarly isolated, in techniques of instrumental music. In order to determine degrees of political influence, however, it is true that the first of these methods is rarely applicable, since, although the determinants of political influence are capable of being changed, they are seldom if ever capable of being changed experimentally. The changes once carried out are not reversible, so that they cannot usually be carried out at all unless there exists a widespread desire to abandon the older state of affairs for good. But the method of historical abstraction is generally applicable and its practical possibilities are greater the greater the accumulation of historical knowledge. There does not seem to me, therefore, to be any valid objection to the use of the present concept on the ground that it is not possible to determine degrees of political influence.

There are, in addition, strong positive reasons for retaining the use of the concept. Questions about influence are as important in politics as questions about legal authority and coercive power. Are the decisions of the legislature, for instance, primarily determined by the interests of a social class, or by the state of trade, or by the opinion of the majority of the electorate formed independently of class interest and in ignorance of world conditions, etc., etc.? All these questions, and many others like them, are questions about political influence. Generalized, they amount to the one question, Where is the influential sovereign located? What the correct answer to this question may be is, of course, a different matter, but that the question itself is an important one seems to me to be beyond doubt. It is important because a correct answer to it would enable one to intervene more effectively in political affairs. If we wish to determine what Acts of Parliament shall be passed, without being ourselves Members of Parliament, it is important to know which is the most effective way of doing so, whether to try and convince the majority of the electorate, or to try and convince or overthrow the ruling class, or to do something else.

There is, however, one important qualification which needs to be stated if the concept is to be successfully used in this way, namely that the strongest political influence has to be a domestic and not a foreign influence. When the persons, or bodies of persons, who exercise a certain influence within a state, normally reside outside that state, then either it is impossible for any citizen to affect their actions or else, if he can do so, he can usually do it only through the legislature. In either case, his knowing where the strongest political influence lies, will not help him to determine the activities of the legislature. The concept is useful, therefore, only when the actions of the legislature can be regarded as being predominantly determined by the actions or wishes of persons who normally reside within the state, whether they be the whole people or a part of them. Its utility is clearest, of course, where there exist political conventions expressly designed to secure the supremacy of a certain kind of influence, as when a government is given a 'mandate' in an election; but its utility may be equally great in practice where there exist no accepted political conventions of this kind, as when the government is, in fact, an instrument of an oligarchy or a priesthood.

Since we must, therefore, as it seems to me, accept the concept, it now remains to define it. This is a difficult matter, since the concept is a residual concept and can only be defined negatively in terms of other concepts. I propose, however, to construct a definition in the following way. To exercise influence, as we have seen, is to determine a person's actions in certain intended ways, by some means other than by a rule of law or a threat of force. But in order that any influence may be regarded as a political influence, it must be an influence on politics, and to say that anything is an influence on politics is to say that it determines the actions, jointly or severally, of the legal and coercive sovereigns. For instance, certain elements of a country's culture, such as knowledge of the country's history, can often in this sense be a means of political influence, in a way in which other elements of its culture, such as a knowledge of mathematics or a taste for good music, very seldom can be. To exercise political influence, therefore, is to determine in certain intended ways the actions, jointly or severally, of the legal and coercive sovereigns, provided always that their actions are determined by some means other than by a rule of law or a threat of force. It is now possible to define what is meant by the exercise of sovereignty in the influential sense. To exercise sovereignty in this sense is to exercise political influence, as now defined, to a greater degree than anyone else, provided that those who exercise it normally reside within the state whose legal or coercive sovereign they are supposed to influence.

Before leaving these definitions, there is one further point to be made. The definitions now given do not define sovereignty, but the exercise of sovereignty; that is, they define different kinds of events or occurrences. Words like 'sovereignty', 'power', 'authority', and 'influence', however, have this peculiarity, that when used in a sentence they do not inform us of any events now happening or about to happen, but of the probability of such events under certain understood conditions. In this respect, they resemble the names of dispositions. To say that x is sovereign, for instance, is to say, among other things, (1) that if a new law were to be enacted, and if no revolution occurred in the meantime, etc., then x would enact it (legal sense); or (2) that if an uprising were to take place, and x was not itself disaffected, etc., then x would suppress it (coercive sense); or (3) that if a new law were to be enacted, then x would determine the kind of law which the legislators would enact (influential sense). To say that a certain body of persons is sovereign, therefore, is not to say that it now determines the actions of persons in certain intended ways, etc., but that it recurrently succeeds in doing this under certain understood conditions, and will continue to do so under the same conditions in the future. This is the element of truth in the otherwise misleading view that sovereignty implies permanence. Sovereignty does imply recurrent activities of a certain kind under certain understood conditions, but it implies nothing about the duration of the conditions. It is also the much larger element of truth in the still somewhat misleading view of Austin, that sovereignty implies *habitual* obedience on the part of the bulk of the subjects. To say that sovereignty implies habitual obedience is false, if by 'habit' we mean a disposition of which the occurrent manifestations are voluntary and automatic, as in the case of smoking and swearing. Sovereignty does, however, imply recurrent acts of obedience, as distinct from habitual obedience in the strict sense, and to this extent Austin was right. Once we understand the proper logical function of words like 'sovereignty', 'power', 'authority', etc., we can easily embrace the element of truth in these views, without at the same time committing ourselves to the errors which they have helped to propagate.

3

We are now in a position to deploy the results of the above discussion. The main purpose of the discussion so far has been to simplify the theory of sovereignty as analysed in the first part of this paper, while at the same time avoiding the logical ambiguities of the traditional theory. This has been done by reducing the six concepts, mixed up in the traditional theory, to three concepts, now systematically defined and analysed. These three concepts, taken together, constitute an analysis of the concept of power as used in political theory. If this analysis is in general correct, then the applicability of the theory of sovereignty to modern political conditions should follow as a matter of course. A test of its correctness, therefore, is whether its applicability to these conditions does in fact follow.

The usual objections raised against the theory of sovereignty on the score of its inapplicability to modern political conditions, are the following: (1) that the theory is inapplicable to the most important political developments of the last hundred years, namely, political democracy, political federalism, and public law as represented in welfare legislation; (2) that it is incompatible with belief in international law, and (3) that it is powerless as a theoretical device to safeguard the individual against despotism. I shall now briefly consider whether the above analysis of the concept does in fact meet these objections.

In the case of democracy, not only is the theory outlined above consistent with the facts of the case, but it enables a classification of democratic systems which, in itself, it seems to me, is both interesting and useful. If democracy is defined as majority rule, we may distinguish the different species of democracy by distinguishing the relations which may exist (1) between the majority and the legal sovereign, and (2) between the majority and the coercive sovereign. In both cases, there are two relations which may exist between them: (a) the majority may itself constitute the sovereign or (b) it may be the strongest influence on the sovereign (i.e. may itself constitute the influential sovereign). These are the relations commonly referred to, more especially when used with reference to the state's legal functions, as direct democracy and indirect democracy respectively. Since, however, every state has both legal and coercive functions, and since either function may be characterized by either of these two relations, we have four ideal forms of democracy, as follows: (1) Direct legal and direct coercive democracy, e.g. the political organization of some highly developed tribal societies; (2) Direct legal and indirect coercive democracy, e.g. the political organization of some of the Greek city states; (3) Indirect legal and direct coercive democracy, e.g. the state of affairs existing on the American frontier during the last century, approximately; (4) Indirect legal and indirect coercive democracy, e.g. Parliamentary democracy where it exists at its best. Whatever the merits of this classification, it demonstrates, at least, that the theory of sovereignty now presented is fully applicable to the general conditions of political democracy.

We may turn, then, to the argument from federalism. This has been held to be fatal, in particular, to the concept of legal sovereignty. Where in the United States, for instance, is the legal sovereign located? One school replies that the legal sovereign is the constitution; but since the constitution can be legally amended by both Houses of Congress acting in conjunction with three-fourths of the States of the Union, this is hardly plausible. Another school consequently replies that the legal sovereign is both Houses of Congress acting in conjunction with three-fourths of the States of the Union. But since this body has acted as a body only on twenty-one occasions in a hundred and sixty years, and since both Houses of Congress, in any case, derive their own legal existence from the constitution, this is even less plausible. The question is clearly an embarrassing one, and becomes even more embarrassing once it is realized that there is nothing in the nature of the dilemma which makes it one peculiar to federal states. It is a dilemma which arises whenever we have to deal with legal systems which distinguish between ordinary law and constitutional law, whether the constitution be federal or otherwise. What, then, is the answer to this dilemma?

There is, of course, a perfectly simple answer, namely: that in constitutions of this kind—and in almost any constitution, for that matter—there exist at least two supreme legal authorities, one having supreme authority in one set of decisions, on one level of generality, and the other supreme authority in another, on a different level of generality. The traditional objection to this straightforward answer has been that legal sovereignty is not, in that case, necessarily indivisible. But as has been previously shown in this article, the phrase 'sovereignty is indivisible' can mean in this context two quite different things. In one sense it is logically necessary that sovereignty should be indivisible, namely in the sense that it would be self-contradictory to hold that there could be more than one final decision on any one legal question, but it is neither logically nor causally necessary that the sovereign should be indivisible in the sense that every legal question should be finally decided by one and the same legal authority. Although traditional theory was right, therefore, in holding that sovereignty is in some sense indivisible, it is not indivisible in the sense necessary to sustain the above objection. In which case, there is no further difficulty.

The argument from welfare legislation has again been held, with greater apparent justification, to be fatal to the concept of legal sovereignty. The argument is put by Duguit as follows (p. 31):

> If the state is not sovereign in one only of its activities it is never sovereign.
> Yet in those great state services which increase every day—educational, the Poor law, public works, lighting, the postal, telegraph and telephone systems, the railways—the state intervenes, but it intervenes in a manner that has to be regulated and ordered by a system of public law. But this can no longer be based on the theory of sovereignty. It is applied to acts where no trace of power to command is to be found.

In this statement, two criticisms of the theory of legal sovereignty are implied. In the first place, it is implied that since all welfare legislation *legally* binds the government to provide certain services for the community, such a government can no longer be regarded as *legally* sovereign. Secondly, it is implied that the theory of legal sovereignty requires one to hold a command theory of law, whereas in welfare legislation there is, in fact, no trace of command to be found.

The first of these criticisms is much the more important of the two. To meet it at all, it is necessary seriously to face the question: How can a supreme legal authority be *legally* subject to its own rules? Hitherto it has been well-nigh universally held that to admit the implication in this question would be tantamount to asserting a self-contradiction. All political theorists have found it logically necessary, therefore, either to deny the existence of legal duties on the part of the government so as to be able to maintain its legal sovereignty, as with Austin, or else to deny its legal sovereignty in order to assert its legal duties, as with Duguit. But neither of these standpoints appears to me to be in the least plausible. In fact, it is quite clear that both standpoints are the opposite poles of one and the same antinomy, and one of the chief merits which can be claimed for the theory of sovereignty now presented here is that it enables us to discover the conceptual source of this antinomy and thus to dispose of it once and for all. The antinomy arises from a failure to distinguish between legal and coercive sovereignty. If these two concepts are identified, it does become logically self-contradictory to hold that a supreme legal authority can be legally subject to its own rules. For if a genuine sovereign is, by definition, a composite sovereign having both legal and coercive functions, and if this composite sovereign prescribes rules to itself, then either those rules cannot be enforced against the sovereign, in which case they are not genuine laws, or else, if they are genuine laws and can be so enforced, the so-called sovereign is not a genuine sovereign. But if the concepts of legal and coercive sovereignty are not identified in this way, this self-contradiction does not arise and the antinomy disappears. For in this case, the rules prescribed by the legal sovereign to itself may be enforced against itself by the coercive sovereign, and may thus be correctly called laws, while the legal sovereign, which is thus subjected to its own rules, is subjected only in virtue of the enforcement of the rules by the coercive sovereign and not in virtue of their prescription, in which case it is still no less sovereign legally. In short, just as the distinction between the legal and coercive sovereigns enabled us to show how constitutional law can be positive law, so also it enables us to show how a supreme legal authority can be legally subject to its own rules. To this extent the argument from welfare legislation can be turned into an argument in favour of the theory of sovereignty presented here.

The second criticism is less important, and there are, in any case, two replies which may be made to it. In the first place, although it is logically necessary that a person who holds a command theory of law should also hold a theory of sovereignty of some kind, since the existence of a command implies the existence of a commander, there is no such necessity for a person who holds a theory of sovereignty to hold a command theory of law. Even if it is true that the rules of a supreme legal authority cannot be correctly interpreted as commands, this is not the slightest evidence for believing that they are not the rules of a supreme legal authority. In the second place, even if one were obliged to hold a command theory of law, this need no longer be embarrassing. On the above theory of sovereignty, an advocate of the command theory of law need no longer argue that acts of welfare legislation consist of commands issued by the legal sovereign, whether addressed to itself or to anyone else. He can now argue that in so far as these rules are genuine laws and not self-imposed moral precepts, they consist of the commands of the coercive sovereign addressed to the legal sovereign. This is at least plausible. Indeed, on this view, it can hardly be now said that the existence of welfare legislation presents any serious difficulty for a command theory of law.

And now the argument from international law. It has been said that the growth of international law is incompatible with the sovereignty of the state, but this is a vague criticism, and in order to give it some precision it is necessary to clarify its terms. It is necessary, in particular, to distinguish two uses of the word 'law'. It may mean (*a*) a body of rules enforceable by institutions having supreme coercive power, i.e. positive law in the strict sense; or it may mean (*b*) a body of formal and solemn agreements, usually between states, the maintenance of which is solely dependent upon the recognition of an interest or a duty by the contracting parties. I shall call it agreement law. The argument that the growth of international law is incompatible with the sovereignty of the state may, therefore, mean any one of four different things. It may mean (1) that the existence of a supreme legal authority within a state is incompatible with the existence of a world positive law; or (2) that it is incompatible with the existence of an inter-state agreement law; or (3) that the existence of an inter-state agreement law is incompatible with the existence within a state of a sovereign in the influential sense; or (4) that the existence within a state of a sovereign, whether in the legal, coercive or influential sense, is a practical obstacle to the free development of inter-state agreement law and/or universal positive law. What now, then, may be said of these four arguments?

Of the first argument, namely that the existence of a supreme legal authority within a state is incompatible with the existence of a world positive law, there are two things to be said. (*a*) Since such a thing as a world positive law does not as yet exist, any incompatibility which there may be between its own existence and that of a supreme legal authority within a state, does not, in present circumstances, argue the non-existence of the supreme legal authority. (*b*) Even if a universal positive law did exist, its existence would be incompatible, not with the existence of a supreme legal authority within the state, but with the existence of *more than one* legally sovereign state, which is quite another matter. Of the second argument, that the existence of a supreme legal authority within the state is incompatible with the existence of an inter-state agreement law, it must be said that this is no argument at all. The alleged incompatibility simply does not exist. If two bodies, both of which are legally sovereign within different territories, reach certain solemn agreements with each other, it is simply false to assume that they thereby cease to be legally sovereign within their own respective territories. The third argument, however, is valid criticism of most traditional theories of sovereignty. It is often true, although not always, that the existence of an international law is incompatible with the sovereignty of the state in the influential sense. The existence of an international agreement may in practice be as binding upon a government as any positive law, although in a different way, and to ignore this would be to ignore a fact of very great political importance. Whether it is so or not, however, is an empirical question. It is entirely a question of fact whether the strongest influence on the legal sovereign is an international or a domestic influence. But assuming that it is in fact an international influence, this implies no criticism of the theory of sovereignty advocated here, since it is not essential to this theory to hold that it is either logically or causally necessary that there should exist in any state a sovereign in the influential sense. The fourth argument was the argument that the existence of sovereignty in any sense is a practical hindrance to the free development of inter-state agreement law and/or universal positive law. In this case, the contention itself may well be both true and important, but even if true it does not in the

G

least deny the existence within the state of a sovereign in any of the senses indicated. The fact, if it is a fact, that these things hinder the growth of international law, is no proof, unfortunately, that these things do not exist.

Lastly, is it true that the theory of sovereignty is powerless to safeguard the individual against despotism? Undoubtedly, as against much the greater part of traditional theory, this charge is justified. The traditional theory has been extremely liable to slip into one of two positions, either (1) of identifying sovereignty in a legal or coercive sense with sovereignty in a moral sense, or (2) of ignoring sovereignty in the influential sense. The first standpoint is exemplified in the Rousseau-Hegel-Bosanquet tradition, the second in the Bodin-Hobbes-Austin tradition. The effect of the former was to prejudge all questions of political obligation in favour of the despotic claims of the state, while the effect of the latter was to put the law and the coercive forces of the state, for theoretical purposes, beyond the possibility of control by society. The one told the subject, in effect, that he ought to have absolute government because it is good for him, the other that he must have absolute government if he is to have any government at all. Either standpoint is vicious, whether from a theoretical or a practical point of view. But, equally clearly, neither standpoint is essential to a theory of sovereignty. They are simply by-products of ambiguities in the statement of the theory, and can be easily removed once the proper distinctions are drawn. The purpose of this article has been to draw these distinctions, and thus to safeguard the theory against this as well as the other charges.

V

ON PUNISHMENT

by A. M. Quinton

Fellow of New College, Oxford

I

Introductory

THERE is a prevailing antinomy about the philosophical justification of punishment. The two great theories—retributive and utilitarian—seem, and at least are understood by their defenders, to stand in open and flagrant contradiction. Both sides have arguments at their disposal to demonstrate the atrocious consequences of the rival theory. Retributivists, who seem to hold that there are circumstances in which the infliction of suffering is a good thing in itself, are charged by their opponents with vindictive barbarousness. Utilitarians, who seem to hold that punishment is always and only justified by the good consequences it produces, are accused of vicious opportunism. Where the former insists on suffering for suffering's sake, the latter permits the punishment of the innocent. Yet, if the hope of justifying punishment is not to be abandoned altogether, one of these apparently unsavoury alternatives must be embraced. For they exhaust the possibilities. Either punishment must be self-justifying, as the retributivists claim, or it must depend for its justification on something other than itself, the general formula of 'utilitarianism' in the wide sense appropriate here.

In this paper I shall argue that the antinomy can be resolved, since retributivism, properly understood, is not a moral but a logical doctrine, and that it does not provide a moral justification of the infliction of punishment but an elucidation of the use of the word. Utilitarianism, on the other hand, embraces a number of possible moral attitudes towards punishment, none of which necessarily involves the objectionable consequences commonly adduced by retributivists, provided that the word 'punishment' is understood in the way that the essential retributivist thesis lays down. The antinomy arises from a confusion of modalities, of logical and moral necessity and possibility, of 'must' and 'can' with 'ought' and 'may'. In brief, the two theories answer different questions: retributivism the question 'when (logically) *can* we punish?', utilitarianism the question 'when (morally) *may* we or *ought* we to punish?'. I shall also describe circumstances in which there is an answer to the question 'when (logically) *must* we punish?'. Finally, I shall attempt to account for this difference in terms of a distinction between the establishment of rules whose infringement involves punishment from the application of these rules to particular cases.

2

The Retributive Theory

The essential contention of retributivism is that punishment is only justified by guilt. There is a certain compellingness about the repudiation of utilitarianism that this involves. We feel that whatever other considerations may be taken into account, the primary and indispensable matter is to establish the guilt of the person to be punished. I shall try to show that the peculiar outrageousness of the rejection of this principle is a consequence, not of the brutality that such rejection might seem to permit, but of the fact that it involves a kind of lying. At any rate the first principle of retributivism is that it is necessary that a man be guilty if he is to be punished.

But this doctrine is normally held in conjunction with some or all of three others which are logically, if not altogether psychologically, independent of it. These are that the function of punishment is the negation or annulment of evil or wrongdoing, that punishment must fit the crime (the *lex talionis*) and that offenders have a right to punishment, as moral agents they ought to be treated as ends not means.

The doctrine of 'annulment', however carefully wrapped up in obscure phraseology, is clearly utilitarian in principle. For it holds that the function of punishment is to bring about a state of affairs in which it is as if the wrongful act had never happened. This is to justify punishment by its effects, by the desirable future consequences which it brings about. It certainly goes beyond the demand that only the guilty be punished. For, unlike this demand, it seeks to prescribe exactly what the punishment should be. Holding that whenever wrong has been done it must be annulled, it makes guilt —the state of one who has done wrong—the sufficient as well as the necessary condition of punishment. While the original thesis is essentially negative, ruling out the punishment of the innocent, the annulment doctrine is positive, insisting on the punishment and determining the degree of punishment of the guilty. But the doctrine is only applicable to a restricted class of cases, the order of nature is inhospitable to attempts to put the clock back. Theft and fraud can be compensated, but not murder, wounding, alienation of affection or the destruction of property or reputation.

Realizing that things cannot always be made what they were, retributivists have extended the notion of annulment to cover the infliction on the offender of an injury equal to that which he has caused. This is sometimes argued for by reference to Moore's theory of organic wholes, the view that sometimes two blacks make a white. That this, the *lex talionis*, revered by Kant, does not follow from the original thesis is proved by the fact that we can always refrain from punishing the innocent but that we cannot always find a punishment to fit the crime. Some indeed would argue that we can never fit punishment to wrongdoing, for how are either, especially wrongdoing, to be measured? (Though, as Ross has pointed out, we can make ordinal judgments of more or less about both punishment and wrongdoing.)

Both of these views depend on a mysterious extension of the original thesis to mean that punishment and wrongdoing must necessarily be somehow equal and opposite. But this is to go even further than to regard guilt and punishment as necessitating one another. For this maintains that only the guilty are to be punished and that the guilty are always to be punished. The equal and opposite view maintains further that they are to be punished to just the extent that they have done wrong.

Finally retributivism has been associated with the view that if we are to treat offenders as moral agents, as ends and not as means, we must recognize their right to punishment. It is an odd sort of right whose holders would strenuously resist its recognition. Strictly interpreted, this view would entail that the sole relevant consideration in determining whether and how a man should be punished is his own moral regeneration. This is utilitarian and it is also immoral, since it neglects the rights of an offender's victims to compensation and of society in general to protection. A less extreme interpretation would be that we should never treat offenders merely as means in inflicting punishment but should take into account their right to treatment as moral agents. This is reasonable enough; most people would prefer a penal system which did not ignore the reformation of offenders. But it is not the most obvious correlate of the possible view that if a man is guilty he ought to be punished. We should more naturally allot the correlative right to have him punished to his victims or society in general and not to him himself.

3

The Retributivist Thesis

So far I have attempted to extricate the essentials of retributivism by excluding some traditional but logically irrelevant associates. A more direct approach consists in seeing what is the essential principle which retributivists hold utilitarians to deny. Their crucial charge is that utilitarians permit the punishment of the innocent. So their fundamental thesis must be that only the guilty are to be punished, that guilt is a necessary condition of punishment. This hardly lies open to the utilitarian countercharge of pointless and vindictive barbarity, which could only find a foothold in the doctrine of annulment and in the *lex talionis*. (For that matter, it is by no means obvious that the charge can be sustained even against them, except in so far as the problems of estimating the measure of guilt lead to the adoption of a purely formal and external criterion which would not distinguish between the doing of deliberate and accidental injuries.)

Essentially, then, retributivism is the view that only the guilty are to be punished. Excluding the punishment of the innocent, it permits the other three possibilities: the punishment of the guilty, the non-punishment of the guilty and the non-punishment of the innocent. To add that guilt is also the sufficient condition of punishment, and thus to exclude the non-punishment of the guilty, is another matter altogether. It is not entailed by the retributivist attack on utilitarianism and has none of the immediate compulsiveness of the doctrine that guilt is the necessary condition of punishment.

There is a very good reason for this difference in force. For the necessity of not punishing the innocent is not moral but logical. It is not, as some retributivists think, that we *may* not punish the innocent and *ought* only to punish the guilty, but that we *cannot* punish the innocent and *must* only punish the guilty. Of course, the suffering or harm in which punishment consists can be and is inflicted on innocent people, but this is not punishment, it is judicial error or terrorism or, in Bradley's characteristically repellent phrase, 'social surgery'. The infliction of suffering on a person is only properly described as punishment if that person is guilty. The retributivist thesis, therefore, is not a moral doctrine, but an account of the meaning of the word 'punishment'. Typhoid carriers and criminal lunatics are treated physically in much the same way as ordinary criminals; they are shut up in institutions. The essential difference is that no blame is implied by their imprisonment, for there is no guilt to which the blame can attach. 'Punishment' resembles the word 'murder'; it is infliction of suffering on the guilty and not simply infliction of suffering, just as murder is wrongful killing and not simply killing. Typhoid carriers are no more (usually) criminals than surgeons are (usually) murderers. This accounts for the flavour of moral outrage attending the notion of punishment of the innocent. In a sense a contradiction in terms, it applies to the common enough practice of inflicting the suffering involved in punishment on innocent people and of sentencing them to punishment with a lying imputation of their responsibility and guilt. Punishment *cannot* be inflicted on the innocent; the suffering associated with punishment *may* not be inflicted on them, firstly, as brutal and secondly, if it is represented as punishment, as involving a lie.

This can be shown by the fact that punishment is always *for* something. If a man says to another 'I am going to punish you' and is asked 'what for?', he cannot reply 'nothing at all' or 'something you have not done'. At best, he is using 'punish' here as a more or less elegant synonym for 'cause to suffer'. Either that or he does not understand the meaning of 'punish'. 'I am going to punish you for something you have not done' is as absurd a statement as 'I blame you for this event for which you were not responsible'. 'Punishment implies guilt' is the same sort of assertion as 'ought implies can'. It is not *pointless* to punish or blame the innocent, as some have argued, for it is often very useful. Rather the very conditions of punishment and blame do not obtain in these circumstances.

4

An Objection

But how can it be useful to do what is impossible? The innocent can be punished and scapegoats are not logical impossibilities. We do say 'they punished him for something he did not do'. For A to be said to have punished B it is surely enough that A thought or said he was punishing B and ensured that suffering was inflicted on B. However innocent B may be of the offence adduced by A, there is no question that, in these circumstances, he has been punished by A. So guilt cannot be more than a *moral* precondition of punishment.

The answer to this objection is that 'punish' is a member of that now familiar class of verbs whose first-person-present use is significantly different from the rest. The absurdity of 'I am punishing you for something you have not done' is analogous to that of 'I promise to do something which is not in my power'. Unless you are guilty I am no more in a position to punish you than I am in a position to promise what is not in my power. So it is improper to say 'I am going to punish you' unless you are guilty, just as it is improper to say 'I promise to do this' unless it is in my power to do it. But it is only *morally* improper if I do not *think* that you are guilty or that I can do the promised act. Yet, just as it is perfectly proper to say of another 'he promised to do this', whether he thought he could do it or not, provided that he *said* 'I promise to do this', so it is perfectly proper to say 'they punished him', whether they thought him guilty or not, provided that they *said* 'we are going to punish you' and inflicted suffering on him. By the first-person-present use of these verbs we *prescribe* punishment and *make* promises; these activities involve the satisfaction of conditions over and above what is required for *reports* or *descriptions* of what their prescribers or makers represent as punishments and promises.

Understandably 'reward' and 'forgive' closely resemble 'punish'. Guilt is a precondition of forgiveness, desert—its contrary—of reward. One cannot properly say 'I am going to reward you' or 'I forgive you' to a man who has done nothing. Reward and forgiveness are always *for* something. But, again, one can say 'they rewarded (or forgave) him for something he had not done'. There is an interesting difference here between 'forgive' and 'punish' or 'reward'. In this last kind of assertion 'forgive' seems more peculiar, more inviting to inverted commas, than the other two. The three undertakings denoted by these verbs can be divided into the utterance of a more or less ritual formula and the consequences authorized by this utterance. With punishment and reward the consequences are more noticeable than the formula, so they come to be sufficient occasion for the use of the word even if the formula is inapplicable and so improperly used. But, since the consequences of forgiveness are negative, the absence of punishment, no such shift occurs. To reward involves giving a reward, to punish inflicting a punishment, but to forgive involves no palpable consequence, e.g. handing over a written certificate of pardon.

Within these limitations, then, guilt is a *logically* necessary condition of punishment and, with some exceptions, it might be held, a morally necessary condition of the infliction of suffering. Is it in either way a sufficient condition? As will be shown in the last section there are circumstances, though they do not obtain in our legal system, nor generally in extra-legal penal systems (e.g. parental), in which guilt is a logically sufficient condition of at least a sentence of punishment. The parallel moral doctrine would be that if anyone is guilty of wrongdoing he ought morally to be punished. This rather futile rigourism is not embodied in our legal system with its relaxations of penalties for first offenders. Since it entails that offenders should never be forgiven it is hardly likely to commend itself in the extra-legal sphere.

5

The Utilitarian Theory

Utilitarianism holds that punishment must always be justified by the value of its consequences. I shall refer to this as 'utility' for convenience without any implication that utility must consist in pleasure. The view that punishment is justified by the value of its consequences is compatible with any ethical theory which allows meaning to be attached to moral judgments. It holds merely that the infliction of suffering is of no value or of negative value and that it must therefore be justified by further considerations. These will be such things as prevention of and deterrence from wrongdoing, compensation of victims, reformation of offenders and satisfaction of vindictive impulses. It is indifferent for our purposes whether these are valued as intuitively good, as productive of general happiness, as conducive to the survival of the human race or are just normatively laid down as valuable or derived from such a norm.

Clearly there is no *logical* relation between punishment and its actual or expected utility. Punishment *can* be inflicted when it is neither expected, nor turns out, to be of value and, on the other hand, it can be foregone when it is either expected, or would turn out, to be of value.

But that utility is the morally necessary or sufficient condition, or both, of punishment are perfectly reputable moral attitudes. The first would hold that no one should be punished unless the punishment would have valuable consequences; the second that if valuable consequences would result punishment ought to be inflicted (without excluding the moral permissibility of utility-less punishment). Most people would no doubt accept the first, apart from the rigorists who regard guilt as a morally sufficient condition of punishment. Few would maintain the second except in conjunction with the first. The first says when you may not but not when you ought to punish, the second when you ought to but not when you may not.

Neither permits or encourages the punishment of the innocent, for this is only logically possible if the word 'punishment' is used in an unnatural way, for example as meaning any kind of deliberate infliction of suffering. But in that case they cease to be moral doctrines about punishment as we understand the word and become moral doctrines (respectively platitudinous and inhuman) about something else.

So the retributivist case against the utilitarians falls to the ground as soon as what is true and essential in retributivism is extracted from the rest. This may be unwelcome to retributivists since it leaves the moral field in the possession of the utilitarians. But there is a compensation in the fact that what is essential in retributivism can at least be definitely established.

6

Rules and Cases

So far what has been established is that guilt and the value or utility of consequences are relevant to punishment in different ways. A further understanding of this difference can be gained by making use of a distinction made by Sir David Ross in the appendix on punishment in *The Right and the Good*. This will also help to elucidate the notion of guilt which has hitherto been applied uncritically.

The distinction is between laying down a rule which attaches punishment to actions of a certain kind and the application of that rule to particular cases. It might be maintained that the utilitarian theory was an answer to the question 'What kinds of action should be punished?' and the retributive theory an answer to the question 'On what particular occasions should we punish?' On this view both punishment and guilt are defined by reference to these rules. Punishment is the infliction of suffering attached by these rules to certain kinds of action, guilt the condition of a person to whom such a rule applies. This accounts for the logically necessary relation holding between guilt and punishment. Only the guilty can be punished because unless a person is guilty, unless a rule applies to him, no infliction of suffering on him is properly called punishment, since punishment is infliction of suffering as laid down by such a rule. Considerations of utility, then, are alone relevant to the determination of what in general, what *kinds* of action, to punish. The outcome of this is a set of rules. Given these rules, the question of whom in particular to punish has a definite and necessary answer. Not only will guilt be the logically necessary but also the logically sufficient condition of punishment or, more exactly, of a sentence of punishment. For declaration of guilt will be a declaration that a rule applies and, if the rule applies, what the rule enjoins—a sentence of punishment—applies also.

The distinction between setting up and applying penal rules helps to explain the different parts played by utility and guilt in the justification of punishment, in particular the fact that where utility is a moral, guilt is a logical, justification. Guilt is irrelevant to the setting up of rules, for until they have been set up the notion of guilt is undefined and without application. Utility is irrelevant to the application of rules, for once the rules have been set up punishment is determined by guilt; once they are seen to apply, the rule makes a sentence of punishment necessarily follow.

But this account is not an accurate description of the very complex penal systems actually employed by states, institutions and parents. It is, rather, a schema, a possible limiting case. For it ignores an almost universal feature of penal systems (and of games, for that matter, where penalties attend infractions of the rules)—discretion. For few offences against the law is one and only one fixed and definite punishment laid down. Normally only an upper limit is set. If guilt, the applicability of the rule, is established no fixed punishment is entailed but rather, for example, one not exceeding a fine of forty shillings or fourteen days' imprisonment. This is even more evident in the administration of such institutions as clubs or libraries and yet more again in the matter of parental discipline. The establishment of guilt does not close the matter; at best it entails some punishment or other. Precisely how much is appropriate must be determined by reference to considerations of utility. The variety of things is too great for any manageably concise penal code to dispense altogether with discretionary judgment in particular cases.

But this fact only shows that guilt is not a logically *sufficient* condition of punishment; it does not affect the thesis that punishment entails guilt. A man cannot be guilty unless his action falls under a penal rule and he can only be properly said to be punished if the rule in question prescribes or permits some punishment or other. So all applications of the notion of guilt necessarily contain or include all applications of the notion of punishment.

VI

IS THERE A CASE FOR THE GENERAL WILL?

by Bernard Mayo

Lecturer in Philosophy, University of Birmingham

IT is fashionable nowadays to discredit the theory of the general will, and an attempt to rehabilitate it is not likely to receive much sympathy. Nevertheless, I propose to give some reasons for adopting a more lenient attitude towards the theory, and to indicate some possible lines along which a rehabilitation might be conducted.

Orthodox refutations of the general will theory proceed somewhat as follows. It is pointed out that the term, as used, for example, by Rousseau, is ambiguous. Sometimes the generality of the general will seems to reside in the subject of the will, and sometimes in the object. In the first case, the objector disposes of the general subject, showing that this would entail a super-organism over and above the individual; and that, in the absence of any such organism, the general will could mean only the sum of individual wills. In the second case, a typical line of attack is to show that, even if there is a common object of willing—which is itself held to be highly problematical—yet the individual attitudes to this common object will be all different, so that here again there is only a sum of different individual wills.

I wish to maintain that this ambiguity, so far from constituting a fatal weakness in the theory of the general will, is actually a source of strength. But first I shall examine a more fundamental objection, resting on the assertion that there is no such thing as a will. For the type of objections mentioned above assume that the notion of 'will' is not itself in question. They amount to the statement that, even if there is such a thing as the will, it can only be an individual and not a general will. But the objection I am now considering removes this assumption and denies the existence of a will—and, *a fortiori*, of the general will.

Fortunately, there is no need to examine the ground of this objection to the notion of 'will'. For the very existence of this objection is itself a powerful support for the general will. Whatever grounds are alleged for the assertion that the will does not exist, some reasons must be found for the utility of supposing that it does. However doubtful the status of the 'facts' to which it is assumed to refer, the word 'will' has performed, and still performs, a useful function. I wish to suggest that whatever reasons may be found to account for the utility of the concept of the individual will may also account for the utility of the concept of the general will. Let us now examine these reasons.

At the common-sense level, the will is assumed to be something which precedes, and causes, an individual voluntary action. But such an action, on analysis, fails to reveal anything corresponding to the will. Introspection does not reveal a consciousness of 'willing' as a separate mental activity leading to acting. Nor does a critical observation by another person of the particular action reveal anything more than the factual physical changes in the external world (though much more may, of course, be inferred). These discoveries have the effect of relegating the will to the realm of metaphysics. But the practical utility of the concept demands analysis. We then find that the division of an act into intention and result gives us a greater power of prediction than does the examination of the act as a whole. The intention is more characteristic of the act than is the actual physical result; more important, it is more characteristic of the agent. It implies an element of permanence and reliability, on which we base our forecasts of future events. This is called knowledge of a person's character. In other words, this hypothetical division of an act into intention and result increases our control over our environment. The intention we call the 'will', and a series of such intentions exhibits the element of permanence which enters into individual character.

It is essential to distinguish 'intention' from 'motivation'. Both terms have their uses, but the dangers of confusing them can be seen, for example, in the shortcomings of the utilitarian political philosophers. By dwelling on 'motives' as if this were the only way of referring to the significant element of action, and especially on the motives of pleasure and pain, these philosophers tended to regard the human being as a bundle of desires and fears—just as later exponents of psychological theories of the state spoke of him as if he were a bundle of complexes. Now we can hardly state dogmatically that the human being is a unity or is a plurality. But there are at least certain purposes for which it is convenient to regard him as a unity and not as a plurality. And it is because it shows him as a unit in action that the term 'will' is often useful. This last point is so important that I think it would hardly be overstating the case to say that the will 'is' this unity. For the unity, from the standpoint of a person's actions, cannot be completely described in any other terms, and certainly not in physical ones: for a person's actions are not confined to the particular region of physical space occupied by the body.

We have thus arrived at what may be called a pragmatic justification for the use of the term 'will' as applied to the individual. Firstly, it establishes a criterion for judging character and forecasting actions; secondly, it emphasizes the importance of intention as distinct from practical consequences; and thirdly, and most significantly, it represents the individual as a unity.

Now the reasons which justify the use of the term 'will' as applied to a society are the same as those which justify it as applied to the individual. What a society does is made up of what individuals do. But to leave the matter there is to acquiesce in a condition parallel to that in which individual actions might be regarded as mere changes in the physical world. The actions of a society, like those of an individual, cannot be usefully correlated without a similar division into intention and result. To say this is to say much more than the commonplace dictum, that institutions can only be described in terms of the ends for which they exist. For it entails that the ends are not the ends of individuals. The intention of the society cannot be equated with any combination of the intentions of its members. We saw that for some purposes it is convenient to regard the human being as a unity, and for others as a plurality, and that neither of these views was 'true' in any sense other than a pragmatic one. The same applies to the state and to all less comprehensive societies. States and societies do act; or, to be more precise, there are facts which it is convenient to describe as acts of the state rather than as acts of individual citizens. The statement that the act of a society is 'really' equivalent to a collection of particular acts of particular members may be logically irrefutable, but it is not of greater value than the statement that the act of an individual is 'really' equivalent to a collection of psychological events. If it is permissible, and even essential, for certain purposes to regard the individual as a unit in action, it is equally permissible to regard a society as such.

It may be objected that the unity of the individual is at any rate factual, while that of the state is hypothetical—even, it may be said, an empty hypothesis. But I am arguing that the unity of the individual, in the sense in which we speak of the will or the self, is also hypothetical. I shall make this point clearer by dealing with a further objection. It will be objected that the application of the terms 'unity' and 'will' to both individual and state entirely blurs the distinction usually made between an organism and an organization. I shall reply by distinguishing between three types of unity. Two of these apply to the human body, which is both a material and an organic unity: for the human body can be described both in material-istic terms as a single piece of matter and in biological terms as a single organism. The third type of unity is psychological. It is in reference to this type of unity that the will unifies the self. The coincidence between biological and psychological unity is only a contingent one. Cases of 'divided personality' illustrate this. Now the difference between the individual and the state consists at any rate partly in this, that the individual can practically always be regarded as a unit in all three senses, whereas the state can be regarded, for certain purposes, as a unit only in the third or psycho-logical sense. It follows that, just as there is no necessary connection between will and organism in the case of the individual, so there is no necessary connection between will and organism in the case of the state. Consequently, the concept of the general will is not incom-patible with the very proper distinction between organisms and organizations.

But where, it may be asked, is the unity of a society located? It is even clearer than in the case of the individual that the unity is discoverable not in the physical effects of the actions but in the intention. What makes a society one society is the end for the sake of which it came into existence and continues to exist. This is easily seen in the case of small and well-defined societies, such as a tennis club or the Council for the Preservation of Rural England. But in larger societies, such as the churches and the trade unions, and especially in the most comprehensive of all societies, the state, the unity becomes hard to discover, because it becomes difficult to say what the common purpose is. But this need only mean that different individuals will give differing accounts of the purpose of such a society. And this makes it still more obvious that the purpose of a society is not identifiable with any combination of the recognized purposes of individuals.

But the unity of the individual was grasped and put to use for purposes of correlating experience only by means of the concept of the will. In the same way, the essential unity of the state is clarified by the concept of the general will. In fact, as in the case of the

individual, there is reason for claiming that the general will 'is' the
unity of the state. Both the terms 'individual will' and 'general will'
have a pragmatic justification, and do not entail any necessary
conclusion as to the metaphysical status of any entity. The important thing is to recognize that the individual will and the general
will have exactly equal claims to recognition. Any grounds there
may be for denying the one will be grounds for denying the other.

This account cannot be complete without an empirical justification of my point, and I can give only the barest summary of one.
The task would be to produce evidence that the general will is in
fact a concept in current use, either under another name or as an
implicit assumption. I can find no explanation for some of the
problems of political obligation except by assuming that there are
facts answering to the requirements of the general will theory. Are
there such facts? Political obligation implies a duty to obey the
laws of the state, which are enacted and promulgated by persons.
It also implies a duty to obey the executors of the law, such as police
and Ministry officials, who are also persons. Yet there is no duty to
obey a person with whom I have not entered into a voluntary
obligation. My reason for obeying him is not that he is a certain
person—I have no duty to him as such—but that he holds a certain
office. And this implies, among other things, that I recognize that
he will act according to the rules governing the tenure of his office
and not in his own personal interest. If it were not known to be
possible that a person could act otherwise than in his own immediate
interest, there could be no obligation to obey him, and therefore no
political obligation.

But if he does not act in his own interest, in whose interest does
he act? The answer is immaterial. He acts according to rules, and
has his own private interest in doing so. Political obligation arises
not because a person in office acts in anyone's interest, but because he
acts in accordance with rules which are embodied in a certain
structure, and because this structure represents the unity of the state
which we have called the general will.

It should now be clear why the ambiguity denounced by the
critics is, as I mentioned at the outset, a source of strength to the
general will theory. I have tried to show that the general will is to
the unity of the state what the individual will is to the unity of the
individual. But the individual will is a unity which can be referred
indifferently either to the individual self or to the end towards which
the acts of the individual are seen to tend. Similarly the general will

ought to imply both that there is something general which wills and that there is a general end which is the object of the will. The critics have seen that this is in fact the case. But their criticism ignores the change of dimension. They assume that the 'something general which wills' could only be a kind of super-individual, a theory which leads to an organic view of the state. But I think I have shown the error in supposing that the subject of the general will would need to be an organism. It would not, however, be paradoxical to attribute to it a kind of 'personality' (defined in a strictly psychological sense) bearing the same relation to the general will as a human personality bears to an individual will. This large-scale 'personality' would be the kind of thing referred to in such expressions as 'the English character' or 'the American way of life'.

The further objection noted, that there cannot be an object of the general will because the individual attitudes to a so-called common object would be all different, assumes what it sets out to prove, that there cannot be a will distinct from combinations of individual wills. But it seems to me that, if there were such a will, it would have an object, the existence of which would be quite compatible with the variety of individual attitudes to it. No individual will, no individual interpretation, even, of the general will, is identical with the general will. No individual wills the common object. Indeed, as we saw in the case of the state, he may not know what it is. To assert that he does will the common object is a self-contradiction, for he wills what he wills, and the common object is what the society wills.

I have throughout been careful to refrain from assigning any factual existence to the general will. I have been content to suggest that, if there is any pragmatic justification for the use of the term 'will' in ordinary descriptions of persons and their actions, then there is a similar pragmatic justification for the use of this term in the description of societies and their actions. Given the conditions under which it becomes a useful concept, it is quite appropriate that the contrast between individual and society should be expressed in terms of the contrast between the individual and the general will.

H

VII

PLATO'S POLITICAL ANALOGIES

by *Renford Bambrough*

Fellow and Tutor of St. John's College, Cambridge

R ECENT work on the origin of philosophical problems and doctrines has been done mainly in the fields of epistemology and ethics. The concepts of mind, knowledge, belief, perception, right, good, will, intention, responsibility, and some of the concepts of mathematics and the advanced natural sciences, have received the careful and almost the exclusive attention of those philosophers who have trodden the trail blazed by the classical English empiricists, and walked in the more freshly-printed footsteps of Moore, Russell and Wittgenstein.

But in the last few years there have been signs that, in spite of the gloomy prognostications of diehard opponents of the linguistic school, and in spite of the youthful exaggerations of some of its early adherents, its methods can be used outside the areas in which they were at first so effectively applied. The second and third generations of linguistic philosophers are seeking new fields to plough. It is no longer considered either over-ambitious or un-respectable for a linguistic philosopher to apply his techniques to the discussion and characterizing of modes of discourse in which his predecessors were, on principle, not interested. The result is that we can now see in a new light some of the most celebrated of the doctrines that have traditionally been called philosophical; we may not agree with the authors of the doctrines as to their precise characters and effects and consequences; we may believe that their authors seriously misconceived the logic of the doctrines; but philosophers of to-day are increasingly free from the delusion that a doctrine has been finally scotched when it has been shown that it is not what it seems, or not what its author supposed it to be. We are learning that an ugly duckling may be an entirely satisfactory swan.

There are two distinct ways in which philosophers have shown their new and refreshing broadmindedness. In the first place there has been a revival of interest in the philosophers of the past, and such

books as that of Mr. Stuart Hampshire on *Spinoza* are likely to
appear more frequently in future: books which are written from
the standpoint of a modern critical philosopher, but which interpret,
sympathetically as well as with penetration, ethical and metaphysical
doctrines built in an earlier manner and style. The second way in
which philosophers are showing the widening of their interests is by
devoting philosophical time and attention to new kinds of questions,
and, in particular, by examining the vocabulary and the grammar
of historical, political and religious discourse. Among recent work
under these heads may be mentioned Mr. T. D. Weldon's book,
The Vocabulary of Politics, Mr. Patrick Gardiner's account of *The
Nature of Historical Explanation*, and Professor John Wisdom's essay
on the logic of *Gods*.

The present essay on Plato's use of analogies in his discussion of
politics is an attempt to combine the two new types of interest: to
set out as accurately and fairly as possible how Plato was led to his
characteristic doctrines in political philosophy, and also to make
certain comments upon those doctrines, and upon his manner of
supporting them, which may be able to establish points about the
nature of political philosophy in general, and what, and by what
means, it may be expected to achieve. Although only Professor
Gilbert Ryle seems to have acted on it, there is a growing belief
that the interpretation of Plato and the elucidation of philosophical
questions and doctrines can profitably be combined.[1] The following
pages have the dual purpose of making Plato's doctrines clear and
making a contribution to the understanding of the logic of political
theories.

It will prevent misunderstanding, and the awakening of expecta-
tions that this essay will not satisfy, if the following points are
stressed at the outset:

(*a*) It is a commonplace that for Plato and Aristotle the relation
between ethics and politics was so close as to make them virtually
one inquiry. No attempt will be made here to force on Plato a
distinction which could only lead to distortion of his doctrines.

(*b*) There will be no discussion of Plato's concrete and particular
political recommendations, but only of the general principles
according to which he claimed to show the necessity for his concrete
proposals.

(*c*) Attention will be concentrated on certain analogies, pictures,

---

[1] G. Ryle: Plato's Parmenides, *Mind*, 1939.

parallels and metaphors which recur repeatedly in Plato's writings on ethics and politics. An attempt will be made to show:

(i) That these analogies were very influential in shaping and directing Plato's political thought.

(ii) That they are in themselves very plausible, and that they continue to influence philosophical and semi-philosophical thinking on politics.

(iii) That they are, nevertheless, if taken too seriously and pressed too far, radically misleading as to the character of political thinking and political action and decision.

(iv) That it does not follow from conclusion (iii), even if it can be adequately established, that the analogies concerned are entirely vicious and unilluminating. Still less does it follow that analogies must be avoided in writing and thinking philosophically about politics (as, for example, Miss Margaret Macdonald in her article 'The Language of Political Theory' might seem to be suggesting).[1]

. . . . .

The analogies which are most characteristic of Plato's way of thinking about ethics and politics are those between the established arts, crafts and branches of knowledge and a supposed art, craft or branch of knowledge whose exponents would be uniquely qualified to pronounce infallibly on questions of value in ethics, politics and aesthetics. They are derived from a characteristically Socratic mode of argument. Socrates was in the habit of asking his listeners to whom they would go for a new ship or a new pair of shoes. When they said, 'To a shipbuilder, to a shoemaker', Socrates would go on to ask to whom they would turn for an ethical or political decision. The only answer that would satisfy him was that political and ethical decisions must be made by political and ethical specialists or experts. Justice seemed to him to be a *techne* like medicine, mathematics, music, or agriculture. In the shoes and ships of which Socrates was for ever talking we have the origin of Plato's conception of the philosopher-king, and of the virtue that is equated with knowledge. In the *Republic*, the *Politicus* and the *Laws*, as well as in the ethical dialogues which deal less prominently with the political aspects of virtue, Plato consistently maintains that the true statesman must be thought of as the possessor of the knowledge of good and evil, an expert physician of the soul whose prescriptions

[1] M. Macdonald: 'The Language of Political Theory', in Flew, ed., *Logic and Language*, 1st Series, 1951.

for spiritually diseased men and cities carry with them an absolute and unchallengeable authority. The average citizen and even the politician of long and wide experience is no better than a layman or a quack doctor in comparison with the philosopher. We insist on having our shoes and ships made by skilled specialists: surely it is unreasonable to rely on our own untutored judgments, or on those of any unskilled amateur, for commodities infinitely more valuable than any material goods?

All such expressions as 'the body politic' and 'the ship of state', which we now use so freely and easily that we are barely conscious that they are metaphorical, are derived ultimately from these Platonic analogies between politics and the specialized arts, crafts, trades and professions. The word 'government' itself is based on a transliteration of *gubernator*, which is in turn a translation of κυβερνήτης—the helmsman who was one of the favourite illustrations of Socrates and Plato. When Plato used them in his dialogues to elaborate a portrait of the politician as a qualified specialist, these metaphors were striking poetical pictures, which had been used by some of the poets but which were still new and suggestive as the basis for political theorizing. The conception of politics that they could most naturally be used to express, and the only one to which they could lead if they were regarded as more than *mere* figures of speech, was firmly opposed to that of the majority of Plato's fellow-citizens in his own and in the preceding century. Plato puts into the mouth of Protagoras a story which presents the democratic view that all citizens are equally entitled to have political and ethical opinions and to exercise political influence. Although some men have special faculties and skills which others lack, a sense of right and wrong was, by the command of Zeus to his messenger Hermes, given equally to all men. It follows that it is reasonable and right to adopt the Athenian practice of entrusting to skilled and trained specialists the building of ships and the treatment of disease, while at the same time reserving to the whole citizen body all questions calling for political decision.[1] The same political principle is embodied in the Funeral Speech of Pericles as given by Thucydides.[2] Not every citizen can be in charge of his city's affairs, but he is competent and he is entitled to criticize the policies of those who govern him.

Against this democratic view Plato set a theory of ethics and politics whose practical consequences would be radically different.

---

[1] *Protagoras*, 320c–328d, especially 322a–324c.   [2] Thucydides, II, 40.

If the royal art of politics is analogous to the art of the healer or the skill of the navigator, then it follows that it can be practised only by the small minority who have the native ability and the training necessary to master its subtlety and complexity. As Plato says in the *Politicus*, even draughts-players of distinction are few and far between in any community, and so it would be foolishly optimistic to expect to find more than a very few men in any place at any time who were qualified to be true statesmen.[1] It is therefore misguided to entrust the government of a city to the whole body of the citizens, or to any minority party among them, or to any individual man who is not qualified by the possession of true political wisdom.

Even the most severe critics of this Platonic political doctrine have acknowledged that it is very plausible. Many commentators have succumbed to its fascination without resistance. What no commentator appears to have done is to do full justice to its plausibility without accepting too many of its implications, or to subject it to the necessary criticisms without being excessively severe. Disputes about the value of these Platonic political analogies share with many other philosophical disputes a chronic unsettleability which has led men of equal discernment as philosophers and commentators to take up diametrically opposed positions about them. What seems to be needed, if it can be obtained, is a neutral account of the logic of the dispute between Plato and his critics, which may be able to show that the dispute is to be ended, not by a victory of one party or the other, but by a setting out of the just claims of both sides.

A feature which distinguishes this dispute from many others of the same general type is that its unsettleability arises not only from the complexity of the logic of such expressions as 'art', 'science', 'branch of knowledge', when they are used in a variety of metaphorical senses, but also from the fact that very much more is at stake than the application of these words. This is not to say that all disputes about the application of words are trivial. The inclination or disinclination to apply a particular word often goes with an ability or inability to see things in a particular light or from a particular point of view, and there may be scope for sustained rational discussion, for argumentation, between the inclined and the disinclined. But disputes which are at the same time about practical issues are both more bitter and less amenable to resolution by neutral analysis. The dispute about Plato's political analogies is such a dispute. We have seen that Plato's aristocratic and monarchical

[1] 292e.

principles can be derived from his analogies, and that a Protagorean criticism of Plato's imagery can contribute to the defence of democratic institutions. In all disputes about the value of particular political analogies the issue is liable to be not only theoretical (logical) but also practical (political) in character, and the task of the logician is to elucidate and to evaluate the arguments that may be urged on both sides, and not to take up the position of one side against the other. Part of this task of elucidation will consist in showing which concrete political proposals are logically related to the acceptance or rejection of particular metaphorical and analogical ways of speaking about politics and politicians. To call for a neutral account of the logic of political analogies is not to suppose that the account, when given, will be equally acceptable to both parties in a dispute about the analogies; nor is it to ask that the logician, in his capacity as citizen, should refuse to favour one side rather than the other. His analysis would be unacceptably tendentious if it were conditioned by his allegiance, but it would, on the other hand, be useless if it were prevented from issuing in allegiance. The remainder of this essay will be an attempt to set out the logic of Plato's political analogies in the manner here suggested.

.   .   .   .   .   .

The doctrine that political wisdom is analogous to a special skill is nowhere more clearly and succinctly expressed than in the Parable of the Ship in the *Republic*, which it will be convenient to quote in full:

> Imagine this state of affairs on board a ship or a number of ships. The master is bigger and burlier than any of the crew, but a little deaf and short-sighted and no less deficient in seamanship. The sailors are quarrelling over the control of the helm; each thinks he ought to be steering the vessel, though he has never learnt navigation and cannot point to any teacher under whom he has served his apprenticeship; what is more, they assert that navigation is a thing that cannot be taught at all, and are ready to tear in pieces anyone who says it can. Meanwhile they besiege the master himself, begging him urgently to trust them with the helm; and sometimes, when others have been more successful in gaining his ear, they kill them or throw them overboard, and, after somehow stupefying the worthy master with strong drink or an opiate, take control of the ship, make free with its stores, and turn the voyage, as might be expected of such a crew, into a drunken carousal. Besides all this, they cry up as a skilled navigator and master of seamanship anyone clever enough to lend a hand in persuading or forcing the master to set them in command. Every other kind of man they condemn as useless. They do not understand that the genuine navigator can only make himself fit to command a ship by studying the seasons of the year, sky, stars, and winds, and all that belongs to his craft; and they have no idea that, along with

the science of navigation, it is possible for him to gain, by instruction or practice, the skill to keep control of the helm whether some of them like it or not. If a ship were managed in that way, would not those on board be likely to call the expert in navigation a mere star-gazer, who spent his time in idle talk and was useless to them?

I think you understand what I mean and do not need to have my parable interpreted in order to see how it illustrates the attitude of existing states towards the true philosopher.[1]

Before attempting to criticize the suggestions contained in this parable it will be advisable to set them out with all possible clarity and precision. In the first place it is clearly implied that there is a body of knowledge which is indispensable to the ruler in precisely the sense in which the knowledge of 'the seasons of the year, sky, stars, and winds', is indispensable to the navigator. This body of knowledge is recognized to be indispensable by all rulers who are worthy of the name. Only a ruler who was ignorant of it would deny that it was relevant and necessary to the purposes of government, and his ignorance would make his denial of no account, since *either*

(a) He knows that the knowledge which he lacks is necessary, and he *dishonestly* denies that it is necessary, *or*

(b) His ignorance of the knowledge that is necessary blinds him also to its necessity, and he *ignorantly* denies that it is necessary.

The knowledge required by the ruler, like the knowledge required by the navigator, can be passed from master to pupil. Just as we should refuse to entrust our safety at sea to a man who had no training or experience in navigation, so ought we to entrust the government of our cities only to the accredited expert in the art of government. Political conflict, whether it is carried on by force of arms or by rhetoric, is both irrational and wicked, since it consists in attempting to settle by force or by mere persuasion a question which is capable of being settled by rational means, and which must be settled by such means if we are not to be criminally misgoverned. The tyrant, the oligarch or the democratic leader who induces men to accept his rule is an impostor: his desire for political power implies the claim that he has mastered a science of which he is in fact ignorant. Such skill as he has is a mere cleverness which deserves the name neither of knowledge nor of art.

The parable presupposes a distinction between knowledge and skill, or between knowing *that* and knowing *how*. The knowledge

[1] VI, 488a–489a, translated by F. M. Cornford.

of times and seasons and stars and winds, and the knowledge of the routes by which particular destinations can most quickly and safely be reached, together form an indispensable part of the equipment of the navigator, but he must also know how to make use of the knowledge at his disposal. Similarly the statesman's qualifications will consist of both science and skill, of theoretical knowledge and the ability to apply it in practice.

. . . . .

This analogy is sound at so many points that Plato and many of his readers have been misled into supposing that it is sound at all points. The clearest way of showing its fatal limitation is to amend the analogy so as to make it wholly accurate. As soon as we do this, we are able to see at once that the analogy, properly understood, can be held to count against the point of view which Plato expresses through it and claims to derive from it. Plato takes the crucial step in the wrong direction when he draws a parallel between a governor's choice of a policy and a navigator's setting of a course, and this move is all the more dangerous because it is so tempting. The true analogy is between the choice of a policy by a politician and the choice of a destination by the owner or passengers of a ship. The point can be put in the familiar terms of ends and means. Plato represents a question about what is to be done (as an end) as if it were very like a question about what is to be done (as a means) in order to achieve some given or agreed end. He obscures the fact that, in politics as well as at sea, the theoretical knowledge and the practical ability of the navigator do not come into play until the destination has been decided upon; and although navigators may have their own preferences for particular destinations, these preferences have no special status, and are neither better nor worse than those of their masters. It follows that the democrat can state his anti-Platonic case in terms of Plato's analogy. Plato's claim that there is a special *techne* by which the political expert may reach infallibly sound decisions can be disposed of by putting it accurately into the terms of Plato's own picture. He is like a navigator who is not content to accept the fares of his passengers or the fee of his master, and then to conduct them where they wish to go, but who insists on going beyond his professional scope by prescribing the route and the destination as well as the course by which the route can best be traversed and the destination most suitably reached.

This criticism reduces the power of the 'ship of state' parable, but it does not leave it quite powerless. Provided that we do not use it for a purpose which it can only serve when it is tendentiously stated, the parable is an illuminating one. Our governors certainly do need special qualities and qualifications if they are to govern well. Not every citizen in a democratic country is equally suitable to be Prime Minister; and those who are suitably gifted need training and experience before they can safely be entrusted with high political office. But it cannot be shown that these special qualities and qualifications amount to knowledge of an absolutely and universally correct set of ultimate political objectives, or to a special skill at selecting such objectives. There is no body of knowledge such that from it can be derived infallible or even fallible decisions about ultimate political objectives. The bus-driver has his special skill and training, but they do not entitle him or enable him to choose the route along which he is to drive. The decisions which a politician is specially qualified to make are decisions about how a given objective is to be reached. Although it is tempting, it is also misleading to pass from one sense to another of the ambiguous proposition that a politician is specially qualified to make decisions. If this means that he has a certain skill and experience at deciding which measures will produce which desired effects, then it is acceptable and unexciting. But if it means that he is entitled to decide which *ultimate* effects are desirable, then it is spectacular and unacceptable. Plato's version of the parable of the Ship of State commits him to the second sense of this proposition, and to the view that there can be and ought to be accredited experts to answer our questions about moral and political values, wise men who will speak with true authority where actual politicians speak only with the authority of force or rhetoric to back them.

.   .   .   .   .

This suggestion that there can be knowledge of what is good, and therefore experts at determining what is good, both for individual men and for communities, is explicit in Plato's recurrent use of the analogy from which all talk of 'the body politic' is ultimately derived; an analogy between justice and bodily health, and between the politician or moralist and the physician.[1] The basic features of this comparison are very like those of the parable of the ship, but it deserves a full and separate treatment because it is so frequently used by Plato and by theorists who are under his influence, and also because some of its consequences are subtly different from those of the analogy between politics and navigation.

[1] E.g. *Gorgias*, 463b ff.; *Politicus*, 293a.

The dualism of body and soul was well established in Greek language and thought before the time of Socrates, but Socrates and Plato sharpened the opposition between them, and used the contrast as the basis for a picture of man from which they derived their conception of the philosopher-statesman as a 'doctor of souls', a physician qualified to prescribe remedies for the spiritual ills of men and cities. The argument may be summarized as follows. When we are sick in body we entrust ourselves to qualified medical practitioners, who have learned their *techne* from qualified teachers. We do not presume to set up our own untrained judgments against those of the specialist whose business it is to know the difference between health and disease, and who has learned by what specifics health may be preserved or restored, and disease cured or avoided. We very properly mistrust the unqualified quacks who fraudulently set themselves up as physicians. But in matters of spiritual health, or justice, which is infinitely more important than mere bodily health, we do not behave so rationally. We either totally neglect our spiritual ailments, or we write out our own untrustworthy prescriptions, or we trust to some demagogue or sophist who has had no training in spiritual medicine, and who does not know, but only pretends to know, under what laws and by what policies a city may be well governed, and by what rule of life an individual man may be made upright and virtuous. An ignorant orator may be able to persuade an ignorant mob that he knows what is good for them and their city, and that the true philosopher is a rogue or a visionary. But the demagogue is in reality no better than a confectioner who persuades a crowd of children to prefer his own wares to the unpalatable drugs of the physician who really has their welfare at heart and who knows how to minister to their needs.[1]

The persuasive force of this elaborate analogy resides mainly in the insistence that actual politicians have not undergone a special course of training in order to learn the nature of the good and to master the methods by which it may be attained. It is perfectly true that none of us, whether a politician or not, has gone through such a course of training. But it is only in the context of the parallel between ethics-and-politics and medicine that we can be induced to feel ashamed of this deficiency. Because it is obvious that a physician who had no special knowledge and no special skill would be no true physician, we are induced to feel that a politician who has not had an analogous training to that of the physician, leading to the possession

[1] *Gorgias*, 521e.

of an analogous body of knowledge, is no true politician, but a fraudulent pretender to a science that he lacks. It is only when we free ourselves from the toils of the analogy that we can see why politicians lack the special training which Plato wishes to prescribe for them. It is not, as Plato suggests, because they are lazy, or morally perverse, or neglectful of a clear duty, but because there is no such special training, no body of political knowledge, analogous to the medical knowledge of the physician, to which the politician could aspire. The complaint that our governors do not know their job has great force because it suggests that we could go further and specify the knowledge that they regrettably lack. The complaint loses its power as soon as we recognize that no such specification is possible. The physician can learn from other physicians how to preserve and restore our health, and he can teach his art and craft to his successors, because within well-known limits there are agreed standards for determining whether a body is healthy or diseased. When the diagnosis has been made, it then becomes possible for the doctor to apply the remedies which experience has shown to be beneficial in comparable cases in the past. But the diagnosis and treatment of spiritual ills is not on such a firm theoretical or experimental basis. There are no agreed standards for determining whether a soul or a city is healthy or diseased, just or unjust, and this is not because spiritual medicine is an under-developed science, but because it is not a science at all. The lack of agreed standards of justice, which is Plato's main reason for pressing the analogy between justice and health, is also the decisive reason against accepting the analogy. Plato's aim is to suggest that he himself *knows* what is ultimately and absolutely good. If we accept this suggestion, then politics and ethics become, for us, sciences like medicine, learning by experiment and experience how to embody in law and policy the given standards of justice and virtue. But we cannot accept the analogy unless we can accept the suggestion, and we cannot accept the suggestion because Plato can say nothing in its defence that could not equally be said by a rival claimant to ultimate and absolute knowledge of the good, in defence of a different set of 'absolute' standards. Only if there were some conclusive tests by which we could adjudicate in a dispute between Plato and his absolutist rival would it be proper to speak of ethical and political knowledge in the sense required by the Platonic analogies between ethics-and-politics and the *technai* of medicine, navigation, shoemaking and shipbuilding: and there are no such conclusive tests. Ethical and political disagreement is different in logical kind from medical disagreement or disagreement between navigators. Ethical and political disagreement is radical and interminable in a sense in which scientific disagreement, or disagreement about the means for achieving an agreed end, is terminable by recognized procedures; such disagreement remains terminable in principle even when it is not terminated in fact. But ethical and political disagreement in its most characteristic forms is interminable, because it is not about means, but about ends.

This is not to say that none of the disagreements which are commonly and properly called ethical and political are about means rather than ends. The fact that there are such disagreements is one of the main sources of the Platonic doctrine, and is indeed one of the important truths that the doctrine embodies. Still less is it to say that ethical and political discussion is useless or irrational: and it is here that the greatest positive value of the Platonic analogies is to be found. What the analogies teach us, at the cost of certain distortions and exaggerations which may mislead us on other points, is the important lesson that there is scope for sustained rational discussion about the choice of ends and purposes. If we see the analogies at their true value, giving them neither too much nor too little weight, we shall avoid making each of two serious errors:

(i) *The Platonic error*: the error of supposing that, since ethical and political questions are proper themes for rational discussion and inquiry, and in this respect are like questions of fact, they must also be like questions of fact in the further respect that the answers to them will embody *knowledge*, and that to each of the questions there will be one incontrovertibly true or correct answer, if only it can be found.

(ii) *The anti-Platonic error*: the error of supposing that, since the answers to ethical and political questions do not embody knowledge, and are not such that to each of the questions there is one incontrovertibly true or correct answer, and in this respect ethical and political questions differ from factual questions, they must differ *toto caelo* from factual questions, and must be incapable of being rationally discussed and satisfactorily answered.

To see that both these errors are errors is to learn important lessons about the logic of ethical and political questions, statements and disputes, and it will therefore be appropriate to consider generally, and not only in direct connection with the Platonic analogies, certain questions about the logic of choice and decision which a discussion of the analogies has raised. But first it will be convenient to complete the account of the analogies themselves by making some comments on those which have not been considered at length.

.   .   .   .   .

Besides navigation and medicine, Plato illustrates his conception of ethics and politics by reference to mathematics and music, to the arts of manufacture, such as shoemaking, shipbuilding and weaving, and to the tendance of animals. None of these calls for a full and separate treatment, since the comments made above on the analogies with medicine and navigation apply, *mutatis mutandis*, to all the analogies in general. It will be sufficient to indicate those features of each *techne* which make it an unsuitable model for the supposed *techne* of ethics and politics.

The importance of mathematics and music for Plato's purpose is that they are disciplines in which, *par excellence*, we find questions to which there are precisely correct answers, and experts who can find and give those answers as men speaking with authority. For Plato, as for Locke, mathematics was the paradigm of certainty and accuracy to which morals and politics were required to conform.[1] But the ambition is a hopeless one precisely because of those features of ethical discourse of which Plato complained, and without which ethical discourse would not be ethical discourse. We accept the expert's solution of a mathematical problem because we know from experience that he agrees with other experts, and he agrees with other experts because the problem can be precisely stated and there are approved methods of solving it. These conditions do not hold in ethics and politics. There are not even any adequate neutral criteria for determining who are the experts, so that an attempt to appeal to experts simply transforms an ethical or political dispute into an equally unsettleable dispute about who are the ethical or political experts. In such a case as this it has become misleading to speak of experts at all, since it is an important part of the meaning of the word 'expert', in its standard uses, that an expert is a man who can be appealed to by the ignorant or puzzled layman.

The practical skill of the shoemaker, the shipbuilder, or the weaver seems at first sight to be a more promising model for the practical skill of the politician, but here again, as in the cases of navigation and medicine, it is found that Plato has obscured certain important

[1] Locke: *Essay Concerning Human Understanding*, Pringle-Pattison's edition, p. 277.

dissimilarities between the original and the alleged copy. Just as we were allowed to forget that it is the passengers and not the navigator who choose the destination and the route of a ship, although it is the navigator's skilled task to set and steer the course, so are we allowed to forget that the skill of the craftsman is an instrument which serves the purposes of his patron. The craftsman's function is a mastery of the means by which a given end can be achieved; the choosing of the end is no concern of the craftsman *qua* craftsman. There is certainly some analogy between the craftsman's skill and the skill and experience of the politician at managing men and affairs, but the parallel breaks down at the crucial point, since there is wide general agreement on the purposes to be served by shoes or ships or clothes, while there is no such agreement on the ends to which men and affairs are to be manipulated. As soon as we cease to assimilate the choice of ends to the choice of means we also cease to ask that ends should be chosen as only means can be chosen. When the Platonic analogy is fully and accurately stated it no longer inclines us to accept the doctrine it was designed to support, for we then see that it is the unskilled customer who decides, and the skilled craftsman who acts on his instructions. Ethical and political disagreements are disagreements between the customers, and ethical and political skill, in the only sense in which the phrase can properly be used, is incapable of composing such disagreements.

Similarly, the shepherd and the goatherd are skilled at tending flocks and herds for well-known and well-agreed purposes. Their skill at feeding and fattening animals is instrumental to their own or their masters' desire for wool or milk or meat or money; it is a skill not at choosing, but at serving purposes. The shepherd of men is less favourably placed. There is no agreement about the ends to which his skill must be applied, and it is not only his fellow-shepherds, but also the sheep themselves, who justly feel entitled to be taken into his counsels. Despotism is the only political system which can be favoured by those who take this analogy seriously, and even if we mistakenly take the analogy as a valid argument in favour of a despotic form of government, we shall still be faced with all the questions which the analogy was intended to answer. These questions will now take the form, 'Who is to be the despot?' and 'To what ends is the despot to use his power?' To say that philosophers should rule is not to answer those questions *de finibus bonorum et malorum* which Plato claimed to be answering, since they all arise again as questions about the selection and training of the philosophers. The answer is acceptable only so long as it is vacuous; as soon as it acquires any content it is tendentious: and it is dangerously easy to fail to notice the transition from the platitude to the dogma that can be expressed in the same form of words.

Wherever Plato turns among the *technai*, although the word covers a wide variety of skills, studies and pursuits which no modern language would call by one single name, he cannot find what he is seeking, a skill at determining which ends ought and ought not to be pursued. He is conscious of this difficulty, and he attempts to overcome it by distinguishing between the standard, instrumental arts, and a higher, prescriptive art, the kingly art of politics.[1] All the lower arts are means to ends; the royal art, as practised by the true philosopher, prescribes to the lower arts the ends they are to serve. But this is to stop an unbridgeable gap with an empty name. There is no such prescriptive *techne*, not because civilization is in its infancy, but for the inescapable logical reason that anything which can properly be called a *techne* will be by its very nature instrumental, and the decision about the purpose for which it is to be used will lie outside its own scope.

.   .   .   .   .

A critical account of Plato's political analogies has led us to diagnose and treat the Platonic error of over-assimilating questions about ends to questions about means, of demanding that there should be neutral and definitive answers to deliberative questions as well as to questions of logic and questions of fact. But if we take an overdose of the antidote we shall commit the anti-Platonic error of underestimating the similarities between deliberative questions and other kinds of questions. It is not for nothing that they are all called questions, and that the grammatical form of a question of fact is often indistinguishable from the grammatical form of a deliberative question. This similarity in name and form is the prime source of the Platonic error. It seems natural to expect that the question 'Which is the highest mountain on earth?' should be as logically similar as it is grammatically similar to the question 'Which is the best life on earth?' But when we look closely at the methods we adopt in answering these two questions, and at the language in which we conduct and describe our search for the answers, we see the important differences as clearly as we saw at first sight the important similarities. Questions about what is the case are answered

---

[1] See, e.g. *Politicus*, 260c.

by investigation leading to discoveries which are recorded in sentences which are both grammatically and logically indicative. Questions about what is to be done are answered by a process of deliberation leading to decisions which are recorded in sentences which are sometimes grammatically indicative, but whose logical mood is imperative rather than indicative.

The difference in the logical moods of the answers to the different kinds of questions is connected with differences in the logic of the questions themselves. It is also connected with differences in the logic of the procedures and the concepts we use in seeking for and recording the answers. When we have seen that the logic of factual questions both resembles and is different from the logic of deliberative questions, we shall be prepared to find that the logic of any concept which is used in dealing with both types of question will be appropriately different for each type of question; but we shall then need to guard against the danger of taking the differences too seriously, and denying that both types of questions are proper questions. The Platonic error and the anti-Platonic error have a common source in the error of supposing that all proper questions are to be answered in the logical indicative, that all proper questions are questions about what is the case. Plato recognizes that deliberative questions are proper questions and therefore supposes that they must be questions about what is the case. The anti-Platonist recognizes that deliberative questions are not questions about what is the case and therefore supposes that they are not proper questions.

To accept the Platonic analogies unconditionally is to suppose that the concepts of knowledge, truth, right answer, speaking with authority, expert, have the same logical roles in ethics and politics as they have in science and mathematics. To reject the Platonic analogies unconditionally is to suppose that none of these concepts has any place in the logic of ethics and politics. To give due weight to the Platonic analogies is to recognize that some of these concepts have a place in the logic of ethics and politics, but that the logical roles they play in ethics and politics are different from those they play in science and mathematics.

In science one expert agrees with another about the answers to most questions within their field, and the answers on which they agree are usually the right answers. The experts speak with authority, and the answers that they give are the map of a field of knowledge. It would be rash and unreasonable of a layman to disagree with an expert about the shape of the earth or the size of the sun or

I

the ecology of orchids. Even when the experts disagree, they agree at least on the methods by which their dispute could be settled. They know what it would be like for the truth to be discovered, for one of them to be proved wrong. Even if they are both equally right they will not both be right to the same degree on the same question; they may be right about different questions in a cluster of questions; but as long as they are really contradicting each other only one of them can be right. Science is to this extent neat and tidy and safe. To one question, one answer; to one question of fact, one fact.

But in ethics and politics the experts disagree so much and so radically that we hesitate to say that they are experts. The Prime Minister and the Leader of the Opposition disagree as violently as the untutored laymen who sent them to Parliament. Whatever our own political views we shall have experts on our side and experts against us, even if we think that politicians are amateurs and we turn to those dons who *really* know about these things. But how can they know? They cannot all be right, and yet it seems that however long and hard we try we can never show that any of them is wrong. Perhaps they are all really amateurs, even the dons and the ministers, and we need a philosopher-king to teach them. Perhaps we ought to follow Plato and Mrs. Barbara Wootton to that 'entirely new and exciting country' where science is science and politics is also science and where they have a proper disrespect for 'unprofessional political judgment'. In this happy land 'controversies on matters on which at present reasonable men may differ will eventually fall into the category of arguments about the flatness or roundness of the earth'.[1]

But this will never do: and we see why it will never do when we see that the relation of decisions to deliberative questions is different from the relation of discoveries to questions of fact. There is nothing to which my decision must correspond in order to be a reasonable decision in the way that my belief must correspond to what the world is like in order to be a true belief; and so there is nothing to prevent your decision and my decision from both being reasonable although your decision is different from mine. In ethics and politics we can differ and go on differing and still be reasonable men. But of course some men are unreasonable, and they make their decisions without sufficient thought and knowledge, without looking far

[1] Barbara Wootton, 'The Social Sciences and Democratic Political Practice', in *Confluence*, vol. 3, no. 1.

enough back upon experience or far enough forward to the consequences. Plato is right when he urges that we ought to be as careful in deliberation as we ought to be in investigation, even if he is wrong when he presses the point by saying that deliberation *is* investigation. Mrs. Barbara Wootton is right when she says that a good democracy is an educated and well-informed democracy, even if she is wrong when she presses the point by sketching an ideally educated democracy in which Parliament would be a fact-finding commission and the Opposition would never earn their salaries.

In fields where the authorities not only do but *must* disagree, it is tempting either to choose one authority and say that he is the only authority, or to deny that there are any authorities at all: to forget that the great statesman or the great moralist has all the authority conferred by wide knowledge, long experience, clear thought, and above all the tolerant recognition that the search for the right solution to a practical problem can never be ended by a Q.E.D.

VIII

LIBERAL MORALITY AND SOCIALIST MORALITY

by W. B. Gallie

Professor of Philosophy, the Queen's University, Belfast

ONE morality or many? Liberal Morality and Socialist Morality; bourgeois morality and Georges Sorel's 'morality of producers'; Protestant morality and Catholic; Greek morality and Christian; 'aristocratic' morality and 'slave' morality, 'open' morality and 'closed' morality—what, if any, is the relevance of such distinctions as these to moral philosophy?

Looked at from one angle they suggest something obvious enough; the fact that in different times and places different systems or aggregates of moral belief have prevailed, and the fact that sometimes in one and the same community different groups of people have adhered to different, in some cases to violently conflicting, moral beliefs. While no intelligent and informed person has ever denied these facts, moral philosophers have disagreed greatly as to their interpretation: I think, however, that their disagreements can be fairly summed up under the four following lines of interpretation.

First, what I shall call the 'monarchic' view explains the existence of moral cleavages and conflicts in a very simple way. It points out that, although in every moral situation there is only one right judgment to be made or action to be chosen, yet the possibilities of moral error or failure are in every case enormous; and this simple fact explains all the real or basic differences in men's moral beliefs which history discloses. It may, of course, be granted on the monarchic view, that in any actual situation the right moral judgment or decision must take notice of many 'non-moral' (factual) features of that situation, and that, since adequate knowledge of these is not always equally available to different (and let us assume equally conscientious) agents, apparent (but only apparent) moral disagreements may be inevitable between them. And it may further be granted that differences in the non-moral features of situations typical of two different communities, e.g. differences in respect of the experimental knowledge and administrative skill possessed by them, may be so great, and may affect all moral questions arising within either community so profoundly, that it is perfectly natural (though it can be dangerously misleading) to talk about two different moralities, and to label them with the names of the communities or types of community, in which they are found. But these admissions, for the monarchic view, in no way alter the fact that the cardinal moral attributes, right and wrong, good and bad, etc., apply and apply univocally in every situation to which moral considerations are in any way relevant. Thus, on the monarchic view, it should be possible theoretically (for all that it is in fact causally impossible) for a Chinese gentleman of the fifth century B.C., an Athenian citizen of the same period, a medieval monk and a contemporary citizen of Ealing or Nijni-Novgorod, to settle down and reach agreed and valid conclusions as to the duties of *any* man in certain well-defined moral situations, e.g. to decide in what circumstances, if any, a man should actively resist the commands of his Government. On the monarchic view, therefore, phrases such as Liberal morality and Socialist morality are ethically unimportant; since on this view moral philosophy is concerned only with those supreme moral principles and notions which are always applicable in no matter how widely divergent situations.

The monarchic view has, I think, been held by almost every great moral philosopher up to the present century. Certainly it possesses the attraction of logical simplicity and certain tonic properties highly relevant to moral practice; for, as a rule (though there is no logical necessity about this) adherents of the monarchic view assume that the particular moral beliefs to which they subscribe at least exemplify the one and only valid set of moral canons that exists; and surely no higher-order belief could be more important than this for inspiring and sustaining moral steadfastness. On the other hand, I must confess that the almost Augustinian exclusiveness of the monarchic view distresses me. Not so much because I dread being classed with the vast variety of moral goats who roam the wide pastures of error; nor yet because I think that adherents of the view are necessarily committed to a kind of higher-order self-righteousness: but rather because I suspect the parochial narrowness of their moral perspective. How often, I wonder, do adherents of the monarchic view reflect seriously on the range and variety of men's moral experience —from the men of Cro-Magnon to the present day? Moreover, I find highly suspicious the studied lack of interest, shown by most adherents of this view, to our rapidly accumulating knowledge of the different ways in which, in different communities, morality is learnt.

The second line of interpretation I call the polyarchic view. This, as its name suggests, stands in radical opposition to the monarchic view, maintaining that, far from there being one single set of valid moral standards, there are an indefinite number of these, embodied in different moralities whose cardinal principles are not mutually corrigible. Hence our previous happy picture of the Chinese Mandarin and his friends was a wholly misleading one; for the participants in the imaginary discussion would have been simply unable to comprehend each other's moral viewpoints. That there are and have been fundamentally different moralities is, for the polyarchic view, no more surprising than that there are and have been fundamentally different forms of human community, and of human language, art, religion and education: forms so different, that is to say, that even the theoretical possibility of mutual correction and supplementation between them doesn't arise. Within any given morality, different commands, appeals, valuations, etc., may be criticized, may be compared and classified as absolute, conditional, etc.; but between different moralities—well, the commands simply don't carry, the appeals don't work, the valuations and judgments lose their singleness of meaning; consequently comparisons and classifications can be of interest only to ignorant busybodies.

Now this, the polyarchic view, suffers from lack of a distinguished ancestry, although I suspect that something of Aristotle's and much of Hume's view of morality might be retained within a polyarchic framework. Lack of long ancestry should not, however, be counted against the polyarchic view; since the considerations that lend it weight—mainly historical, anthropological and psychological— could hardly have suggested themselves before the nineteenth century. Among recent writers of repute, Bergson, Sorel and Santayana seem to me, in their different ways, to be polyarchic moralists. None of these writers, however, has paid anything like sufficient attention to the logical difficulties that their view involves: in particular the difficulty of deciding at what point divergences in moral practice and belief should be taken as signs of the existence of two or more distinct moralities. In general, it seems to me, the difficulty with the polyarchic view is not to defend it—it is easy enough to appreciate the strength of the evidence that *might* be brought forward in support of it: the difficulty is, rather, first to state it in consistent and logically manageable form, and, secondly, really to believe it, or to 'live with it' if that expression may be allowed, since, if true, the polyarchic view means that we should abandon all hope of settling major moral disagreements by discussion. And this is a conclusion which I, for one, feel very uncomfortable about accepting.

The two remaining lines of interpretation can be dealt with more briefly. The first, ethical relativism, resembles the polyarchic view superficially, since it agrees that there are and have been different moralities which are not mutually corrigible; but, further, it maintains that different moralities are always relative to other and more basic differences between groups, communities, civilizations: they are relative to—and this I suppose means theoretically deducible from if not reducible to—differences in, for instance, experimental and historical knowledge, forms and traditions of tribal and national life, methods of organizing production and distribution of goods, and so on. In effect, then, ethical relativism can be considered as the polyarchic view qualified (or perhaps we should say neutralized) by a very simple-minded and dogmatic theory of scientific and other forms of explanation. From the point of view of theoretical ethics, therefore, ethical relativism is not of great importance: it involves all the difficulties of the polyarchic view, and others which call for criticism from logic and metaphysics rather than from ethics. From the practical standpoint, however, ethical relativism is of the first importance; since one extreme and widely accepted form of it is Marxism.

Lastly, we have the Idealist interpretation which represents morality as essentially one and absolute and eternal, and yet such that it inevitably differentiates itself into radically conflicting forms or phases. Happy reconciliation, it might seem, of the monarchic and polyarchic views, each of which has such obvious attractions and at the same time such apparently inescapable defects. But, alas, few competent thinkers to-day would be willing to accept the arguments (if this word can be used) by which Hegel and his followers advanced their at once uplifting and comfortable conclusions. I mention the Idealist view, however, because it may, however obliquely, throw light on what has become, in my belief, the most important problem facing moral philosophy to-day. Namely: How, or on the basis of what sorts of consideration, should we seek to decide between the monarchic and the polyarchic view of moral differences? Or, more simply, Is Morality one or many?

Recent writers on ethics, it seems to me, have either shirked this question or tried to approach it along altogether unpromising lines. For the last four decades the ablest moral philosophers, in this country at any rate, have been preoccupied almost exclusively with certain problems in the 'logic of ethics': questions as to the definability or indefinability of key ethical expressions, and as to the possibility, or 'correctness', in any language, of combining certain ethical expressions or of analysing certain of these in terms of certain others. Some of these questions are of great logical interest; but if anyone has thought that answers to any of them would suffice to answer our question, 'One morality or many?' then he was certainly mistaken; and if anyone makes the milder claim that answers to the above questions are a necessary prerequisite of answering our question, I would say that he is very probably mistaken. My reason for saying this is simply that the 'logic of ethics' is, like all logic, concerned solely with consistency and inconsistency of meanings and usages—and is concerned, in particular, with meanings and usages used within a given language *to express a given morality*: it is powerless to decide whether or not different languages, or for that matter any one language, can be used to express a number of different moralities. The question, One morality or many?—in this like the questions, One time-series or many? One God or many? One set of aesthetic values or many?—being a question of fact, is one that no amount of logical analysis can ever possibly decide.

What the true answer to this question is I do not know, and what suggestions I could put forward as to the way we should set about trying to answer it are at once vague and unconfident. What perhaps I can do usefully, and shall now attempt, is to suggest how one illustrative instance of it should be presented, so as to serve as starting-point for more ambitious discussion. I ask: Do we, in this country to-day, subscribe to two distinct moralities which might reasonably be labelled Liberal and Socialist? This is my question; but the bulk of what I have to say will be aimed at showing that this question is a real and intelligible one.

THE LIBERAL-SOCIALIST CONFLICT

We have certainly been told by a number of eminent politicians that behind our present political divisions there lie certain fundamental differences in moral outlook. To be sure, those who tell us this (chiefly from the ranks of anti-Socialist parties) would claim that there is in fact only one true morality, viz. 'liberal morality';

just as those who deny it (chiefly from the Socialist ranks) would claim that socialist policies *in this country at any rate* are quite compatible with that 'liberal morality', and are indeed the best means of implementing or 'fulfilling' it. But we should not too seriously take this preference, on the part of active politicians, for the monarchic view; for when our politicians assert or deny a fundamental cleavage in our moral aims and standards they are almost certainly thinking of a cleavage by classes, or at least by 'pressure-groups'. This, however, is not the only form that a fundamental moral cleavage might take. Why shouldn't it exist *within* each one of us? Why shouldn't each one of us, in some degree, be internally divided, pulled this way and that on different issues by the claims and counter-claims of two conflicting moralities? The moral and political heritage of our nation makes this suggestion, to my mind, an extremely plausible one In this country we have a long tradition of letting the other side have its say, and of combining hard-hitting debate with the attempt to understand our opponent's point of view. Thus, assuming that our two (presumptive) moralities have been continuously expressed, however imperfectly and inconsistently, in public debate and discussion over the last seventy odd years, what could be more natural than that the main claims and tenets of each of them—and more, the main springs of appeal and inspiration peculiar to each—should have passed into all or most of us, unobtrusively and perhaps even insensibly, in the course of our education, reading, and day-to-day discussion of political and moral issues? Anyhow, in what follows I am going to assume that any fundamental moral cleavage in *this* country, as between Liberal and Socialist aims and standards, is such that its results are to be found within individuals quite as much as between different groups or classes of individuals.

Two other preliminary points may be made here. Obviously by the choice of the names Liberal and Socialist I intend that my two (to repeat, presumptive) moralities are intimately connected with a familiar political division. Liberal Morality, if it exists as a distinct morality, must be primarily a political morality, i.e. its central principles must be concerned with the relations of State and citizen: and similarly with Socialist Morality. But if either in fact deserves the name of a morality it must evidently extend, or be in the process of extending, to other moral issues which would not ordinarily be said to have any close connection with politics. That this is the case —that the principles of Liberal Morality, for instance, could be disclosed in fields as different as family relations, industrial relations, educational and cultural ideals—could, I think, be quite plausibly suggested. But to elaborate such ideas would be a secondary task and one that I cannot attempt in the present paper. On the other hand, it might reasonably be admitted, by anyone asserting the existence of our two moralities, that a number of moral principles and beliefs (for instance, certain parts of our sexual morality) are such that they can easily be incorporated within both our moralities without, however, destroying their distinctness. The principle of monogamy, and the incest taboo, are obvious examples.

But, secondly, because of the long continuous tradition of our political and social institutions in this country, it is natural to assume that our two moralities may be even more intimately related. And in fact, it seems to me, that Socialist Morality (as I shall represent it) arises from a protest, an almost unwilling protest, against the practical inadequacies of Liberal Morality, from which it retains—or perhaps we should say takes for granted—certain very important moral principles. For this reason the issue which I have chosen to illustrate the question, One morality or many? may seem an unfortunate and muddling one. Would it not have been better to choose, for illustrative purposes, the unmistakable conflict between our so-called Western morality and the morality that prevails in Communist countries? The difficulty about this suggestion is to know what Communist morality is or is like. (Some of us, no doubt, would deny that there is any such thing, would claim that Communism is an a-moral, if not anti-moral, political doctrine.)[1] And the same kind of difficulty would arise if we were to select for comparison and contrast the moralities of two civilizations widely separate in respect of scientific knowledge and administrative skill. On the whole, it is best to begin by considering a conflict of moralities which (as I hope to show can plausibly be held) may well exist at our own doorstep. We can thus be reasonably confident that we know what we are talking about; and may thus get a somewhat clearer appreciation of what polyarchic moralists are talking about, when they insist on the distinctness of different moralities.

How, then, should we try to articulate the hypothesis of the Liberal-Socialist conflict? The best way I can think of is this: I shall try to set out very briefly, for comparison and contrast, the differ-

---

[1] I am convinced that this view is wrong. A morality of a kind exists—i.e. calls out genuinely conscientious effort and action—in Communist countries. And perhaps some of us *do* know what it is like—if, that is, we met during childhood with that morality in which 'being good' means being obedient, working hard, and in particular saying to strangers only the things we have been told to say to them.

ent meanings which three cardinal moral notions, those of justice, liberty and good government, might reasonably be expected to possess within our two moralities, assuming that they exist. And in doing this I shall for simplicity write, in the sections that follow, as though I were fully convinced (as in fact I am not) that Liberal Morality and Socialist Morality really do exist and conflict in our society, and indeed in each one of us.

JUSTICE, LIBERTY AND GOOD GOVERNMENT ACCORDING TO LIBERAL MORALITY

1. For Liberal Morality justice is essentially a *commutative* conception, grounded on the familiar claim that rewards or returns should be proportional to merit. This claim is recognized by men whenever they co-operate, be their motives for co-operation never so selfish: indeed, recognition of it is perfectly compatible with (some would say, is necessarily involved in) a reasoned egoism. The ideas of distributive and retributive justice presuppose the notion of commutation: for instance, in the economic field the idea of fair shares and fair compensation presuppose the idea of a fair or open market in which the relative merits of different products and services are gauged.

For Liberal Morality, then, justice consists primarily in those arrangements whereby the meritorious individual, wherever his work or services are publicly available, shall receive back his (commutative) due.

2. Commutative justice is best assured when each individual is left free to decide in what ways he will use his own capacities and property, subject to the proviso that *his* way shall not prevent others from using their capacities and property in *their* ways; and evidently the system of free contract is an admirable device for ensuring this result wherever men choose to divide and 'mix' their labour. But this account and defence of individual liberty is inadequate, since it presents liberty as a purely instrumental value, a means of achieving commutative justice. The fact is that the idea of commutative justice logically *requires* that the individual shall be a freely choosing agent: otherwise our ideas of the meritorious individual and of rewards proportional to merit would lose an essential part of their meaning. Liberal Morality requires that each of us shall be left free to market or canvass his wares (be they material or intellectual, political or religious) and on *this* condition get back what returns

our wares are proved to deserve. Thus, liberty, for Liberal Morality, means primarily liberty to get what one deserves.

Lest this should seem an unpleasantly hard-headed conception, it may be recalled that Liberal Morality is concerned with men's recognizable claims on one another, not with liberty as an abstract or poetic ideal: it is concerned with those claims that can justify themselves competitively, or, more generally, with claims that deserve to be taken seriously. Freedom, for Liberal Morality, emphatically does not mean, for instance, freedom to live on the back of the community.

3. For Liberal Morality the main functions of a good Government are negative and preventive, e.g. defence of country and protection of life and property. The positive function of government is to safeguard the greatest possible freedom of choice for every citizen; and probably the best way of doing this is to facilitate and simplify the making of free contracts and to enforce these once they are made. (This is perhaps the main reason why Liberal Morality, while admitting that capacity and property—and hence returns on these—may always be unequal between different individuals, insists so emphatically on the principle of equality before the law.)

These limitations on the scope of government are usually urged by Liberals on grounds of efficiency; but they can also be defended on specifically moral grounds. In the first place, 'If legislation interferes in a direct manner, it must be by punishment':[1] but punishment can be morally defended only when there is *already* an offence against the right of the individual to use his capacity and property in his own way. Extension of legislation, however, beyond the tasks already mentioned, inevitably eats into the field in which the individual can exercise this right. To look at the matter from another angle, whenever Governments engage in creative, productive tasks, a number of individuals are not only deprived of their liberty to produce and create, but, since their work is now directed by Government (under the threat of punishment) they are deprived of one of the main conditions of moral dignity, viz. the chance of rewards that will measure the wisdom of their choices and the consistency of their efforts. Thus, whether or not socialistic legislation must result in political tyranny, it will inevitably produce a kind of moral suffocation. Such legislation is always to be resisted, perhaps especially when it is defended under such pretty names as 'action in accordance with the general will' or 'collective action'.

[1] Bentham.

I can only hope that the above 'interpretations' of justice, liberty and good government suggest the kernel of something that can reasonably be named Liberal Morality. Evidently this kernel is made up of four closely interweaving notions: those of justice as primarily commutative, of individual merit, of freedom of choice and contract as morally defensible (indeed as morally necessary) and of the self-limiting character of good government. We shall see how each of these notions, as asserted in Liberal Morality, is not only contradicted but opposed in the most radical manner in Socialist Morality. But before turning to this I want to revert for a moment to my earlier statement that Socialist Morality arises from a 'Socialist Protest' against the inadequacies of Liberal Morality. This protest is lodged largely on *factual* grounds. Thus it complains that the Liberal account of justice is defective or misleading since it suggests that the capacities and property of different individuals are either things given by Nature or else in some way 'meritoriously owned'; whereas, in fact, property—and hence to some extent capacity—are usually the result of inheritance. Similarly, it is protested that the system of free contract does not in fact always or even usually result in the greatest possible fairness in rewards. And, again, it can be argued that the Liberal account of good government rests on the factual (but false) assumption that no important improvements in governmental machinery can ever be devised, and hence that all government or collective action must remain, basically, of a restrictive and repressive kind. It is unnecessary to elaborate these protests which have been repeated so often in Socialist literature. It is important, however, to bear them in mind, for they help to explain, or at least to mitigate, some of the more surprising—at first sight more 'starry-eyed' and unrealistic—features of Socialist Morality.

JUSTICE, LIBERTY AND GOOD GOVERNMENT ACCORDING TO SOCIALIST MORALITY

For Socialist Morality justice is essentially a distributive, not a commutative conception. Nor is it based on any of the *actual* claims men make, or have made, on one another in respect of fair rewards and returns; for all such claims are subject to the taint of non-moral self-interests and pressures, whether from individuals or groups. Justice, like all other strictly moral notions, is derived from an ideal —conceived as realizable in the future and already in some measure affecting men's aspirations—an ideal state of affairs in which moral claims would act as motives entirely without the taint of self-interest. Such is the ideal of Socialist society in which men would co-operate for two main motives: first, to ensure an adequate material basis of life for all, this being conceived as an absolute moral duty; and second, to ensure for all the greatest possible freedom in those departments of life in which freedom is in fact a necessary condition of a good or 'truly human' life. Absolute or ideal justice can be achieved only in Socialist society, which indeed is the embodiment of justice: relative justice, in the meanwhile, consists in those arrangements and policies which aim at realizing the Socialist ideal.

On this view the claims of commutative justice are not forgotten: on the contrary, they are explicitly rejected as misnomers. That men have always desired rewards proportional to merit may be admitted; and that legal recognition of this desire, in certain societies, has contributed to rapid economic advances, may also be admitted. But these admissions do nothing to establish the moral defensibility of the desire or its recognition. In its cruder forms (e.g. 'An eye for an eye, and a tooth for a tooth') the idea of commutation is a morally repulsive one: in more refined forms, e.g. the puritanical quest of rewards for personal merit, it is hardly less objectionable—the old Adam of egoism rationalized into respectability.

2. The idea of commutative justice being rejected, it is clear that the Liberal defence of freedom of choice and contract—generalized in the conception of freedom to get what one deserves—makes no appeal whatever to Socialist Morality. What, then, are the freedoms which Socialist Morality finds necessary to a good or truly human life? It may be noticed, in the first place, that the freedoms to which Liberal Morality gives most attention—freedom of contract and freedom of speech and expression—are of particular interest to three classes of men: entrepreneurs, professional consultants, and 'intellectuals'. But there are, of course, other freedoms which members of these favoured classes usually enjoy—indeed enjoy so plentifully that they usually take their existence for granted—but of which the great mass of men are only too often deprived: in particular the freedoms associated with leisure, freedom to obtain disinterested knowledge, to cultivate tastes of one's own, freedom —or the genuine opportunity—to enjoy one's friendships and family-life: in general, that freedom which consists in moral elbow-room, in the sense of having a life of one's own; freedom to *be*— whatever is worth being for its own sake, rather than freedom to get—that so-called 'fair reward', which is too often got by snatching it from under the nose of one's neighbour. This freedom, freedom

to *be*, cannot be legislated into existence; but it is our duty to ensure by whatever means we can devise, that the most obvious obstacles to it shall be removed. Among these are the economic waste and insecurity involved in every form of competitive (liberal) economy.

The ideals of freedom of thought and expression, like the principle of equality before the law, are things which Socialist Morality gratefully takes over from Liberal Morality; but with the reflection that these principles point beyond the narrow confines in which that morality sets them. It is the privilege of Socialist Morality not simply to inherit these principles, but to generalize and fulfil them. (The great error of Liberal Morality was to consider them as so sacrosanct or so invulnerable that it would be either blasphemous or useless to examine, with a view to enduring, their conditions: this being only one example of the Liberal's failure to see that unless men deliberately control the blind aggregate of social forces, these forces will certainly control *them*.)

3. Legislation in Socialist society, and the kinds of legislation that will bring this society into being, will inevitably be concerned with the direction of economic life. The merits of a socialized economy are commonly urged in terms of efficiency, e.g. the elimination of competitive waste; and the relevance of this line of argument to the Socialist conception of freedom we have already seen. But the moral case for socialized production and distribution can be argued more directly. First, since the provision of material sufficiency for all is an absolute duty, binding on each one of us, we cannot leave its fulfilment to the enterprise—or lack of enterprise—of a number of individuals using their resources in ways that *they* think best. Each one of us, on the contrary, is morally obliged to demand and, when it is established, to support and serve the kind of organization that can fulfil this first demand of Socialist Morality. But secondly, suppose a collective economy in existence and actually meeting this demand: would not this fact be an inspiration to a new kind of 'moral solidarity' that could afford to tolerate—and more, to welcome and foster—such freedom, spontaneity and variety in the lives and tasks of our fellows as are necessary for their enjoyment of a 'truly human' life? Thirdly, a more speculative defence. We all know that certain values and virtues cannot in strictness be counted individual possessions, since they exist only *between* individuals, in friends, marriages, clubs, schools, communities, communions, etc.; now it may well be that a more collective way of living would bring new values of this sort to light, as, for instance, Georges Sorel believed.

Acceptance of these arguments does not mean that we can afford to neglect Liberal warnings of the dangers of excessive or precipitate Government action. Political tyranny and moral suffocation are things which Socialist Morality, more perhaps than any other morality, must abhor, since its aim is to bring into being a society in which moral motives (including love of freedom) will govern men's actions to an extent never before known. And for this reason it is evident that Socialist society can never be brought into existence by force, or even legislated into existence without a continuous effort of persuasion and example.

That this Socialist interpretation of justice, liberty and good government stands in sharp and to all appearances systematic conflict with the Liberal interpretation seems to me perfectly clear. The kernel ideas of Liberal Morality, commutative justice, the meritorious individual, the moral necessity of free choice and contract (especially in economic life) and the self-limiting character of good government are countered by the ideas of distributive justice, the contributing individual, freedom as essentially freedom to *be* not to get, and collective action in economic affairs. It is as if the parable of the talents were countered by the parable of the vineyard. If space permitted, it would no doubt be interesting to go over these crucial points of conflict in more detail, and to suggest further causes and bring out further consequences of them. And it would be of great topical interest to outline a contemporary 'Liberal protest' to the practical inadequacies of Socialist Morality as outlined above. But to attempt either of these things would be premature. The purpose of the comparisons just made was simply to expand our hypothesis, of two distinct moralities conflicting in our society, to the point at which we can begin to ask, knowing sufficiently what we mean by it, Is this hypothesis true? and, as a necessary correlate of this question, By what methods can we verify or refute it?

Methods of Verification

Three methods seem possible. First, we might examine the immediate political scene in this country and ask whether, for instance, the present course of Socialist legislation expresses or appears to be based on Socialist Morality as outlined above? But the course of legislation in this country has seldom or never been explicable in terms of a single set of principles, moral or economic; we pride ourselves on our political empiricism, realism, opportunism even. Besides, every Government of a nation is bound to legislate to a pattern of national interests, standards and traditions, with which its own party principles must somehow accommodate themselves. This line of verification, therefore, seems a rather unpromising one.

Suppose, however, we were to look at the writings of such great moralists and political thinkers as we ordinarily label Liberal and Socialist; should not the general views and most celebrated dicta of Bentham and Stuart Mill, say, and, on the other side, of Robert Owen, William Morris and the Fabian theorists provide clear evidence for or against our hypothesis? But, if I was right in suggesting that the Liberal-Socialist conflict works *within* most of us, then we should expect that the writers I have just mentioned— prescient and morally sensitive men as most of them were— would also have been in some degree affected by it. And that this was the case with Bentham and Mill and, on the other side, with most of the Fabians, could, I think, be very plausibly maintained. On the other hand, these great men all wrote in the express *belief* that there is only one true morality, which everyone will come to recognize if only it is presented clearly enough and reiterated often enough. Consequently it would be idle to look for exact confirmation of our hypothesis in their actual dicta or arguments.

Since these two methods fail, it might be suggested that we should look into our hearts—or examine our consciences—with a view to finding there evidence for or against our hypothesis. But I doubt whether ours is the kind of question in which the answers of the heart or conscience are of much value. I can well imagine a man looking into his heart, in an hour of great bitterness, and saying with a kind of truth, 'I acknowledge no moral obligations' or 'Nothing matters'. And I can imagine a man, suddenly awakened from moral torpor or scepticism, saying on the same kind of evidence, 'Well, at least I acknowledge *some* moral obligations' or '*Some* things matter'. But that a man should be able to decide, on the direct evidence of his heart or conscience, that his moral beliefs and dispositions fall into two or more radically conflicting systems—this seems to me most unlikely. A decision of this kind could hardly result from direct self-examination: our moral self-divisions are revealed, if they are revealed anywhere, 'written large', in the old Socratic phrase, in the world of action and controversy.

Following the lead of this criticism we reach a fourth suggestion: that our hypothesis can best be tested by examining, with all the

K

logical rigour we can command, our own serious discussions of current moral issues, in the first instance those that have a close bearing on political morality. (For instance, the 'closed shop' issue, the rights of scientists to make public their findings, the rights and duties of parents in the education of their children.) And my guess is that if we examined our actual discussions of these questions we should find that the more we endeavour to reach important, well-informed and consistent decisions on them, the more we are subject to a tantalizing and exhausting pull and counter-pull of opposing claims and standards, very like those which I have attributed to Liberal and to Socialist Morality. But one man's guess on this matter isn't even a first step to real verification. Is the proposal, then, that we should organize a nation-wide chain of conscientious discussion groups, to be polled, at some appointed date, by Dr. Gallup and his friends? This suggestion is, perhaps, not quite so silly as some moralists would have us believe; but I admit that it would be pretty useless, unless and until an effective way of direct and presenting the discussions had been agreed to. And how should agreement be reached on this initial, and quite crucial, question?

But, conceivably, Art might here come to our aid where Social Science fails us. Suppose, for instance, one were given a dialogue to read; and suppose that in it there were represented, through the words of artistically well chosen (i.e. for the purpose in hand, representative) characters, the course of a discussion on any serious moral issue of the day. And let us suppose that the questions and answers of the main characters betrayed a kind of systole-diastole movement in allegiance to the claims now of Liberal, now of Socialist Morality. The results reached in the discussion would be of minor importance: doubtless every participant in it would be represented as coming down on one side of the fence or the other, from sheer exhaustion, or from the natural desire to take up and stick to some definite position or to ground that position on some plausible general theory. The important thing would be the move-ment, the oscillation, betrayed by every character in some degree, from one moral position to the other. Let us further suppose that the dialogue to bring out very clearly that this oscillation is not due to mere logical woolliness or moral spinelessness. On the contrary, we may imagine that it is precisely the most morally earnest and intellectually persistent and incisive of the participants that display (somewhat in the manner of Glaucon and Adeimantus in the *Republic*) the painful duality of their moral beliefs and allegiances.

And now I ask: Would not the intelligent reader of such a dialogue be able to say on reflection whether it was true of his own moral experience? I think he would be able to. I don't say that his judgment on this matter would be infallible or that, whichever way it went, it would be sufficient to decide the question 'One morality or many?' but it would be a first step towards answering this question. If our reader decided that the dialogue was true to his own experience, he would possess some initial evidence in favour of a polyarchic interpretation of his moral experience; while, if he found it untrue, this discovery would at once illuminate and, indirectly, strengthen his adherence to a monarchic interpretation.

On the former alternative, our reader would, if at all scientifically minded, proceed to look for further consequences of his (apparent) moral division. He might recall, in the first place, that if most of us are subject to chronic moral frictions and frustrations, we should, on the master hypothesis of modern psychology, expect a consequent falling-off in our effective moral energy and enthusiasm. This, to be sure, is a very vague suggestion which, until specified further, we could hardly hope to verify. It might be suggested, then, that in a society whose members are becoming increasingly aware of a lack of uniform moral standards we should naturally expect the following broad divisions of moral types: on the one hand unreliable opportunists and shilly-shallyers (who might nevertheless retain, in emergencies, considerable moral resilience); and on the other hand, conscientious, heavy-hearted individuals, who suffer the pull and counter-pull of the conflicting standards they seek vainly to serve together and who, in consequence, are too often practically inept and unadaptable. And I will risk saying that, in my experience, this division holds true in alarming measure in this country to-day. But secondly, with regard to these conscientious, heavy-hearted individuals we might expect a second consequence; we might expect them to be unhealthily shy—one might almost say prudish—about expressing publicly their strongest moral convictions and to wince away both from popular statements of 'what every good Britisher stands for' and from the serious (if crude) probings and challenges of contemporary moral evangelists. And I think that few intelligent observers of our present-day society can have failed to notice these traits in a great many of the best, most conscientious individuals they know. Thirdly, following the same psychological lead, we should all of us tend to show at our best when our attention is directed away from those issues that evoke our condition of conflict—

issues that arise whenever we concentrate on setting our own house in order: in other words, we should show at our best when on the defensive, when our whole way of life—internal conflicts and frustrations and all—is threatened by forces which we all consider alien or evil or both.

And in fact most of us do know pretty clearly what we are *against*, and know how to stand up to it. It is when we have to state—or, perhaps more, when we have to listen to—what we are *for*, that our utterances and reactions lack singleness, force and style. Inner conflicts, frictions, frustrations, dissociations even—these can be temporarily overcome when our whole way of life is threatened. But remove the threat, and the conflicts, with their dismal consequences, return.

Concluding Remarks

What I have tried to do in this paper is to urge the importance for moral philosophy of certain facts which, no matter how difficult they are to describe, classify and interpret, do give the polyarchic view of moral differences what plausibility it possesses. And I would urge all adherents to the monarchic view to give these facts their most careful attention; and more, to give the polyarchic interpretation of them—considered as an hypothesis—a fair run for its money. For instance, with regard to the Liberal-Socialist conflict as I have presented it, it seems to me simply useless to say that evidently both sides cannot be right in all they claim, though both may be wrong, but that much the most likely explanation of the conflict is that both sides are right in some of their claims and wrong in others. For this simple-minded solution neglects entirely the systematic character of the conflict. It is not a conflict at one point only (as are most of the conflicts of *prima facie* duties discussed in contemporary ethics), but at a number of intimately related points: conflict along a whole front, so to say. More generally—and more audaciously—I would urge that the monarchic view of moral differences deserves to be taken seriously from now onwards only in so far as it is prepared to meet and counter the polyarchic view on the latter's own ground. Moreover, I would say that this means a pretty well continuous task for adherents to the monarchic view: they must be prepared to examine carefully and fairly any facts, arising from whatever quarter, that can reasonably suggest the existence of two or more conflicting moralities, with their own autonomous, i.e. not mutually corrigible, aims and standards.

Whether the monarchic view could sustain this task I do not know. I will only say here that, in my opinion, it would be quite possible for adherents to the monarchic view to hold that single, absolute morality admits—and perhaps requires—unbridgeable conflicts and cleavages between equally conscientious people on *certain* moral issues. But to say that this is possible is a very different thing from showing, in terms of actual moral conflicts which we can all recognize as important, that this situation obtains; and to show this would, I think, call for an infinitely deeper, more searching examination and illumination of moral life than has been attempted by any moral philosopher in the last hundred years.

This brings me to the last remark I wish to make. I have said that the question 'One morality or many?' is the most important question facing moral philosophy to-day; and the methods of investigation I have been suggesting are, of course, aimed at settling this crucial question, however slowly and painfully. But now it seems perfectly clear to me that the value of a moral philosophy lies less in the conclusions it reaches (and the logic by which it reaches them) than in something which it achieves as it goes along: something which I can only describe as illumination of moral life. This again, I must admit, is a wretchedly vague phrase; but perhaps I can show what I mean by it by saying that it is the function which, to this day, Plato's moral philosophy discharges far more adequately than any other. Plato's dialogues do not explicitly describe, but they do nevertheless illuminate in a remarkable way, the moral world of his contemporaries. That moral world is a vastly different one from our own; and yet it is curiously familiar—we can find our way about it, so to speak, with a surprising confidence. Now I believe that some of the methods I have suggested in particular concentration on current issues relating closely to political morality, and the possibilities of a new kind of discussion aimed at unmasking fundamental differences rather than at reaching superficial agreement— *might* do something towards illuminating our contemporary moral world: *might* help to dispel that thin but bewildering fog which seems to surround so much current ethical discussion and to make its terms and distinctions so unearthly and unreal. This at least is my hope, and my suggestion to those who have that rare combination of gifts which the practice of moral philosophy requires.

Each may think for himself what those qualities are and whether he possesses them.

IX

THE CONTROVERSY CONCERNING THE WORD 'LAW'[1]

by Glanville Williams

Fellow of Jesus College, Cambridge
Lecturer in Law, Cambridge University

SEMANTICS is a great solvent of controversy. In this paper it is proposed to apply linguistic philosophy to what is, perhaps, the largest of all jurisprudential disputes, namely, that as to the word 'law'. Professor Robson expresses a common reaction to this dispute when he says that the question 'What is Law?' remains one of the most insistent and yet elusive problems in the entire range of thought.[2] The position here taken will be that the problem (failing agreement upon the referent) is an unreal one: that it appears to be insoluble because it is verbal.

I

The amount of printed matter on the meaning of the word 'law' is enormous. Thurman Arnold rightly says that any attempt to define this word leads us into a maze of metaphysical literature, perhaps larger than has ever surrounded any other symbol in the history of the world.[3] The outpouring came not only from lawyers but also, in more recent years, from anthropologists and sociologists. This study will be confined to the legal writings; and it will not be necessary to go back farther than the writings of Austin, because the dispute did not reach serious proportions in England until his time.

It is unnecessary to repeat here Austin's theory at any length, and the only feature of it to which attention need be called is his effort to arrive at the 'proper' meaning of the word 'law'. At the outset of his lectures on jurisprudence he set himself to frame a definition of law, the subject of his study, that would effectively confine it to municipal (i.e. state, or positive) law. Austin correctly saw that the distinguishing feature of municipal law as opposed to social observances is that law is, in general, enforced upon the members of the

---

[1] A revised version of a paper originally published in (1945) 22 *British Year Book of International Law* 146.

[2] *Civilization and the Growth of Law* (1935), 3.

[3] *The Symbols of Government* (1935), p. 216.

community by the organized might of the community. Accordingly he seized on this feature of enforcement for his definition of law. Every law properly so called, he said, is a general command, and is subject to an evil in case of disobedience. This does not fit all municipal law; but it is not a bad general description. Unfortunately, when Austin came to define municipal law (which he called 'positive law', and which he thought of as a species of 'law properly so-called'), he thought it necessary to embody also in the definition the theory of sovereignty. Austin made a minor mistake in thus assuming the existence of Austinian sovereigns all over the world; and, moreover, his work did not include the close analysis of legal relations that was later to be made by jurists like Hohfeld. But speaking generally, Austin's insistence upon the test of enforcement was a perfectly sound point, so long as he was speaking of municipal law. His major mistake, and the cause of most of the subsequent trouble, was his assumption that because the test of enforcement satisfied the municipal lawyer (or, at least, the lawyer who was interested in municipal *private* law, as opposed to constitutional law), therefore it was a touchstone of the 'validity' of any and every application of the term 'law'.[1] Acting on this assumption, he constructed a complete table of the uses, 'proper' and 'improper', of of the term 'law'. The table is well known, and it is enough to recapitulate Austin's statement of 'law improperly so called'. This comprises (*a*) 'laws by analogy', i.e. rules of conduct imposed by the general opinion of an indeterminate body, such as the laws of fashion and of honour, the custom of wearing black at funerals, and (we may add) the conventions of the constitution, and (*b*) laws by metaphor, e.g. such scientific uniformities as the law of gravity, and also the laws of a game like bridge, and the laws of art.

Austin's theory has given rise to two main controversies: first, whether he has hit upon a satisfactory test of *municipal* law (which was what he was primarily trying to do); and secondly, whether he was 'right' in saying that what he called 'law by analogy' and 'law by metaphor' are not 'properly' called 'law'. It is unnecessary to say any more about the first question: as to the second, it is my

---

[1] Austin was not the first to assert this. Hobbes had declared that 'law properly is the word of him that by right hath command over others', and he was followed by Bentham, who suggested a doubt 'with what degree of propriety rules [of international law] can come under the appellation of *laws*': *Principles of Morals and Legislation*, 1789 ed., ch. xix, § 25 (Bowring's ed., i, 150), 1823 ed., ch. xvii, § 25; cp. Bentham's *General View etc.*, ch. iv (Bowring's ed., iii, 162).

purpose to show that this question is purely a verbal one, although few of the parties to the controversy seem to have realized it.

The storm-centre was the department of 'laws by analogy'. Lawyers were not likely to lose sleep over Austin's assertion that the laws of bridge and the law of gravity were not properly called law; but 'laws by analogy' were on a different footing. This rubric included, in particular, early customary law and international law, for these were not commanded by a determinate person. Consequently they were, according to Austin, outside the pale of 'law properly so called'.

Now it was not *necessary* for Austin's exposition to assert that early customary law and international law were not 'properly' called law. It was enough for him to say that he did not intend to include them within the term 'law' *for his purpose*—i.e. that he did not intend to draw upon them in fashioning the subject of jurisprudence as he proposed to teach it. But, instead of saying this, he asserted that these bodies of rules were not 'properly' called law, and in so doing he gravely offended some jurists who were interested in these subjects, and had always thought of them as law.

It is or should be clear to us to-day that in thus attempting to dogmatize on the 'proper' meaning of a word Austin was mistaking the function of words. The word 'law' is simply a symbol for an idea. This idea may vary with the person who uses the word. Austin defined what the word meant for him, which he was entitled to do, but he was not entitled to adopt a legislative attitude and declare what the word should mean for other people. The power that Austin assumed for himself, to define the meaning of the words he used, he should have accorded also to others. Everyone is entitled for his own part to use words in any meaning he pleases; there is no such thing as an intrinsically 'proper' or 'improper' meaning of a word. The nearest approach to the 'proper' meaning is the 'usual' meaning;[1] and certainly it is generally desirable to keep to usual meanings, and a person who uses a word in an unusual meaning must state clearly the meaning in which he is using it, on pain of being misunderstood if he does not. But Austin was not seeking the usual meaning of the term 'law'. If he had been, he could hardly have denied that the phrases 'law of nations' and 'law of gravity'

---

[1] A form of the usual meaning is the etymological meaning—i.e. the usual meaning of the word (or of roots from which it is derived) in times past. It may offend our aesthetic susceptibilities if a word is used in such a way as to show ignorance of its origin. But Austin was not speaking of etymology or of aesthetics.

were usual ones, and, moreover, phrases that were usual among the best writers.

Austin's opponents could, therefore, have challenged him on the simple and unassailable ground that he was assuming a power that no man possessed: the power of dictating to others the meanings in which they should use words. But not all of them did this. Instead, some tried to answer the fool according to his folly by contending that other bodies of rules than those recognized by Austin were law 'properly' so called.

It is convenient to start with the objections raised by the historical jurists. They were interested in early customary law, and this Austin's 'command' theory did not fit. Austin had himself demonstrated that it did not fit,[1] so there was no dispute about this. Some of the historians, however, thought that by failing to give a definition of 'law' that would embrace early customary law Austin had made a deep philosophical error in his conception of law. They regarded 'law properly so called' as a broad idea, of which municipal law and early customary law were but particular applications. They asserted that in his 'command' theory of law Austin had failed to make a correct analysis of this idea. So he had, if it be assumed that the term 'law' is to be read as widely as the historians contended. Austin, however, was not concerned to modify his 'command' theory of law, in order to bring in early customary law, because, for him, customary law was not law 'properly' so called. This could be no more than an assertion of personal preference in the use of words, upon which (if these historians had but seen it) scientific argument was not possible.

This criticism of certain of the historians, that they shared Austin's error as to the function of words, cannot be urged against Maine. His treatment of Austin, in Lectures XII and XIII of his *Early History of Institutions* (1875), is moderately worded, and he attempts little more than to show (what Austin did not deny) that early communities governed by customary law knew no Austinian 'sovereign'. Upon Austin's contention that until customs are enforced by courts of justice they are merely 'positive morality', but that as soon as courts of justice enforce them, they became commands of the sovereign, and therefore law, Maine discerningly remarked that this was 'a mere artifice of speech'. He also pointed out that 'nobody is at liberty to censure men or communities of men for using words in any sense they please, or with as many meanings as they please,

[1] *Lectures on Jurisprudence*, 5th edn., vol. i, pp. 101–2, 199–200; vol. ii, pp. 536–43.

but the duty of the scientific inquirer is to distinguish the meanings of an important word from one another, to select the meanings appropriate to his own purposes, and consistently to employ the word during his investigations in this sense and no other'.

It is regrettable to have to take Sir Frederick Pollock as the first representative of the type of objection to Austin that is here being criticized. In an article published in 1872, Pollock wrote of Austin's definition: 'It will be my aim to show that this definition, if exclusively insisted on, errs by elevating what is at most one characteristic of law into its essence; that contrariwise, by losing sight of what is really an essential constituent, it narrows the proper scope of law and tends to an unsatisfactory view of its operation; and that by putting forward the arbitrary and suppressing the necessary aspect of legislation it seriously obscures the organic relation of law to the community.'[1] It is submitted that the question what is the 'essence' of law is not one to be debated as though it were a question of fact. 'Essence' simply means 'important feature', and what is important is a subjective or emotional matter. Also, it is difficult to understand the remark that Austin's definition of law 'tends to an unsatisfactory view of its (i.e. the law's) operation', for the whole question is what is the 'law' that we are talking about, and it is not easy to see how a definition of what we are talking about can tend to an unsatisfactory view of what we are talking about.

Pollock went on to picture the typical Indian village community as seen by an imaginary observer imbued with Austin's theory. He declared: 'Not one of the conditions required by the conception of law which the (Austinian) inquirer brought with him is satisfied; yet it is impossible to say that in such a society there is no law without giving an entirely wrong impression'. That is to say, without giving an entirely wrong impression to a listener *unacquainted with Austin's definition of law*. But this is simply an elaborate way of asserting that the limitation put by Austin upon the meaning of the word 'law' is an unusual one; it is not, and cannot be, a factual refutation of Austin's definition. A statement that this primitive society was not governed by law *in the Austinian sense of the word* would be a true statement, and would not be misleading to a person who knew the Austinian theory.

At the time of this article Pollock was still a young man, but he repeated the substance of his view later in his *First Book of Juris-*

[1] 'Law and Command' (1872), 1 *Law Magazine and Review*, 3rd Ser., 189 at 191.

prudence,[1] where he declared that the Austinian view was 'hard to reconcile with the witness of history'. Bryce kept him company by asserting that the imperative theory was 'untrue as a matter of history'.[2] The theme was also taken up and embroidered by Clark in his book called (and very improperly so called!) *Practical Jurisprudence*, published in 1883. About a hundred pages of this book were devoted to the derivation of the word 'law' and of certain corresponding words in other languages. Summarizing his own work, Clark wrote: 'In the unconscious definitions of law furnished by those early names for it, which I have been examining, . . . the nearest approximation to a uniform or pervading idea is certainly not so much that of *enactment, position* and *command*, as of *antiquity, general approval* and *usage*: where an original notion of *ordinance* does appear, it is not human but divine' (p. 90). The study certainly throws an interesting light upon the primitive attitude to law—i.e. to early customary law—and indicates the psychological conditions that helped it to secure obedience. But Clark seems to have thought that his work did something more than this, viz. refute Austin. At p. 94 he says: 'I have been mainly occupied in showing that the original conception of law, in several very important instances, by no means agrees with the fundamental part of his [Austin's] definition'. To this we may reply for Austin that he was not interested in the original conception of what Clark chose to call 'law', and that in fact he (Austin) chose not to call this original conception 'law'. Etymological meanings are no more than the usual meanings of words in past ages, and Austin did not regard himself as bound by usual meanings whether belonging to the past or to the present.[3]

In the next hundred pages of his book, Clark examined multitudinous definitions of law framed by philosophers and lawyers. This initiated in England the sterile discussion of definitions of the word 'law' that has done so much to discredit jurisprudence. Clark, like Austin, seemed to think that there was a proper definition of the word 'law', but he disagreed with Austin as to what that definition was, and he thought that he could vindicate his opinion by examining the definitions given by others. He did not seem to

---

[1] 6th edn. (1929), pp. 23–4.

[2] *Studies in History and Jurisprudence* (1901), vol. ii, p. 44; cp. ibid., p. 249.

[3] Three other writers to inject etymology into jurisprudence were T. E. Walker (*The Science of International Law*, 1893, pp. 21–5), W. G. Miller (*Data of Jurisprudence*, 1903), and Salmond (*Jurisprudence*, 7th edn., 1924, App. I). Salmond's statement of his purpose in doing so is moderately worded and hardly open to objection, but Walker, like Clark, evidently thought that his study provided a refutation of Austin.

realize that this process could only indicate the usual meaning of the word 'law' and could not prevent Austin from using it in a restricted meaning.

Clark also followed Pollock in supposing that he could disprove Austin by reference to the facts of history. Thus at p. 154 he declared that there is a 'fact to be observed in the case of the Indian village communities, and which bears in a very direct manner upon Austin's definition of law. These small bodies have from time immemorial been under successive conquerors or their descendants, despotically ruling vast tracts of country. They cannot, therefore, to anticipate a little, be called *independent states*; and Austin would logically deny them the name of *political society* at all. But it would be mere perverseness, for want of "position" by a sovereign, internal or external, to deny the name of law to the rules which have regulated the conduct of their members for so long, and which no prince, however despotic, could conceivably to the Indian mind have altered.' Austin's reply to this could have been that no fact to be observed in the case of the Indian village communities could bear upon his definition of law, for the simple reason that he had excluded the custom of the Indian village communities from his definition of law.[1] I do not quite know what Austin would have said to the charge of 'perverseness', but we at any rate can make his defence for him. In the classic words of Humpty Dumpty, 'The question is which is to be the master—that's all'.[2]

In the course of time a new champion of Austin's attitude towards early customary law emerged in the person of Salmond. Salmond directed himself against the proposition of Pollock and Bryce that law cannot be the creature of the state, because it existed before the state. His answer is well known. 'If there are any rules prior to, and independent of the state, they may greatly resemble law; they may be the primeval substitutes for law; they may be the historical source from which law is developed and proceeds; but they are not themselves law. There may have been a time in the far past when a man was not distinguishable from the anthropoid ape, but that is no reason for now defining a man in such manner as to include an ape.'[3] The validity of this argument depends upon what it was

---

[1] Holland, indeed, tried to support Austin by arguing that the custom of the village communities might in some circumstances fall within Austin's definition (*Jurisprudence*, 13th edn. (1924), pp. 53–4). But whether it did or did not could not affect Austin's definition as a definition of what Austin meant by law.

[2] Lewis Carroll: *Alice through the Looking-Glass*, ch. 6.

[3] *Jurisprudence*, 7th edn. (1924), p. 51.

intended to convey. If Salmond meant that arbitrary lines have to be drawn in the application of words, that he himself intended to use the word 'law' to mean only modern municipal law, and that it was no objection to his usage that modern municipal law had grown out of early customary law, then his argument was perfectly sound. But if Salmond meant that the word 'law' has some one intrinsically-proper meaning which can be discovered by the use of reason and in particular by examining the analogies of other word-meanings, such as the meaning of 'man', then his argument was palpably false. To take Salmond's own illustration, the student of pre-history is wasting his time if he gets involved in an argument whether the word 'man' may properly be applied to any particular creature that comes in the line of Adam's ancestors. All that matters is how many resemblances this creature bears to modern man, and what are the points of difference. If anthropologists discover enough about *Pithecanthropus erectus* ('Java man') to be able to affirm that in most respects he was more like modern man than he was like the common ancestor of man and ape, they have made a contribution to knowledge. But if, in consequence, they decide to confer the label 'man' upon *Pithecanthropus erectus*, they add nothing to our knowledge. Their decision will be of importance only in the selection and arrangement of their own particular subject-matter; and it certainly will not mean that you or I, when we speak of 'man', will necessarily intend to include in the meaning of that term such a creature as *Pithecanthropus erectus*.

It is the same with early customary law. By all means let us examine the characteristics of early customary law, and compare and contrast it with modern law. But let us not argue about the propriety of calling it 'law'. If we dispute about the latter we shall not (whatever we think) be discussing the nature of law, but shall simply be arguing about each other's peculiarities of expression.

In fairness to Salmond it must be added that, put in its setting, his remark about early custom not being law is logically defensible, though misleading to the youthful student for whom his book was designed. The setting just referred to was as follows. Salmond began his book by enumerating a number of kinds of law (in the wide sense), including the uniformities of nature and international law, and made upon them the following very sensible observation. 'Any discussion as to the rightful claims of any of those classes of rules to be called laws—any attempt to distinguish laws properly so called from laws improperly so called—would seem to be nothing more than a purposeless dispute about words. Our business is to recognize that they are in fact called laws, and to distinguish accurately between the different classes of rules that are thus known by the same name' (p. 20). Then at page 33 he came to the subject of municipal law, which he preferred to call 'civil law', and announced that 'in the absence of any indication in the context of a different intention, the term law, when used *simpliciter*, means civil law and nothing else, and in this sense the term is used in future throughout this book'. Thus when, later in the book, Salmond declared, in the words already quoted, that 'if there are any rules prior to, and independent of the state, . . . they are not themselves law', he must have meant by the last word, in accordance with his own previous statement, civil (i.e. state) law and nothing else. So read, his proposition that there is no (state) law independent of the state becomes merely a negative reformulation of his own definition. Although a careful reading shows what was meant, the passage is misleading to the student, who is led to suppose that Salmond is advancing a factual proposition as to the so-called 'nature' of law.

Admittedly it may be asserted that there *was* a significant issue between Austin and the historians, namely an issue as to the 'central feature' of 'law', and that the issue was whether this 'central feature' was the force of the governor, or the consent of the governed. Put in this way the question does sound as though it is a factual one. But the difficulty is that a question so formulated cannot be significantly debated unless the debaters agree upon the meaning (i.e. the referent) of the word 'law'. This the Austinians and such of the historians as debated the issue stubbornly refused to do. Had they come to a working agreement upon the meaning of the word 'law' for the purpose of their debate, they would instantly have discovered that there was practically nothing left for them to debate, for there were no facts in issue between them. The most they could have debated would have been whether this or that feature of an agreed referent of 'law' was 'central'. But this debate again would have verged upon meaninglessness, for 'central' in this context is simply a synonym for 'important', and what is 'important' is a subjective matter. Importance lies in the eye of the beholder. No operation can be performed to test whether one feature of a referent is more important than the others, nor is such an operation conceivable. To debate what is important and what unimportant is, therefore, to enter upon a controversy that can only be settled by the emotional conversion of one of the parties.

So much for the legal historians. Turning now to the international lawyers, some of them were even more disturbed by Austin than were the historians. It seemed to these writers that if Austin's theory were accepted it would rock their subject to its foundations. They were not at all of the opinion that international law by any other name would smell as sweet; on the contrary, they assumed, quite rightly, that if it ceased to go by the name of law it would lose caste among the governments that were supposed to respect it. Difficult as was their task in persuading the chancelleries of the world to obey the rules they formulated, it would be even more difficult if they once admitted that what they wrote was no more than 'positive morality'.

International lawyers quite genuinely thought of themselves as lawyers, not as moralists. They wanted to see created a system of arbitral tribunals to settle disputes between nations, with lawyers appearing and arguing the cases; they wanted their subject to be developed in a legal way, working from legal sources and using analogies from private law, and not simply as a body of moral exhortations. What morality required might be disputed, and some might be disposed to argue that the interest of their own state was supreme over ordinary moral principles, whereas international law was thought to be a fixed system binding upon states and developed by reference to authority. The effect of getting people to agree that international law is law is to get them to agree to observe the rules of international law. On the other hand, to allow international law to be called morality means reducing it to shifting formlessness, with no possibility of final settlement.

In short, these international lawyers saw that the word 'law' is not only a symbol for a reference; it also evokes a powerful emotional response. The word 'law' stimulates in us the attitude of obedience to authoritative rules that we have come through our upbringing to associate with the idea of municipal law. Change the word for some other and the magic evaporated.[1] Accordingly these writers felt

---

[1] Clark recognized the importance to international law of catching the emotional associations of the word 'law' when he wrote: 'Who does not know the damning effect of a popular nickname or epigram? The glibly-repeated definition, that denies to International Law the name of *law* at all, must of necessity cast a certain slur upon the principles which still go by that name' (*Practical Jurisprudence*, p. 187). So also Walker: *The Science of International Law* (1893), p. 35: 'To refuse any rule the mere name of Law, on whatever ground, would be, in the popular mind, to deprive it of all that peculiar halo of respectful reverence which has undoubtedly attached to the term in the passing of the ages'. Timasheff: *Introduction to the Sociology of Law* (1939), p. 254: 'The words "law", "statute", "court" and a thousand others have gradually become stimuli of submission'.

obliged to embark upon the unprofitable discussion as to the 'proper' meaning of the term 'law'.

The foregoing statement of the position taken by some international lawyers does not apply at all. Some even swallowed Austin's terminology and conceded that international law was not properly called law, or at any rate was not called law in the strict sense of the word.[1] Others, less docile but still restrained and moderate, pointed out that Austin had no authority to act the law-giver in regard to the meanings of words. Thus W. Oke Manning, in his *Commentaries on the Law of Nations*, published in 1839, seven years after Austin's *Province of Jurisprudence Determined*, sagely observed: 'My objection is that the word *law*, which has, in our language, so long been employed in a much wider sense, should, by a single writer, be declared to be only "properly" used with this restricted meaning' (p. 5). Pollock, in the article already quoted, wittily pointed out the incongruous results of Austin's definition by observing: 'If we are not to be allowed to give the name of law to the Declaration of Paris, for instance, we may console ourselves if we choose by giving it to an ultimatum addressed, say, by Monaco to Russia'. This was legitimate argument as to the desirable use of words, not open to objection so long as it was not disguised as an argument on a point of fact. Hall's treatment of the subject may be regarded as open to criticism on the latter score, for after conceding 'an element of truth' to Austin's view, he observed: 'It is now fully recognized that the proper scope of the term law transcends the limits of the more perfect examples of law'.[2] This is unobjectionable if it means merely that the word 'law' is not limited in its ordinary usage to municipal law, but then Austin had never denied the fact. One rather feels that Hall in this and later sentences joined Austin in the search for objective proper meanings other than usual meanings, and if so he laid himself open to the same charge as Austin.

[1] Wheaton: *International Law*, 8th edn. (1866), pp. 18–19, quotes Austin with approval. In Halleck's *International Law*, 1st edn. (1861), pp. 51–2, it is said that 'these rules cannot, perhaps, with strict propriety be called laws, in the sense of commands..., but... they are... properly termed *laws*'. This is either badly expressed or self-contradictory. Maine: *International Law*, 2nd edn. (1894) (lectures delivered in 1887), p. 49, thought that Austin's views on international law were 'very interesting and quite innocuous', adding: 'It is very convenient, when the main subject of thought is positive law, that we should remember that International Law has but slender connection with it, and that it has less analogy to the laws which are the commands of sovereigns than to rules of conduct, which, whatever be their origin, are to a very great extent enforced by the disapprobation which attends their neglect'. Writers on jurisprudence who followed Austin's view of international law were Gray, *Nature and Sources of Law*, 2nd edn. (1921), p. 130; Holland: *Jurisprudence*, 13th edn. (1924), p. 133; cp. Holland: *Lectures on International Law* (1933), p. 6.

[2] *International Law*, 4th edn. (1895), pp. 14–15.

In 1884 Lawrence published a paper entitled 'Is there a true International Law?'[1] He summed up the matter neatly by saying that 'everything depends upon the definition of law which we choose to adopt. The controversy is really a logomachy—a dispute about words, not things' (p. 29). Yet one cannot help feeling that Lawrence himself did not realize the full import of his assertion. Had he done so, he would have made the assertion earlier in his paper, and have rested his case upon that point alone. In that event he might have damped down the controversy. As it was, he succumbed to the temptation of producing arguments against Austin, and thus poured oil instead of water upon the flames. One of his arguments was that there are other motives of obedience to municipal law besides force (e.g. religion, superstition, morality, self-interest, lethargy); also, municipal law would break down if every rule had to be enforced. These are true propositions of fact, but they cannot be used to prove or disprove a definition.

Objection also attaches to part of Walker's discussion in his *Science of International Law* (1893). Walker began excellently by pointing out that though Austin was free to limit his treatment to some alone of those rules that commonly go by the name 'laws', he was not free to play the dictator as to the use of words by other people (p. 8). Walker also pointed out that the ordinary meaning of the word 'law' was wider than Austin's. Had he stopped there he would have earned nothing but applause. But then, with an excess of enthusiasm for his subject, he went on to copy the historians by appealing to history and philology, arguing that Austin could be confuted by 'the hard facts of history' and 'the history of words'. As I have said before, and do not mind repeating, neither of these can in logic destroy a definition.

In a later paper Pollock argued that the difficulty or impossibility of enforcing a rule of international law is no objection to regarding international law as having a 'legal' character, because 'in the early history of all jurisdictions the executive power at the disposal of the courts has been rudimentary, if indeed, they had such power at all'.[2] This is another attempt to prove a definition by reference to the facts of history.

The question was again taken up by J. B. Scott in an article entitled 'The Legal Nature of International Law'.[3] Two of his

---

[1] *Some Disputed Questions in Modern International Law* (1884), p. 1.
[2] 'The Sources of International Law' (1902), 2 *Columbia Law Review*, 511 at 514–15, reprinted in Dickinson, *The Law of Nations* (1929), p. 36.
[3] (1907), 1 *American Journal of International Law*, 831.

L

arguments were as follows. (1) It is no objection to the legal nature of international law that it is unenforceable, because certain duties imposed by municipal law upon the superior organs of government in a state are equally unenforceable. The conclusion follows from the premise, but the premise assumes a particular definition of 'law'. If one were to deny this definition, asserting (as Austin did[1]) that the duties imposed upon a government are only quasi-legal, one could logically deny the conclusion. (2) International law is law because it is part of the law of every state. Here the premise is not quite true,[2] and even if wholly true it would not yield the conclusion that international law is a law binding states towards each other.

Coming to more modern times, Keith,[3] in a discussion of Austin's definition, remarks that it 'has no general validity'—as if a definition can be valid for any purpose except the purpose of the person who advances it.

It is not only the English who concern themselves with the pseudo-problem of the legal character of international law. Dr. Lauterpacht[4] summarizes the view of several Continental writers (Bergbohm, Bluntschli, Heilborn, Fauchille, De Louter, Strupp, Walz) who argue that international law is law notwithstanding the absence of compulsory jurisdiction in international courts, for the reason that as a matter of history law preceded the establishment of tribunals. Dr. Lauterpacht's comment on this theory is that 'it assumes the existence of law in communities in which, on its own showing, such existence may legitimately be the object of controversy'. While agreeing with the substance of this comment I should like to alter its wording, for to speak of the theory as being concerned with 'the existence of law' may lead the unwary reader to believe that a question of fact is involved, when all that is involved is the application of words. I should therefore prefer to say that the theory seeks to prove the 'validity' of a particular application of a word by the artifice of using the same word in a similar way in another context. In fact no proof of the 'validity' of a linguistic usage is necessary or possible.

---

[1] *Lectures*, 5th edn., i, 288. Austin, however, spoke only of a *sovereign* government; he admitted that the English monarch, not being sovereign, could logically be under duties.

[2] See Lauterpacht: 'Is International Law part of the Law of England?' (1939), p. 25, *Transactions of the Grotius Society* 51; Dias: 'Mechanism of Definition as Applied to International Law', [1954] *Cambridge Law Journal* 215.

[3] In his edition of Wheaton, *International Law*, 6th edn., i, 6.

[4] *The Function of Law in the International Community* (1933), p. 424. For a further bibliography of Continental literature see Charles Rousseau: *Principes Généraux du Droit International Public* (1944), i, 6–7.

Modern international lawyers who enter the lists in the controversy usually do so by trying to frame a definition of 'law' that will include international law. A favourite definition is that of Westlake,[1] tying the idea of law to that of society or community. Every society, according to this school of thought, necessarily has a system of law. Beginning with this formula, all that is necessary to prove that international law exists is to prove that an international society exists. But, of course, this again is a verbal question, depending upon one's definition of the word 'society', which is so vague in its ordinary meaning that one can give it any twist one pleases. Westlake was quite certain that an international society existed; Dr. A. L. Goodhart, a later recruit to the theory, was not so confident.[2] Consequently Dr. Goodhart could not decide whether international law was properly named or not.

One rather remarkable turn taken by the controversy is the way in which some writers seize upon the institution of war to prove the legal character of international law. It might have been thought that even limited war was, to say the least, a blemish in international relations. But instead of describing it as a blemish, some writers introduce it into the discussion almost with an appearance of relief, as constituting the legal sanction behind international law and so as proving its 'legal' character. Thus Jhering, having postulated the element of coercion in his definition of law, found that he could save the 'legal' character of international law only by arguing that it was maintained by unorganized force, i.e. by war.[3] Other distinguished writers taking the same line were Sidgwick, Scott, Oppenheim, and Fischer Williams.[4] So also Westlake distinguished a moral from a legal international claim as one that states 'do not feel justified in supporting with the last degree of pressure'.[5] This last definition is extremely difficult to apply, and is open to the objection that it makes legality depend upon bellicosity. Nor need

---

[1] *Collected Papers* (1914), ch. 1.

[2] 'The Nature of International Law' (1936), 22 *Trans. Grot. Soc.* 31. Cp. Zimmern: 'The Decline of International Standards' (1938) 17 *International Affairs* 1; Schwarzenberger: 'The Rule of Law and the Disintegration of International Society' (1939) 33 *American Journal of International Law* 56; Brierly: *The Outlook for International Law* (1944), pp. 4–5. Dr. Schwarzenberger carries the matter of nomenclature into yet more refined realms, distinguishing between community law and society law and saying that international law is the second but not the first.

[3] *Der Zweck im Recht*, tr. under title *Law as a Means to an End* (1913), pp. 242 ff.

[4] Sidgwick: *Elements of Politics*, 4th edn., pp. 286–7; Scott, op. cit., at pp. 863–4; Oppenheim, *International Law*, 5th edn., i, p. 13; Fischer Williams: *Aspects of Modern International Law* (1939), p. 92. Cp. the criticism of Salmond: *Jurisprudence*, 7th edn., p. 559.

[5] *Collected Papers*, pp. 2–3, 7, 12–13.

we stop to consider the difficulty in the way of the theory resulting from the fact that customary international law appears to draw no distinction between a sanctioning and an aggressive war. It may, however, be pointed out that, quite apart from all these difficulties, the supposed analogy to municipal law does not hold, because a rule would not be regarded as part of municipal law merely because it was supported by a threat of unorganized enforcement, e.g. revolution, or even organized but non-state enforcement, e.g. strikes or gangsterism. Enforcement in municipal law means enforcement through a fixed social mechanism, and nobody pretends that that exists on the international plane.

During the present century some international lawyers, perceiving the disastrous consequences of the unorganized enforcement of international law, and feeling strongly that international law should be strengthened on the municipal model, have taken to arguing that international law as it now stands does not deserve the name 'law'.[1] The sentiment is admirable, but to express it in this particular way is simply to conceal the value-judgment involved and to invite verbal opposition.

2

It will be seen from the foregoing account that the error as to the 'proper' meaning of words and as to 'true' definitions is still widespread. For this there seem to be several reasons. For convenience of discussion they will here be considered in separate numbered sections, though to prevent possible misunderstanding it must be premised that some of the sections are simply different aspects of each other.

(1) The first misconception is the idea that a controversy as to concepts is not a verbal but a scientific controversy. Thus Lauterpacht quotes Somló as denying that international law partakes of

[1] Thus C. Van Vollenhoven: 'A servile science of jurisprudence, *ancilla potestatis*, instead of directing attention all the time to the shortcomings of a "law" possessing no sanctions or guarantees, and instead of cleaving to a man like Grotius who had the courage to face up to the truth, contracted the habit of pleading that a law of peace which is continually ignored was none the less a "law" of spotless character and beyond reproach; what is more, these scholars adopted the tactics of concealing from themselves the dangers of that situation:' *The Law of Peace* (1936), pp. 135–6. 'To acquiesce in the permanent absence [of the objective ascertainment of rights by the courts] is to strain its legal character to the breaking-point': Lauterpacht: *The Function of Law in the International Community*, p. 426. 'It is of the essence of the dignity of legal science—including the science of international law—to resist the temptation to lower the standard of law to the low level of an avowedly rudimentary practice': ibid., p. 434. 'The conclusion seems inescapable that positive international law, so-called, has no claim to the name of law': Zimmern (1938) 17 *International Affairs* 12. Lundstedt: *Superstition or Rationality in Action for Peace?* (1925), pp. 161 ff.

the character of law, while maintaining that this is not merely a matter of terminology, 'for (Somló says), if we describe the rules of so-called international law as rules of law we thereby obscure the conception of law as generally used'.[1] Before considering this, let us get clear what we mean by a concept or conception. A concept is simply a universal notion (such as *space, time, causality, bird, law*) symbolized by a word.[2] 'Investigating (or analysing) concepts' means exactly the same thing as defining the corresponding words. Now when Somló refers to 'the conception of law as generally used' he evidently means by the word 'law' municipal law. But this is only one use of the word; there is also its use to symbolize international law, which has many affinities to municipal law. It is easy to construct a concept that will cover both municipal and international law. Why should we not symbolize this concept by the word 'law'? Somló objects; he wishes to confine the term 'law' to municipal law. But this is a mere matter of terminology, a fact that Somló expressly refuses to admit.

(2) The second reason for the misunderstanding considered in this paper is the concealment in language of the difference between a verbal and a scientific (factual) question. Four words that tend to hide this difference are the copula ('to be'), 'exist', 'nature', and 'theory'.

As to the first, a sentence beginning 'Law is . . .' may seem to state a fact; but it can practically always be translated by the words 'The word "law" means . . .', when it clearly introduces a definition. The only case where this translation is not permissible is where the word 'law' is independently defined.

Then, as to the word 'exist', consider its use in the proposition: 'International law does not exist'. This may mean two different things: (i) that states do not observe any normative rules in their mutual dealings, at least in matters of major concern, or (ii) that, although states observe such rules in their mutual dealings, the rules are not to be given the name 'law'. The first assertion is a factual one; it can be verified or disproved by looking at the conduct of states. The second is purely verbal. Yet both assertions alike can be expressed by reference to the 'existence' of international law.

[1] Lauterpacht: *The Function of Law in the International Community*, p. 403, quoting Somló: *Juristische Grundlehre*, 2nd edn. (1927), pp. 153–73.

[2] This definition is sufficient for present purposes, though it is possible for a concept to exist without words. 'A cat will watch for a long time at a mousehole, with her tail swishing in savage expectation; in such a case, one should say (so I hold) that the smell of mouse stimulates the "idea" of the rest of what makes up an actual mouse': B. Russell, *Human Knowledge: Its Scope and Limits* (London, 1948), pp. 109–10; cp. ibid., p. 111.

This word 'existence' seems to refer to a matter of fact, and may well in some contexts mislead the reader into thinking that a mere definition of terms is a scientific proposition.[1]

Again, an inquiry into the 'nature' of a concept like 'law' is simply a search for a definition of a word. But the word 'nature' seems to refer to a matter of empirical fact, and is therefore misleading.

The fourth offender is the word 'theory'. A scientific theory is a formula for correlating the facts of experience; in other words it is a statement of fact of a generalized kind. But a 'theory of law' or 'legal theory' is not a statement of fact; it is a definition of words, or a value-judgment as to what the law ought to be or do, or both.

In a recent article, Mr. Richard Wollheim has advanced the argument that an inquiry into the criterion of the validity of law is not a search for a definition, because it is necessarily relative to a particular legal system.[2] This may be answered by saying that the term defined by this method is not law in general but, say, English law. The proposition that English law is a body of rules laid down in Acts of Parliament, judicial decisions, etc., is a definition of 'English law'.

(3) The third reason is our tendency to conceal the difference between a verbal question and a question of value-judgment. No one would be awarded a doctorate for asserting that in his opinion a state ought to rest on the consent of its subjects. Yet if he writes a book asserting that a state *is* an association resting on the consent of its subjects, academic honours may well follow. What is in truth a value-judgment is disguised as a definition of terms, and the definition of terms is itself erroneously regarded by the academic world as a scientific investigation.

The result of this strange technique of argument may be surprising, as T. H. Green discovered when he found himself obliged by his own terminology to affirm that Czarist Russia could be counted as a State only 'by a sort of courtesy'.[3] A similar difficulty is experienced with definitions of law, advanced by theorists like Duguit and Krabbe, which link it with natural law, 'social soli-

---

[1] Again to prevent misunderstanding it may be pointed out that there is a sense in which a definition is a statement of fact. A definition may be understood as stating the way in which the speaker chooses to use words, and the way in which one chooses to use words is a fact. Or again, a definition may state the way in which the word is ordinarily used, which is also a question of fact. Nevertheless, a definition is not in ordinary discussions advanced as a proposition about a datum: it is a proposition which is itself a datum.

[2] 'The Nature of Law' (1954), 2 *Political Studies*, p. 128.

[3] *Lectures on the Principles of Political Obligation*, 1927 reprint, p. 137.

darity', the 'sense of right', or such-like. The consequence is that any particular rule that happens to be unjust, or anti-social, has to be denied the name 'law', even though it be enforced by the tribunals of a state. On the other hand, to define law, with Marx, as an instrument of class domination, has the peculiar and inconvenient result that the Protection of Animals Act is not law.

Definitions may not only reflect but may sometimes affect emotional attitudes. However, this is not necessarily the case. Positivist definitions of law (like those of Austin, Holmes and Kelsen, which eliminate the moral aspect) have been advanced and accepted by men who did not regard the law-maker as free from moral duties.

(4) A fourth reason is our tendency to hypostatize (objectify) abstractions. We take a word like 'bird' or 'law' and assume that somewhere in the universe there must be some entity corresponding to the word, an investigation into which is just as scientific and factual as the dissection of an individual sparrow in a laboratory. We assume, further, that our definition of the word must be an 'accurate' word-picture of this 'thing' in the universe to which the word belongs. It is this idea that causes us to speak so frequently of 'true' definitions. As soon as we realize that *bird* and *law* are simply mental abstractions from the raw material of the universe, and that they do not exist by themselves separately anywhere, we realize that the idea of a true definition is a superstition. A description of an individual bird now before us, or of an agreed legal system, may be true or untrue, because we can verify it by reference to the facts; but a definition of 'bird' or 'law' cannot be true or untrue, because we do not start with any facts by which it can be checked. A definition can indeed be true in the sense that it is a representation of the ordinary meaning of the word: but the use of the adjective 'true' in this context is so likely to cause misconception that it is better to avoid it.

Philosophers of the so-called 'realist' school have a great deal to answer for in this matter, for it is they who have stuck so stubbornly to the idea of the 'reality' of universals, and consequently to the idea of 'true' definitions and 'true' meaning. Writing in the volume entitled *Modern Theories of Law*,[1] Professor C. A. W. Manning says: ' "What is philosophy?" is doubtless a philosophical question: for amongst other things philosophy concerns itself with the true meaning of terms'. This must mean that philosophy concerns itself

[1] (1933), p. 184.

with the ordinary meaning of terms, or with suggested new meanings, or both. There is no other possibility. This is not to disparage
philosophy, for much useful work can be done in investigating the
ordinary meanings of words (e.g. the functions of the copula), and
making suggestions for improvement. What is true for philosophy
is true for more specialized investigations of a kindred nature, such
as analytical jurisprudence. The point to insist on is that such studies
must start from words as they are actually used; it is unhelpful to
frame definitions *a priori* and immediately to proceed to pronounce
them 'true' or 'proper'.

(5) Arising out of the proper-meaning fallacy is the idea that
words have not only a proper meaning but a single proper meaning.
This involves a denial of the fact that words change their meanings
from one context to another. To illustrate the difficulties into which
this idea lands one: we commonly speak of 'early customary law',
yet a municipal lawyer refuses to say that all social customs at the
present day are law. Conventions of the constitution, for instance,
are not usually called 'law' by the modern lawyer. Now it is a fact
that it is practically impossible to frame a definition of 'law' in
short and simple terms that will *both* include early customary law *and*
exclude modern conventions of the constitution. If it includes the
one it will include the other, and if it excludes the one it will exclude
the other. This leads the single-proper-meaning theorists to argue
among themselves whether conventions are to be put in or early
custom to be left out. The misconception again comes from
supposing that there is an entity suspended somewhere in the
universe called 'law', which cannot truthfully be described as both
including custom and excluding custom. When we get rid of the
entity idea and realize that we are defining words, we see also that
there is no absolute need to use words consistently. The word
'law' has one meaning in relation to early customary law and a
different meaning in relation to municipal law.[1]

On this question of consistency of meaning a reservation should
perhaps be made, though it is sufficiently obvious. Consistency is
always in some degree desirable, and inconsistency may be a positive

---

[1] An illustration of this error is Timasheff's *Introduction to the Sociology of Law* (1939). The
author first advances what he calls a 'working hypothesis' of what law is, and then proceeds
to try to 'prove' this 'hypothesis' by reference to the 'facts'. He does not perceive that his
'hypothesis' is a definition and that a definition can neither be proved nor refuted. Thus he
is led to challenge Malinowski's definition of law (advanced in a discussion of primitive
law), arguing that it does not 'work' as applied to later societies because it would turn rules
regulating duels into legal rules (p. 277). The error is well pointed out by Kantorowicz in
(1940) 56 *L.Q.R.* 115.

vice. A government that varies its definition of 'aggression' according as its own conduct or somebody else's is being considered cannot be called honest. Honesty demands that words of praise and blame should be used consistently. Even in referential uses one could get muddled by inconsistency of language. However, owing to the inadequacy of language the same words sometimes have to be used in different meanings, and this need not cause confusion if the contexts are quite different. This is so, it is submitted, in the instance discussed in the previous paragraph.

(6) Closely connected with the last misconception is the idea that there are natural differences of 'kind' quite independent of human classification. Thus Leslie Stephen, in a discussion of Austin, asks whether the fact that Austin's 'laws improperly so called' do not conform to his definition of law 'corresponds to a vital difference in their real nature. Is he simply saying, "I do not call them laws", or really pointing out an essential and relevant difference of "kind"?' And again: 'The question then arises whether the distinction between laws and customs is essential or superficial—a real distinction of kinds or only important in classification.'[1] This language is misleading because it overlooks the fact that the concept of kind results from the process of classification, and that all classification is a man-made affair. An inquiry into whether a given difference is one of kind or of degree is a verbal, not a scientific, inquiry.

(7) This error as to the existence of natural kinds is again closely connected with, if not simply an aspect of, the error as to the existence of natural essences. The latter error consists in the idea that the search for 'essences' or 'fundamental features' is in some way a factual investigation, and not merely an inquiry into the meaning of words. Enough has been said in general opposition to this idea, but it may be useful to examine in detail certain contentions of an influential text-book on logic by Cohen and Nagel.[2] The deserved esteem of this book makes the views expressed in it worthy of serious consideration.

After pointing out that disputes over definitions are frequently the result of a conflict of emotional attitudes, the authors go on to say:

However, issues other than emotional ones may also be involved. Religion, for example, has sometimes been defined in terms of some dogma, sometimes in terms of a social organization and ritual, and sometimes in terms of emotional

[1] *The English Utilitarians* (1900), iii, pp. 322, 324.
[2] *Introduction to Logic and Scientific Method*, 2nd edn. (1943), p. 233.

experiences. The resulting conflicts over the meaning or essence of religion have been regarded, perhaps not without some justice, as conflicts over words. But this is only a half-truth. For the disputants frequently have their eye on a concrete phenomenon which presents all these aspects. The quarrels over the right definition of religion are attempts to locate the fundamental features of a social phenomenon. For if those features are taken as the definition of religion, it is possible to deduce many important consequences from it. Thus if belief in some doctrine is the essence of religion, other things follow than if some type of emotional experience is taken as defining religion: in the one case there is an emphasis upon intellectual discipline and conformity, in the other, an emphasis upon aesthetic elements and a neglect of theology.

It is submitted that 'attempts to locate the fundamental features of a social phenomenon' are matters of emotion, not of scientific observation, unless some objective meaning can be given to the word 'fundamental' in connection with the particular inquiry. Therefore the proposition in which these words appear does not advance the authors' argument that the conflict over the meaning of religion is over something other than words and emotion. Also, it is difficult to understand what 'consequences' can be deduced from definitions, other than consequences as to the use of words. The authors say that if belief in some doctrine is regarded as the essence of religion, the 'consequence' will be an emphasis upon intellectual discipline and conformity. But this is in effect a tautology, for it simply means that those who desire to see religion maintained, and heretics cast out, and who think that religion involves fixed tenets, necessarily desire to see these tenets maintained, and those who disbelieve them rejected. The 'consequence' follows not simply from the idea that religion involves fixed tenets, but from that idea plus the desire to see religion maintained; and the consequence is only a consequence in the logical sense, being in fact contained already in the premises. To put this in another way, the fact that a particular sect in real life insists upon, say, baptism, is not the effect of a particular definition of the word 'religion'. On the contrary, the word 'religion' is merely a symbol for the practices of such a sect.

Cohen and Nagel proceed:

The age-long dispute about the nature of law involves similar issues. Is 'law' to be construed as a command, as a principle certified by reason, or as an agreement? The controversy is not simply about words. It is concerned with making one rather than another aspect of law central, so that the appropriate consequences may be drawn from it. A schoolroom illustration is the question, 'Is a bat a bird?' The two parties to the dispute concerning the answer may agree that a bird is a warm-blooded vertebrate having its fore limbs modified as wings, and yet not agree as to whether a bat is a bird. Why? Because one party to the dispute may believe that there is a closer affinity of the bat to rodents than to birds, and may wish to regard those common features of rodents as central to the bat.

Again I do not follow. The 'schoolroom illustration' seems to be plainly a dispute over verbal classification (as Locke held[1]) and thus to prove the opposite of what the authors contend. We are given the fact that there is no dispute over any of the features of the bat; so what is the dispute about if it be not over the application of words? It is difficult to see what is meant by 'making one rather than another aspect of law central' unless the phrase have reference to the application of words. Those who construe law as command refuse to apply the *word* law to any system of rules that cannot be regarded as a command. Those who construe law as a principle certified by reason refuse to apply the *word* law to any system of rules that cannot be regarded as certified by reason. And so on. In each case the controversy is simply as to the application of a word, not as to the characteristics of any particular system of rules under dispute.

The answer to the argument that 'consequences' can be drawn from the definition of 'law' is the same as before: such consequences are only consequences as to the use of words. For instance, if 'law' be construed as a command, the consequence will be that international law will not be called 'law'; but this will not in itself wipe out the body of rules that are now accepted for determining the conduct of states. It is true that if the phrase 'international law' be replaced in current usage by some such phrase as 'international custom', these international rules may lose some of the respect in which they are now held. But this consequence will not follow merely from the definition of law as a command. It will follow from the fact that the word 'law' is nowadays more highly charged with a certain kind of emotion (namely the emotion of unquestioning obedience) than the word 'custom'.

Must these dusty disputes last for ever? They will unless we bring ourselves to realize that definitions have no importance in themselves, no importance apart from the expression and ascertainment of meaning. The only intelligent way to deal with the definition of a word of multiple meaning like 'law' is to recognize that the definition, if intended to be of the ordinary meaning, must itself be multiple.

[1] *Essay Concerning the Human Understanding* (1690), 3, 9, 15–16; 3, 11. 6–7.

There is, of course, no objection to a discussion of the suitability of words for a given purpose, even though it may be difficult to reach agreement. The term 'verbal controversy' is in this respect rather ambiguous, for whereas it always means one in which both parties agree on the facts and differ only on their language, it has two forms. The first is where the parties do not realize that the dispute is only over words, but confuse words and things. This mistake seems to have been made by most of the writers discussed in this paper. The second form is where the parties realize that the dispute is only over words, but deliberate the question which language is the more convenient for expressing the facts. This second type of controversy is unexceptionable on philosophical grounds, though even an argument of this kind, if carried on beyond a certain point, is a sad employment of time. The aim of a discussion as to the suitability of words is to produce agreement upon future verbal conventions; any such discussion that does not have this agreement as its outcome is a failure. If there is a breakdown in the talks, as has happened with the word 'law', the only practical course is for each side to proceed to use the word as it wishes and let time show which is the more convenient.

When jurisprudence comes to disembarrass itself of verbal controversies, in either (but particularly the first) sense of the expression, there will still be some questions, hitherto discussed in connection with verbal ones, that may usefully be saved for discussion on their own account. Thus a comparison of international law with municipal law would be a factual, not a verbal, discussion. Again, one may usefully hold debate over the reasons why men observe rules; how far rules are observed; the reasons for non-observance; how far a particular rule-system is adequate to the needs of society; and how its sanctions can be improved. Any of these matters may be discussed in its own right; but to discuss it as incident to the question whether a system of rules is properly called law is to consign the issue to sterility.

X

THE FACE TO FACE SOCIETY

by Peter Laslett

Lecturer in History, Cambridge University

O N a dull Sunday afternoon the situation of most Englishmen is likely to be that of sitting at home in his family, and there is the coincidence that at one time a large part of the population is in that identical situation. It is the claim of this essay that political and social theory too often tries to understand the coincidence between all these situations as if it were itself one of those situations.

Now the family is a face to face society. All its activities either are, or can be, carried on by means of conversation, conversation between members of the family. When such conversations are no longer possible the family is said to be broken up, or the person now absent from the conversations is regarded as outside the family. He is kept within the potential family by letters. But these letters are only understandable by the absent member in terms of the past conversations which have taken place between him and the man who writes them, and between him and the other members of his family. When he reads them he is confident that he knows what sort of conversations will be taking place within the family as a result of the events which these letters record. He also knows how he himself would be talking if he were present. If a crisis occurs in the affairs of his family, the absent member may well feel that his letters are not enough, that he knows no longer quite what is going on, or what may happen. But he is still quite sure that when he is again face to face with the others in the family, he will understand the new situation, and after some conversations, he will know what to expect. It is further claimed here that works on political theory tend to take on the nature of such letters from within the family, but that we understand them as if they were objective and exhaustive descriptions of the situation within the family, understandable from themselves alone.

The features of the family as a face to face society[1] which are important for this discussion are these. First, that everyone in it *knows* everyone else in it (know, *connaître*, the suggestion which this

---

[1] The words 'society' and 'group' are here used as the feel of the sentence seems to require, and in no technical sense.

word contains of 'being born together' is illuminating if entirely unjustified). He is never called upon to co-operate in any other way than by being present at what is going on. This means that members of a family respond with their whole personality, conscious and unconscious, covert and overt, in all situations, and they behave with the knowledge that the other members do exactly the same. Secondly, that all situations of crisis, when a decision has to be made and individuals do not know what to do, if they can be resolved at all, are resolved by people meeting and talking. In such a meeting, everyone will get to know the situation and will discover what his appropriate behaviour is. The process of solving the crisis and making the decision, will be to some degree one of ratiocination, analysing the situation in terms of propositions, relating these propositions logically, and deciding to act in the way which logic lays down. But to a large degree it will be a matter of personal response, expressed not in propositions, but in exclamations, apostrophes, laughter and silences. All conversations are of this character, as anyone will recognize who has overheard a telephone conversation or listened to a recording of spontaneous discussion. Once more it is a question of total intercourse between personalities, conscious and unconscious, and it may well be that the solution of the crisis takes place as much as a result of what is neither formulated nor expressed, as of what has been called ratiocination.

It should be noted that the situation of crisis, the circumstances requiring a decision, is never entirely an internal situation, and may be to a large extent an external one. This draws attention to the very important fact that no society, even a face to face society of the special domestic sort, lives completely to itself and of its own, Because the external relations of a society, face to face or otherwise, cannot be apprehended in the face to face fashion, they are necessarily apprehended to the greatest possible extent by ratiocination. This means that they can be, and mostly are, a matter of record; the family meeting will begin by the reading out of a letter or a will, perhaps more often a report will be made by one or other of its members describing the circumstances which confront it. In the society of a family, at least, this is as far as record is usually necessary, and the extent to which any society has to rely on written record rather than on the remembered experience of its members, is a rough measure of the extent to which it falls short of being a face to face society. It is worth noticing that documents of this sort, even if they belong to the executive committee of a voluntary association, or to a Board of Directors, to a Cabinet or to a Security Council, are only to a small degree the record of descriptive and analytic propositions. For the most part they are historical records, explaining by chronology. Moreover, that proportion of the covert activity of a face to face society which can readily be made overt, is also chronological; anyone taking part in a family conversation can respond to a challenge to give the reasons in terms of his past experience for his taking up a particular position. What he cannot do, and what he is most unlikely to be asked to do, is to give a description of his exact relation with the family group and what, in analytic terms, explains his whole attitude to the others and so enables him to share in the final conviction of the whole group which issues in the family's decision. The reason why he will not be asked and could not easily respond is important. It is that the psychology of the face to face society is intuitive psychology.

The relevance of this to politics and to the situation with which we began may not be obvious. It is not my purpose to set up the face to face society as the model of all societies, political or otherwise, and to claim, for example, that the society of Great Britain is only to be understood in terms of that model. Quite the reverse. It is to draw attention to the possibility that it is because the politicians themselves do tend to understand the society 'Great Britain' on that model, and proceed as if the intuitive psychology which is appropriate to the family at the fireside is the same as that which is assumed by their behaviour as politicians, that the political theorists have been led astray. Great Britain is not a face to face society. It is an example of what will be called in contrast to it a territorial society. The descriptive psychology appropriate to it is not the same as that appropriate to a face to face society, even though in both cases it may be a matter of intuition, at least on the part of fathers and politicians. Nor is it intended to imply that because the successful behaviour of both of these classes of people is best described as intuitive, it cannot therefore be itself objectively and scientifically analysed. It is only on the condition that both these psychological systems can be reduced to descriptive and analytic propositions that a successful political theory can be contemplated. By 'successful' here is meant what is meant by it in the common-sense language of natural scientists: one capable of accurate prediction. One further safeguard against misinterpretation may be necessary. It is not necessary to believe that these respective analyses can in principle be entirely accurate and absolutely exhaustive in order to recognize that they must be undertaken before we can have a workable theory of politics.

To accept the analysis to be developed here, therefore, the idealistic scepticism of Michael Oakeshott, the politics of metaphor and paradox, must be set aside. But we need not proceed as if all the optimistic implications of Karl Popper's famous phrase 'piecemeal, social engineering' were justifiable. An important step in the argument has been foreshadowed when the directive groups of voluntary bodies, of industrial enterprises, of nation states and of international organizations were ranged alongside the family as face to face societies. We could have added the central and local committees of political parties, of soviets and of the whole class of parliamentary and representative bodies. It seems to be the case that any given sample of individuals capable of acting collectively has only one procedure open to it. It must discover from within itself, or have discovered for it, a group of a critical size which can act, and act continuously, as a face to face society: which is capable, that is, of proceeding by means of conversation between its members, permitting mutual response in terms of the whole personalities of those who compose it, resolving its crises and making its decisions by that combination of ratiocination and of conscious and unconscious response which has already been described. This is, in fact, the nature of representation and of representative bodies defined in the psychological terms used here. A traditional monarchy is, or was, where the face to face society of a particular family organized in an authoritarian way is the representative of a territorial, political society. In this definition the word 'representative' is used in the Hobbesian sense, and it has meaning only in terms of the psychology which describes the relation between that Royal Family and the society at large. A parliamentary democracy, if that is the way to describe Great Britain to-day, is where a synthetic face to face society—the House of Commons—is felt to represent in an arithmetic or rational way our territorial, political society. Here the word synthetic is used to make a contrast between the initially unstructured aggregate of individuals found in the House of Commons, and the 'natural' society of a Royal Family, Court and Council.

In this way the whole of the traditional subject-matter of constitutional criticism can be brought within our criteria, together with many of the problems which political theorists have concerned themselves with. These considerations could be used to give substance and a more exact meaning to such phrases as 'the sense of the House' (or the meeting), and such indispensable words as 'leadership'. They might help the analyst and the historian when he finds, as he always will, that Cabinets and Committees, Military Staffs and Judicial Courts, Boards of Directors and Trade Union Councils, all have what is so often called 'a life of their own', which goes on quite independently of their defined functions and of their fixed positions within a hierarchy or a general system. Such an approach, by allotting a function to the total response of individuals in the face to face situation, allows for the supremely undefinable element of personality. But the object here is not to sketch out in detail, or even in general terms, a political psychology. It is rather to lay down a definition of the type of question which such a psychology should be called upon to answer. And the specific question which is raised in an imperative form by the examples we have considered is this. Given that the psychology of a Legislature or an Executive is to such an extent a psychology of face to face contact, what is the psychology describing their relationships to the society at large? We have seen that the members of such decision-making groups will apprehend these relationships, because they are to them external, as far as they can ratiocinatively, and as a matter of record, though the role of unconscious response must not be neglected even here. But this affects the reciprocal relationship of those for whom they are acting—the voters, the citizens, the country—only by implication. In some respects, moreover, this implication is misleading: it is not the case that a territorial society can be exhaustively described as a galaxy of face to face societies, having a relationship of a particular psychological quality with that group which acts for it and in control of it. The formulation of this critical question requires that we analyse the politics of the face to face society more closely, and more within the context of traditional political theory.

The family is a face to face society of a very special sort, and it has the disadvantage as an example that it is never a political society, at least of the character that contemporary political theorists have to take account of. Nevertheless, our persistent habit of distinguishing between the physiological and the mental, associates with the family some further conceptions which it may be useful to mention. The possibility of co-operation by physiological response and symmetry rather than by mental collaboration is vividly illustrated by the marriage of persons unable to speak each other's language. Such collaboration seems more animal than human, and it is a

M

fact that animal communities collaborate in a very similar way. Social insects, herding mammals, birds and fish in migration do understand each other, do play upon each other's responses, but the condition that they must all be in company, all face to face with each other is inescapable for them. It is one of the attributes of our humanity then that we can co-operate in groupings which are not face to face societies, and at first sight it would seem extraordinary that any theory of human politics which overlooked this truism could have been accepted as complete or could have appeared at all workable. Such an account of political behaviour fails to answer the question raised by Aristotle's first political proposition ἄνθρωπος φύσει πολιτικὸν ζῷον, the question of what does relate the terms 'animal' and 'political' in the statement that man is a political animal.

To understand why this question does not seem to have been raised in quite this form, it is necessary to remember that Aristotle made his proposition under very special circumstances, circumstances which can be pretty exactly defined in the terms we have been using. The whole of Greek political thought was conditioned by the fact that the polis was a political society which was also a face to face society. It may be that it was only because of the coincidence which allowed a society of this size and nature to be independent, to conceive of itself as a whole contrasted with other wholes to become conscious that it possessed those characteristics which we have now agreed to call political, that Greek political thought was possible at all. And European political thought begins with the Greeks. We cannot now go backwards beyond them to recover their inheritance from the Near Eastern Empires, Monarchies, Cities and tribal societies which preceded them, though we can and must recognize that the political lives of their forerunners were amongst the presuppositions of the Greeks. It is not what came before, but what comes after Greek political thinking which interests us, and what comes after the Greeks is ourselves. Ourselves, that is, dating our appearance at the Renaissance, which was, it might be remarked, also a time when the society of cities, cities in Northern Italy, also happened to enjoy political independence, and leaving out of account the political life of the Middle Ages which had come between, the relevance of which to ourselves we have never been able fully to understand. The matrix of our political thinking, then, is Greek, and from these historical generalizations we can go further and state once more the hypothesis with which we began. It may be because we have never been able to transcend the face to face assumptions of Greek political thinking that we are unable to develop a political analysis appropriate to our true situation. In historical high relief, this is why we understand the working of our territorial, political society as if it were the working of a face to face society.

An abbreviated, developmental argument of this sort carries very little conviction, and the rough generalizations about Greek politics and Greek thought will have to be given greater substance. It will surely be readily admitted that the polis is the best possible example of the face to face society defined in purely political, classically political terms. It is not simply that the number of its citizens was always small, never more than 10,000 and often no more than 1,000, small enough, that is, to permit of all their communal business to be transacted by a meeting of the whole. It is also that the Greek thinkers always assumed that every citizen would know every other citizen: there was never a necessity for a synthetic face to face grouping to be created. The ideal political society of Plato's *Laws*, with its exact and constant number of 5,040 citizens, or that in Aristotle's *Politics* which must be able to be called to arms by the shouting of a single herald in normal voice, societies like these obviously had the characteristics which we have remarked upon in the special case of the face to face society of a family. Its activities could be carried on by conversation between all of its citizens, who could, if need be, assemble as a whole for the purpose. In such assemblies, indeed in all situations of political significance, each individual would display the attitudes appropriate to intercourse where experience is shared, not perhaps totally as in the case of a family, but to a far greater extent than can be imagined of any political or quasi-political occasion with which we are now familiar.

This recognition of assumed shared experience in Greek political life draws our attention to a difficulty which always confronts those who try to explain the polis in terms which we can now understand. An assemblage, a cohabitation of a number of people whose whole experience has gone forward in contact one with another, who share not simply a language, a history, and a defined area, but all conceivable, isolable social purposes, resembles nothing which any of us has ever seen, except, perhaps, the working anthropologist in the field. It is like a family, an enormously large family, a whole kin living together—such an impression comes repeatedly into the imagination when you read the *Republic*—but it is not a family. It has an infinitely longer continuous history, with no break at the generations: its purposes are ever so much wider; they are, in fact, the totality of purposes. It is like the annual general meeting of a particularly active and important voluntary association—the Communist Party, for example—but it is even more obviously not such a thing. It is like an Oxford college, and here we meet the well-worn academic simile, but is emphatically not such a body: its members have not joined it from elsewhere, and they will not leave it to go elsewhere: they have always been together and always will be. It is important to recognize these things in order to appreciate how profound was the level at which the conditioning of Greek political thinking went on. In terms of the psychology of groups, Aristotle's word 'nature', the physis which links animal and political in such a way as to make a man, covers a concept which we can only appreciate by making a strenuous effort of the imagination and the understanding.

Because this was their situation and this was their conditioning, the Greeks had no impelling motive to recognize the importance of the truism which we used to distinguish the politics of the herd from the politics of the human group. They did not, of course, disregard it, and their thinking tended to falter at just the points we might expect if its effect had been recognized but its implications had not fully grasped. These points of discontinuity are to be seen at three points in Aristotle's system. The first is in his discussion of those socially and economically within the polis, but politically outside it, the metics and the slaves that is: the second is when he talks of the barbaroi, those outside the Greek area. But the third is the most important, for Aristotle was evidently defeated by political organization on the large scale: as we shall see, cosmopolis went beyond his range.

Nevertheless, the Greeks were able to lay down principles of action which would work, or work for them, and to make ethical pronouncements which their contemporaries found convincing and which have been of overwhelming, constricting influence ever since. That they were able to do this serves to bring into view two further defining characteristics of the ideal face to face society in its political form, both of which are implied by the primary characteristics we have considered so far. The first of these is that the area, the territory covered, should be its least important feature: it is always small and its nucleus is almost necessarily urban. In fact, the most useful negative feature of the face to face society which distinguishes it from the territorial society is the limitation of area it can cover—human and geographical. It is not suited to, not capable of, performing the work of giving political consciousness by itself to the inhabitants of any area larger than a city and its environs. We might seek in this for some insight into the puzzling change which came over the political thinking of the Ancient World when, after Alexander the Great, the polis ceased to be able to enjoy independence, autarkeia, a change which is often regarded as the most important single event, if the word 'event' is permissible, in the whole history of European political thought. This must not be taken to imply that territoriality, extended area and the tendency of its inhabitants to identify their social and political organization with it, is the only necessary feature distinguishing types of social and political solidarity.

The other secondary defining characteristic of the polis must be presented in terms of metaphorical language drawn from neurophysiology, and concerns what may be called the synaptic contact between individuals within it. Synapse is the term used for the interval, spatial distance, between neurons, and the ease, speed, direction and quality with which a synapse can be 'made'—bridged, that is, or traversed—are all of the utmost importance in the study of consciousness. In a face to face society like the polis, social synaptic contact, as we may call it, can obviously be made at the maximum ease, speed and continuity, both ways between each unit and in all directions over the whole mass. The analogy breaks down at the point when it is recognized that the individuals within a society can move, whilst neurons are motionless, but it is, after all, only in a territorial society that such motion is necessary. The polis could be continuously conscious of itself without any individual stirring out of the ordinary area of his everyday business. A territorial society cannot, and though our developed instruments of communication make our situation very different from that in a medieval European monarchy, it is still very distant in the quality of its synapses from the Athens of Plato and Aristotle. For if we press our metaphor to its limit, it is only when individuals are in the presence of each other that the social synapse can be bridged with anything like completeness. Of course, such contact is an important feature of the workings of the political society we live in now. It goes on between rulers and the ruled, as well as between the citizens. It even has to be brought about synthetically by broadcasting and television, now politically indispensable. Nevertheless, the broadcast situation is not fully a face to face situation, since it does not permit of mutual response and interaction. And it is perfectly obvious that social synaptic contact, partial or complete, natural or synthetic, is not the only and obvious pathway of relationship amongst us, as it was amongst the Greeks.

Our contention, then, is that both these two very rare and special conditions, that of a fully developed political society insignificant in geographic area and that of the maximum social synaptic contact, happened to be present amongst the Greeks. This did not make Greek political society any simpler than other societies, for it was in fact highly sophisticated, not in any sense more 'natural' or 'basic'. But this peculiar psychological situation amongst the Greeks is critical from our point of view, because it made possible their intense social and political awareness and so permitted the creation by Greek thinkers of our tradition of political speculation. Its other consequence, however, was that they never felt obliged to concern themselves as such with political awareness which arose under other conditions.

It will not be expected that all the consequences of this conditioning of Greek political thinking upon them and upon their successors to our day should be examined here. All that will be attempted is a few desultory remarks upon the definition of the individual, upon the universality of political ethics, and, in passing, a very obvious illustration from the theory of the general will.

We must begin our examination of the definition of the individual by pointing out what has often been demonstrated before, that the Greeks did not have one. Since they were only concerned with, could only conceive of, the problems of a face to face society, they never felt the necessity of defining or describing the individual in empirical terms. Under these circumstances they could rely for the solution of all political difficulties on the fact that in a given situation a man, any man, knew intuitively what the situation meant and what behaviour was appropriate to it. Now as we have seen it is only under face to face conditions that such intuitive behaviour—putting yourself in the position of the man you are face to face with—is both continuously possible, appropriate, and sufficient. If everyone can be expected to join a situation, respond to it, that is, with that mixture of ratiocination and of conscious and unconscious adjustment we have already described, then there can be no occasion for an exact description of the situation itself. The only information which is likely to be recorded about such a situation, therefore, must take the form of one of those 'letters from the family' which have been referred to, not of an analytic description of the situation itself, of the relations between the individuals within it and so finally of the objective character of any one individual. And the dis-advantage of this type of communication, it will be remembered, is that it is liable to complete breakdown when the correspondents no longer share enough knowledge of each other's experience, a breakdown which can only be repaired by the renewal of shared situations. For this reason we understand both the objective psycho-logical situation within the polis and the psychology of the Greek in so far as we citizens understand them at all, not from the analytic writing of the Greek thinkers, but from the total assistance which Greek literature gives us in imagining ourselves as members of the polis.

All this is part of the common-sense assumptions of the historian and of the political and social commentator. If there is anything new about it, it is the fastening of our attention on the fact that men can give accounts of their activity which they find convincing, and which convince their readers hundreds or thousands of years later, without being at all clear what they are like as individuals, or of what any individual is like. They can do this because of the mechan-ism of face to face relationships, which work perfectly well without anyone caught up in them being called upon to formulate a psycho-logical system of any coherence whatsoever. Greek psychology was, in fact, pure fantasy, and the various improbable theories of the division of the soul found in Plato and Aristotle, could not possibly find a place in any objective account of political relationships. There were certainly reasons for this other than the fact that the Greeks felt it safe to assume that the intuitive psychology of personal relationships was all that was required for the working of their face to face society. The content of Greek religion was one of them.

But the Greeks are not the only political thinkers who succeed in giving the impression that they understand what goes on between individuals whilst holding a more or less irrelevant view of the psychology of individuals. The mechanistic and utilitarian psycho-logy of Hobbes, for example, and perhaps of all those whose political analysis can be classified as 'individualistic' or 'contrac-tarian', is obviously a caricature of the objective behaviour of human individuals. It attempts to understand the individual by regarding his outward, socially oriented attitudes as a skin, or a succession of skins, which must be peeled off if his behaviour is to become intelligible. But it only succeeds in demonstrating that if you approach it in this way, the individual personality turns out to be an onion, consisting entirely in this succession of metaphorical layers, so that when you have separated skin from skin you are left with nothing individual at all. The psychology, then, implied by the political analysis which begins with the indivisible, individual human unit, ends by stripping down each unit as an artificer strips down a machine, into a chaos of unrelated fragments—'will', 'desire', 'passions', and so on.

No doubt, as in the case of the Greeks, the reasons why this individual and social psychology was unsatisfactory must be sought in many places, in the condition of physical and medical knowledge, in the current philosophical systems, and once more in religion. But the particular question we must ask is this—In what arena did Hobbes and company assume that the individual being described, in fact, carried on his activities? Was it in the scattered village settlements of rural England in Stuart times, where an appeal to each individual's fear or will or desire would have been an ineluctably slow and unsatisfactory process? Or are we to take seriously the picture on the title-page of *Leviathan*, in which all Englishmen appear as cells in a body politic, all in physical contact one with another, all nourished by the same blood stream of circulating wealth? Does not, indeed, the whole general metaphor of a living organism rest on the assumption of quick, easy and complete social synaptic contact? The presence of this metaphor is, indeed, somewhat paradoxical in Hobbes, whose individuals were constructed so as to behave ratiocinatively. But are not the very features of the individualistic personality the features to be observed in men talking to each other, responding to each other face to face, like beasts at a feeding-trough? For all their much emphasized discovery of the individual where the Greeks had found no individual to discover, the early individualists observed his behaviour in very much the Greek context. Analysing a man's characteristics when he is in the specified situation of reacting to the physical presence of his fellows, then constructing an individual out of the sum total of those characteristics, this is not the creation of an objective political psychology. There is a confusing circularity in the individualist position. From the initial and obvious error that solitary behaviour is possible to humans, they proceeded to analyse society as if it were an aggregation of solitary individuals. But their solitary individual is really an abstraction from individual behaviour in the face to face situation, and they proceed to associate him with his fellows in a territorial society as if that were itself a face to face society. In this way they manage to make the misapprehension we are considering not once but twice over.

But what of those to whom the state as a physical organism was not simply an irrelevant metaphor? What of the organic theory of the state? Are such entities as Rousseau's General Will, Hegel's Spirit of the Nation, Bosanquet's Real and Apparent Wills, or Gierke's Real Personality of Groups any more realistic? There is no need to dwell for very long on the physiological metaphor itself. It is useful to just the extent that the psychology of national political societies is analogous to the psychology of a human organism, and the resemblance is very restricted. Indeed its persuasiveness and persistence are probably due to the implication which it makes possible, that as an individual mind can have a will, so can a State, a Society or a Nation. For the concept of a General Will which is, nevertheless, the will of all those composing the generality, has straightforward advantages for political analysis, especially for the ethical problems. A first observation about it can be that the philosophers of our time are busying themselves about the concept as applied to individuals, and Professor Ryle and his followers range it along with the rest of the psychological double talk which makes nonsense of most discussions of the mind. Obviously, if nothing but confusion can come from separating off some attributes of the intelligence of a man and calling it his will, it is at least probable that nothing better can be expected from doing just this thing with a collectivity of men.

It is Rousseau who initiated the General Will for political theorists, and Rousseau was a face to face man. There is no need to appeal to his obsession with the city state politics of Geneva or to his insistence that an ethically approved political society can only exist on the small scale in order to demonstrate this about him. Hobbes called the will the last act of deliberation, and this description fits the decision-making process of the face to face group remarkably well. When we attend the meeting of a committee, hear and take part in the discussion, vote for or against the final resolution, and afterwards find ourselves obliged to defend that resolution whether we agreed with it or not at the time, then the phrase 'general will' does seem to mean something to us. We can concede that something embodied in the decision is general in the sense that the will of all is not general; we can even concede that this something is, or began by being, a minority opinion, or held by one man alone.

N

Surprisingly often it corresponds to no one's opinion at all. The interplay between the group of personalities in committee, in fact, can discover a consensus which all of them feel to be outside their own personalities, and after the decision is made it is remarkable how often it is accepted as if each personality had 'willed' it for himself. It is significant, too, that this 'general will' is felt to be rational, in a sense of that word which is important to our discussion. It is rational to those taking part in it because they feel that they know how it came into being; it represents the only possible appropriate reaction of that group to that situation at that time. In this way all the attributes of the general will as conceived of by Rousseau and perhaps by the Idealist thinkers in general, can be given a first rough psychological characterization, and could, I believe, be analysed much more exactly with the use of these criteria.

Directly the concept of the general will is applied to a grouping of a different sort the psychological situation is entirely different. If we take the case of a representative assembly, perhaps a constituent assembly, trying to embody the 'general will' of the political society at large in a series of decisions, this fact becomes obvious. They are quite well aware that however intense the public feeling may be on certain issues and however well organized and powerful may be the pressure behind certain attitudes, consensus of the type they can expect to discover within their own group cannot exist over the whole society. A general will analysis of political society, in fact, can only proceed on the assumption that the quality of the psychological relationships between the directive group and society at large is the same as it is within the directive group itself. This is simply our misapprehension all over again.

Neither Idealism nor Individualism, then, goes very far to provide what their Greek predecessors lack, a workable and useful definition of the individual, and their insufficiency may well be due to their failure to appreciate the distinction we are discussing. As we have seen, Rousseau's man and Hobbesian or Benthamite man work in certain chosen contexts, and our claim is that the contexts are not those in which he must be defined if we are to understand territorial political society. Which ought, perhaps, to make us ask ourselves the question whether a unitary definition of the individual is necessary to a political theory. Could we get on without one, as Mr. Weldon does in the case of the State?

The answer here must be no. It is true that the effort to give substance to the conception 'individual' ought not to be the informing principle of a social and political inquiry; it would almost certainly be misleading if it were. It is not necessary for us to know who the individual is in order to make assertions about his behaviour, and we should not shrink from making selective generalizations about all individuals, even at the risk of saying that all individuals have a characteristic which is not present in its typical form in any individual we have met. It is even possible to contemplate a theory of politics which would satisfy some of the essential criteria, which would, for example, make possible some predictive statements about political behaviour, in which the individual appeared only as a point of reference, the point from which stretches outwards the whole of political and social experience and the point at which must be focused inwards all that can be objectively observed of the way in which societies work. Such a formal scheme would enable us to make use of the swelling volume of statistical studies; it would make psephology[1] a respectable occupation, and perhaps permit us to get our share of the practical applications of the mathematical theory of probability and of symbolic logic.

Whatever we feel about this, and whatever the formal place we decide to reserve for a definition of the individual in a general political theory, there are two features of his descriptive psychology which we cannot overlook if the argument we are pursuing is to be taken seriously. The two things our individual must be able to do are these: respond as he is observed to respond in the presence of his fellows, and co-operate as he is observed to co-operate with people whom he never meets but who share his membership in a territorial society. And in this way his position and his function are fixed with unexpected clarity and some completeness. He is always the whole man: he has to be to respond with his whole self in the face to face situation. This should prevent us from falling victims to the partial caricatures which come out of the wholly individualistic view of human personality. But he is also capable of every degree of partial and ephemeral response which make possible his sense of citizenship and his activities as a citizen. He can conceive of separate interests and identities, and provide for them in voluntary associations bewildering in their variety, or have them provided for him in the local political organization whose exact relation with the central one has been such an intricate puzzle for so long. It need not be if we remember the psychological facts; that a man does not

---

[1] Psephology is the statistical study of voting behaviour, now so enthusiastically undertaken at Oxford.

range his 'memberships' as we call them, thus giving an exclusively transitive sense to a process which is intransitive too, in any logical or intellectually conceived order. There is no limit to their number, there is a wide variety in their quality—psychological quality— there is only a very rough hierarchy in their disposition, a hierarchy which places purposes to which final compulsion is always felt to be necessary (these are what we call political purposes) above those to which compulsion is normally irrelevant. There is one joker in the pack, which is the fundamental psychological need or tendency which individuals have to identify themselves with an overriding, supreme or sovereign authority, which in the men we have to deal with is almost always given a locality somewhere at the head of the territorial association, and which has as one of its attributes the utterance and administration of law. This is not only of direct relevance to the great 'problem' of sovereignty and the confusion coming out of the controversy over pluralism. It also should put us on our guard against idealistic or total accounts of the individual, who can only appear in the presence of, or as the secretion of, that total organization of all purposes—the State.

The inquiry, then, which begins in the necessity of defining the individual, ends in the examination of some of the psychological machinery of that territorial society which we have so far referred to only in apposition to the face to face society. But some of the terms which have been used are the terms not of psychology only, but also of political ethics. We must now return to the face to face society of the Greek polis and examine the case for supposing that Greek political ethics were determined too, determined in such a way that a truly universal system of political ethics could not be developed from them, any more than a useful definition of the individual.

It is not easy to lay down a line of formal analysis here. If, as has been asserted, the individual is represented by a lacuna in the Greek system, then it is difficult to see how Greek political ethics can be given any substance at all, for the subject-matter of political ethics is so largely that of the individual's obligations to other individuals and to the collectivity of other individuals which he is called upon to obey, or which he may feel disposed to resist. Greek political ethics, then, consists in the main of the statements which their general position implies, and it is on the implications of such a work as Aristotle's assemblage—the *Nicomachean Ethics* and its continuation the *Politics*—that we shall concentrate our attention. And the first implication is this, that everything which Aristotle says implies that all citizens know all other citizens, and all citizens know their rulers, indeed, any citizen may be called upon at any moment to be one of the rulers. All this is jejune enough: Greek political ethics are personal ethics and in no separate category at all. The next step is obvious too; Greek ethics are the ethics of a face to face society. This comes out clearly in the rather unexciting norms of behaviour recommended for those in authority. Moderation, large-mindedness, even Speculative Wisdom are the attributes of a man in daily, personal contact with those for whose welfare he is responsible, and because he is under such close and unremitting observation he is really obliged to possess these virtues; he cannot simply strike an attitude and get away with it. It is possible to be cynical about this, of course, and even possible that Aristotle realized it: certainly Machiavelli did, and the strikingly similar personal virtues of his Prince were clearly intended to be feigned, if necessary, for their political advantages—they might be a handicap if they were genuine. But in both cases the contrast between the ethical characteristics of the good ruler and what we in our situation expect our governors to be like is a striking one. Heads of states, party leaders, prime ministers may have attributed to them the commonplace personal virtues, but that is not their important ethical characteristic. What we expect them to be efficient at is the carryings out of a trust, an impersonal, generalized responsibility, and we do not really mind if through the imperfections of propaganda we sometimes recognize that as persons our rulers are worse men than we are ourselves.

Now the conception of trust is a Lockeian conception, and, as everybody knows, it is the result of a typical ethical and analytical muddle. Its immense importance since Locke's day, however, may point to a difference between ethical attitude and psychological assumption amongst the Greeks and amongst ourselves which has a bearing on our discussion. There is no need for a political trust in a face to face society, but it may play a conspicuous role in reconciling a territorial society to the face to face group which undertakes the responsibility of governing it. In our language this means that we are prepared to disregard the Greek claim that personal ethics and political ethics are inseparable; we are prepared, in fact, to recognize that our relationship with our rulers is not wholly a face to face relationship. But we are not ready to go very far in this direction. The most famous of all ethical definitions of our political society is Burke's, 'a partnership in all science; a partnership in all art; a partnership in every virtue and in all perfection'. This definition differs somewhat from Aristotle's description of political association as an association for living the good life. But in both cases the description is inaccurate, or at least it suggests an ethical status for political association, a status which gives it an overriding claim on our allegiance, which is blankly unjustifiable.

For Athens did not create Athenian art, Athenian science, Athenian virtue and Athenian perfection. Although it was true that Athenian culture was different from Theban or Corinthian culture, and although it may have been true that the Athenians could only have carried on their cultural life by means of their own peculiar, local aesthetic institutions, it is nevertheless quite untrue to say that the community of citizens of Athens was the unit which created the literature and the music which was performed at Athens, or the virtues which were esteemed there, or the statuary which adorned those superb Athenian buildings. If we try to give a name to the matrix from which these things finally came, we find ourselves in difficulties. We might make a pause at some such vaguely-defined community as 'Greek civilization' or 'Greek culture', or even the 'Classical Mediterranean World'. It is obvious that this general cultural background was a presupposition of Athenian achievement which would have been impossible without it. But even this wider and vaguer community implies communities and cultural areas outside itself, such as Persia, for example, or even the barbarian Europe to the North. It also implies communities chronologically preceding it in the successive cultural epochs of the Nile delta and the rivers Tigris and Euphrates. Again the point is so obvious that it would be easy to labour at it too much. Aristotle's polis did not create the whole man, and it could not on that ground claim the allegiance of the whole man for itself. No more can any other community, whether or not it is a community to which we should find it easy to attach the adjective political. There is only one unit to which a universal political ethic could possibly apply, and that is the unit of the whole of humanity.

Of all the parables in Greek political literature, this is perhaps the most telling for us now. For Athens or Thebes we could read Britain or France, and for Greek culture the civilization of the West. It might be objected that Burke's word 'partnership' does not mean something which creates, and that it was deliberately chosen to suggest an association in things already in existence. Locke, indeed, in a passage too often overlooked, deliberately makes the point that political association is only partial association, and the necessity for partnerships smaller than a partnership of all mankind is an unfortunate accident, the result of corruption, viciousness and degeneracy. Nevertheless, both Burke and Locke go on to talk as if a political association could enshrine within itself universal ethical values, and with Rousseau it is a dogma that a political grouping is capable of willing universal ends and must be obeyed because it can do so. Our political practice since Rousseau has certainly implied this possibility, and when it comes to a conflict between nation states it is boldly asserted as a dogma. Since the time of the Greeks, moreover, there has existed in the European world a community which can claim that it creates universal values, or at least gives expression to them, the community of the Universal Christian Church. But this claim rests on the same basis as Locke's statement about human corruption, on the basis of Christian Revelation. Revelation, in fact, seems to have played a continuing role in the writings of European political thinkers, not always orthodox Christian Revelation, and not always, perhaps, recognized as such. It can be seen at play in this tendency to proceed from the attributes of the whole of humanity to the ethical qualities of a particular society.

All this makes it clear that the problem of a universal political ethic is not to be solved simply by the manipulation of our selected criteria. But one of the advantages of Greek thinking is the extent to which it was independent of revelation of any kind, and it can be shown, I believe, that it was because the polis did possess the qualities we have described that Greek thinkers could be deceived into thinking that its ethical attributes were universal attributes. The mechanism by which it was done is a simple one. Aristotle's ethics, and this is a quality which they share with very many other ethical systems, give the impression of being not the subject of ethics itself, but the introduction to that subject, its prolegomena. A situation is described, the choices before a man in that situation are hinted at, but only very rarely does he maintain that one choice and one choice only would be the right one, and right because of universal ethical principle. It nearly always 'depends on the circumstances'. If we ask why Aristotle was satisfied to stop short at this point so often, the answer would be common sense. 'You', Aristotle is saying, 'you, my fellow-citizen in Athens, would know what to do in such a case; you do not expect me to tell you that'. And his confidence was not misplaced, for it was perfectly possible for an

Athenian citizen to imagine himself in the situation described, and quite justifiable to allow him to act in it instinctively, just as he was prompted. This, once again, was because Athens was a face to face political society, in which all situations were totally shared situations and the only appropriate behaviour that mixture of the instinctual and the ratiocinative which has already been defined.

It was, perhaps, to give the wrong emphasis when we said that the Greeks supposed the ethical attributes of their political society were universal. Rather it was that their polis was organized in such a way that the issue of universal or partial could not arise. Nothing specifically political could call into question whether or not to act in the traditional manner was to act rightly. What, under such circumstances, is left for the ethical commentator to do? It is to suggest, in the manner of the writer of letters from the family, such general features of situations in which an ethical crux is likely to arise as will enable his reader to feel that a solution would suggest itself to him and to the others who were present if he actually found himself sharing such a situation. It is, in fact, to assume that it is justifiable to regard all political contact as understandable on the face to face model. If this was an analytical error for the Greeks, it was an error easy to understand because of the peculiar conditioning of the societies in which they lived. But, as in the case of the definition of the individual and of the extraordinary notion of the General Will, this misapprehension has been shared to some extent, anyway, by the political theorists of modern Europe, and an exposition at greater length could be made to include examples from their ethical writing which rest on the assumption that all that has to be done is to set up a situation which the reader feels he shares, and then appeal to his common sense. The position seems to have been that systems of political ethics have either been partial or universal, and never both at the same time. Political theorists have either asked us to pretend that the political society, which we do believe we understand, is really the whole of humanity, or they have asked us to recognize our obligation to all of humanity, a conception which is very difficult to understand and leaves us puzzled about the status of our own political society.

We have characterized a political society like our own as territorial, and it is to the workings, the psychological workings, of a territorial society that we must now return. Though we have seized upon territoriality as its distinguishing feature, and though identification with a particular area is a highly important characteristic of what we call nation states, it is not thereby exhaustively defined. A society of this sort need not be settled within a particular area; it can be nomadic. It need have no defined geographical frontier. Moreover, the psychological texture we are to examine is not confined to political societies as such, for all voluntary societies in our social world display it in their looser-knit, less complete way.

In the course of his remarks on the size of the ideal polis, Aristotle says: 'To give order to an excessively large number would surely be a task for divine power'. We can see him stepping here from the tiny political area in which everything and everybody could be known about, into the larger region where these things cannot be done, and yet political consciousness is maintained. To Aristotle it would seem that the working of such units was a mystery, which is why he leaves it to divine power; it could not be brought into the analytical spotlight focused by the city-state. Yet his suggestion that it would be to religion that we must look to find how the thing is done is a penetrating one. It would seem that the features of human psychology which make possible collaboration between individuals who are not in company with each other are the same as those which give rise to religious activity. There is the same sense of community with others unseen and unknown, the same identification with a supreme source of authority and security, the same play upon symbols. It would be possible to pursue the parallel much further, and talk of politicians as a priesthood, the political drama of a coronation or an election as a sacrament, and the body of shared belief which we recognize as holding a community together as revelation. We could use the evidence on the sacramental character of Medieval European Kingship to further the argument, and pursue it through the later European doctrine of the Divine Right of Kings which is particularly rich with psychological symbol when it is found in its patriarchal form, as I have tried to show elsewhere.[1] It is hardest to recognize the process at work in the so-called rational political organizations of the contemporary world, whose leaders and critics consciously reject any suggestion that the body politic is a mystic body in the eyes of those who offer it their allegiance and who are struggling still, as they have struggled in the past, to keep any suggestion of revelation out of political discussion. But here the findings of those contemporary psychological analysts who have given their attention to politics suggest

[1] In the introduction to *Patriarcha* and the other political works of Sir Robert Filmer, Oxford (Blackwells), 1948.

that our generalization still holds good, and can be extended to cover areas which the conventional political theorist might regard as outside his province. For they tell us that the conscience, on which legislators and administrators finally rely, is nothing else but society and its regulations written within the individual personality. The 'internalization of social norms' is the inelegant phrase which they use to describe the process. Although we must be careful of our phraseology, the psychology of the workings of the conscience undoubtedly belongs to what we think of as the psychology of religion.

But it is necessary to proceed from this point with great care. The statements we have made are not intended to be exclusive. If it is the greater emphasis on what we have called the religious mechanism which distinguishes territorial association from association face to face, it does not follow that there is no religious strain in such a social unit as the polis, or even in a modern committee. The capacity for response which we think of as religious is a truly universal human attribute, and it was fulfilling its mediatory and cohesive function in the world of Plato and Aristotle just as it was in the world of St. Augustine and of Gregory VII. In this last situation, moreover, in such a political, social, ecclesiastical and historical continuum as Medieval European Christendom, it is not the fact of deep-seated and universal religious sentiment which by itself ensures that the form of political society shall be so predominantly territorial. Where you have a condition in which a political and an ecclesiastical authority co-exist in parallel in the peculiar way in which they did then, you also have the coincidence that both systems make use of psychological presuppositions felt by contemporaries to arise from an identical revelation. In such a case the problem which they posed as that of the proper relation of the two parallel authorities was bound to be a crucial one.

The medievals themselves, of course, saw it as the logical outcome of the content of revelation itself, but we cannot concern ourselves with the content of any particular revelation, interestingly as the differences between religions affect the psychological texture of various political societies. Our concern is psychological mechanism alone, and we cannot here concern ourselves with the results even of the refusal to recognize the role of 'religious' sentiment in political psychology which is so persistent in the modern world. Our position must stop short at the assertion that the societies of the European Middle Age provide for us their successors the classic examples of territorial organization in which the architectonic position of religion is unmistakable, just as the Greek polis provides the classic example of the face to face political society. That is the objective importance to us of medieval political life.

The reciprocal misunderstanding of the position is, perhaps, even more dangerous. If the psychology of religion enters into the workings of face to face relationships, then even more emphatically does the psychology of personal contact have to be recognized in territorial society. The misapprehension which we have under examination, it must be remembered, is that all relationships are to be understood on the face to face model, and in order to do this we must not imply that none of them can be. Those human units which are, or ought to be, the primary objects of our study, are territorial political societies such as France, Great Britain, the United States, and Russia, and in each of them face to face relationships exist and are important; face to face units exist, very large numbers of them, and, above all, the directive body is itself a face to face society, because, as we have said, that is the inescapable condition of co-operative activity. And we have already laid it down that the important question which the social psychologist has to answer is on the nature of the relationship in such a society of the directive unit to the whole. The limited suggestion we are making here is that it is to those attributes of human personalities and groups which make religious activity possible that he should look for his evidence, as well as to those which can be seen at play when individuals are in company. Which leads to the further suggestion that in the varying relationship from society to society of these two complementary methods of social understanding we may find a useful way of classifying the units which are our subject-matter, classifying them, that is, by internal psychological structure. This can be regarded as an extension in the direction of typology of the general notion of social synaptic contact.

The repeated insistence on this particular question will not be taken to mean that it is the only one which calls for an answer. It has not been our purpose here to do more than hint, for example, at the delineation of our primary term, the face to face society itself. The task of giving exactness and substance to it must be left to the psychologist, the social anthropologist, the sociologist, to all who co-operate in that unsatisfactorily named activity, the pursuit of the social sciences. So must all those other enterprises which would have to be undertaken if this attempt at a formal descriptive analysis were to be turned into a body of evidence for the political theorist, and even for the historian. It seems to me that the techniques which are beginning to be worked out for purposes of this sort, the statistical techniques or even the methods of interviewing and the analysis of individual reactions, could be used perfectly legitimately to this end.

It is unfortunate that a statement of this sort has to be made in an atmosphere of barrenness, almost of futility. This has been the inevitable result of the creation of system upon general system of social analysis, all with their own peculiar vocabulary and their own complicated criteria, all intended to be tested by just such empirical methods, and all equally sterile, so much so that their special terms have been forgotten before the testing process has even begun. There is no intention here to set out just such another general hypothesis to go in its turn on the way to this universal bonfire. Rather the attempt has been to demonstrate that there is an appropriate area for the activity called the scientific study of society, the area between the internal workings of groups on which political theorists have so far tended to base their generalizations and the inclusive arena of territorial society in which the activity of such groups goes forward. In our day the political theorist needs an objective sociology because without it the model on which he is working is an inappropriate one, special and not general. No amount of intuitive insight will reveal to him what are in fact the psychological interrelations between a directive face to face group and the territorial society it directs. Aristotle could intuitively apprehend the workings of the polis because its workings were intuitive; no such automatic guidance from the social atmosphere we breathe is available to us.

There are two further features of the psychological mechanism of territorial society which require notice. The first of them arises from what was said earlier about the single procedure open to a collectivity of human beings acting as a whole, that it shall discover for itself, or rather have discovered for it, a group capable of acting as a face to face society. If it is asked how such a group is discovered and how it maintains itself, an issue is raised which has been a perpetual pre-occupation of political theory, the issue of power and consent. For there is no doubt that the men who succeed in establishing any one group in that position are exercising power over the whole society, and in certain situations they can be said to be conquering it. Nor is there any doubt that the men belonging to the directive unit are in positions of power, and all that is known of human psychology goes to show that these men will tend perpetually to maintain and increase the power they possess, both collectively and as individuals, and by the manipulation of all the psychological instruments we have described. Politicians know how to do these things; they know how to gather to themselves the leadership which arises from the 'religious' life of a territorial community and how to combine it with their personal activity in company with citizens. They can do all this without being able to give an analytical account of what they are doing and how they are doing it, and without the political analyst being able to do so either, so far at least. And if this is what they are doing, it is not obvious at first sight how it can be said of any society that political power can be made to depend on the consent of individual citizens, and in a democracy must be made to do so, especially if the actual relation of subject individuals to the wielders of collective power is anything like what has been described here. The facts of psychological mechanism seem to make an impossibility out of the classic picture of a community of rational individuals, rationally deciding which of their number shall exercise political power for what rational ends and within what limits.

All that can be attempted here must concern itself with the concept of power, power which is so often equated with rationality as if in pursuit of it or in possession of it men were always perfectly clear-headed. This has led to an over-emphasis on power as a sort of electric current flowing between points of negative and positive charge, unitary, undifferentiated. This may to some extent describe its nature, but it is not its whole function. Though freedom to exercise power may be the distinguishing feature of the directive unit of any society and may have had a great deal to do with its establishment, to say this is not to say everything. It was not the possession of undifferentiated power which decided that those particular men should belong to that group, it is not simply power which holds the group together, or which maintains its domination, it is not often power which holds the society together as a whole. Indeed, the manifestation of power is a rare event in our world, reserved for extreme legal occasions and for war, though it is customary to say that the threat to use it explains all authority, nevertheless. The universal recognition that there is a point in a political society, a central and superior point, from which supreme power emanates, is an apparent feature of political solidarity and obedience. But it is the pre-occupation with this obvious fact that has made the recognition of the other features in the map of political psychology so difficult to show up, and one of them is the network of pathways through which this influence flows. In insisting on the difference in psychological texture between face to face and other relationships, we have tried to show that to take part in the exercise of political power a man must act in intricate response to a highly complicated psychological situation. His behaviour, in fact, must be exceedingly conventional if he is to succeed at all. It is within the conventions which must govern his behaviour that the influence of the constituent parts of the society is to be found, its beliefs, its traditions, its institutions of all sorts and finally the individuals themselves, all of them. There is room, therefore, for a doctrine which insists on the rule of law, and that rights shall be respected, individuals shall be treated as ends, and genuine respect, not lip-service, shall be paid to consent. Freedom is not a condition, it is a duty, and representative democracy not an established situation so much as a challenge to the rational use of the instruments of social control.

A final word must be reserved for this adjective 'rational'. It is already a commonplace that political behaviour is not to be understood as rational in the way which was implied a little while ago. British electors do not behave rationally in front of the wireless, or the stump speaker, or the ballot box: diplomats do not behave rationally at the United Nations: at no point where it has been examined, even in that area where it is in closest touch with reality, the area of economic interest, does human behaviour proceed at all consistently 'as calm reason doth dictate'. In its extreme form, the thesis put forward here could be said to be an attempt to account for the 'illusion of rationality' in political behaviour as it is found in the writings of political thinkers. The reason suggested is that they have tended to analyse all societies on the model of the face to face society, which they, like the Greeks, do assume to be rational or ratiocinative in its functioning. We have tried to show why this has been found satisfactory, and how natural it is for men to assume that when they have reduced a situation to one which they feel they could themselves share, and respond to with their whole personalities, they have then demonstrated that it can be understood as rationally constructed. But we also laid it down that the psychology of face to face co-operation is not wholly ratiocinative, and that because you share a situation and are confident you know how to respond to it, you do not therefore understand it in the properly rational fashion. We have still to consider to what extent the complementary mode of social co-operation, the 'religious' mode, can be described as rational.

It is clear that political writers have tended to assume that the rational element in the over-all psychology of a political society is much less prominent than it is in smaller groups. In doing this they may imply a recognition of its 'religious' character, and react away from it because to them, as to most people, religion connotes revelation, the supremely irrational. At the same time, as we have hinted, they seem to introduce revelation themselves when they wish to make their theories consistent and inclusive, though for revelation here they seem to read a nation's history, tradition or collective experience. This attractive little quirk peeps out when they make historical statements. They may say, they are bound to say, that the process whereby Mr. Churchill and his government were thrown out by the British electorate in 1945 was an almost entirely irrational one. Yet they will talk of the long-term good sense of the electorate's decision, and produce all sorts of historical considerations to prove it. We may call this cowardice, even if at the same time we are unable to propose a formula for deciding whether an act of this sort on the part of a territorial society can or cannot be described as rational.

In fact, our attitude to such an issue must be a pragmaticist attitude, as, indeed, it was when we contrasted the intuitive with the ratiocinative element in personal co-operation. We all know that overtly religious societies, believing in revelation and consisting of convinced believers, are able to make decisions of policy and decisions on doctrine. We might appeal to the fruitful distinction put forward a generation ago by Karl Mannheim, the distinction between total rationality, in which revelation can have no part, and functional rationality, which is perfectly accessible to a convinced believer however fantastic his total view of the universe may seem to the outsider. The overriding feature of the psychological mechanism which the national society shares with the religious community is that it works, and it works alongside of, in the absence of, the conditions in which face to face co-operation goes forward. What is important for us to know is how it works, and that I believe we can expect to learn from the psychologist, the social anthropologist, and the sociologist. We can expect to do so, that is, if we pose our questions to them in a way in which they will find it possible to answer them, and in which their answers would be useful to us.

What we should not do is to believe that we have to wait until our own problems are solved at the philosophical level before we consider what further evidence and in what form is obviously necessary in order to work out a workable analysis of society. It would be different if the position were what for so long it has been assumed to be, if, in fact, we had to deal with small, close-knit human units in which intuitive behaviour was appropriate behaviour. Because it is not, because the face to face society is a special society with a specific function and not the universal description of society, we cannot proceed without an anthropology, a psychology, and a sociology.

But above all we must not mistake the recognition that we are faced with the irrational if we are to understand political behaviour for the necessity of proclaiming ourselves as irrational. This is to confuse the obstinacy of our material with the limitations of our methods. Rational demonstration may not be the predominant method of getting things done in politics, but it must be the only method which those who analyse society shall use to demonstrate to each other and everybody else what the issues are.

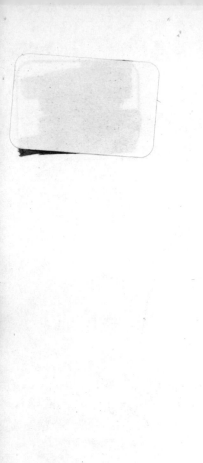